Loving
TIARA

Memoir

TIFFANI GOFF

Published by
TWIG DÉCOR PRESS

PRAISE FOR *LOVING TIARA*

"*Loving Tiara* is the kind of memoir that both breaks your heart and fills it up with hope and inspiration. Tiffani Goff is a fierce and faithful mother who is determined to give her daughter a good life. Her story shows us how a family can overcome extraordinary obstacles, and how a mom can be a superhero." Candi Sary, author of *Black Crow White Lie*

"In an era of instant gratification, excess materialism, and superficial happiness, the author poignantly reveals the deeper gifts that pain and struggle offer all of us. Through a series of losses, including the heart-wrenching death of a child, Goff reminds us the power of resilience, love and intuition to support life's biggest challenges. This is an inspiring, authentic and touching read for anyone seeking more meaning from adversity, and a deeper personal connection to love and life." Melissa Joy Jonsson, best-selling author of *The Art of Limitless Living* and four other life-transformational books.

"*Loving Tiara* is the raw and honest story of the strength of a mother's love that looms bright in spite of crushing realities. Tiffani Goff takes you on a journey through two decades filled with heartbreak, triumph, destiny, and relinquishment. Hers is every parent's nightmare, and her story offers a rare glimpse into how imperfect people can endure overwhelming odds with humor, honesty, and candor." Noelle Cablay, author of *Pieces of Sky*, a memoir

"*Loving Tiara* is recommended not only for any parent whose child or children suffer from significant handicaps or disorders, but for any reader who is interested in a heartfelt tale of struggle against long odds and coping with both the fear of losing hope, but ultimately finding it. It is a contemporary tale of love, frustration, compassion, fear, and myriad other emotions facing a mother who desperately loves a child afflicted with an unforgiving condition that can only be combatted through unwavering persistence, effort, and, ultimately, unconditional love." Dr. Tom Hunter, author

"TT is a boisterous, strong-willed, funny, caring girl who, as I read, stole my heart and inspired me with her strength and resilience. Most inspiring, is her love for her momma and her momma's love for her, a relationship tied and bound by a heart-wrenching, awe inspiring journey they travel together." Liz Mckibbin, Newport Beach Public Library Circulation Manager

"It takes courage to step out of the highlight reel of life, take off the filters and write about life as it truly is. With *Loving Tiara,* Tiffani has done just that. She has bared it all for the reader-raw honesty, brutal reality, and an endless love and fighting spirit for her daughter. A daughter whose health challenges were more than most of us can ever imagine. The true beauty of this book is in its honesty about all of the beautiful messiness that was loving Tiara." Kate Lyon Osher, Business Owner, Writer, Mental Health & Suicide Prevention Advocate

For speaking and appearance information please visit:
www.tiffanigoff.com

Published by TWIG DÉCOR PRESS
Costa Mesa, CA 92626
twigdecorpress@gmail.com

ISBN: 978-1-7342695-0-5 (paperback)
ISBN: 978-1-7342695-1-2 (epub)
ISBN: 978-1-7342695-2-9 (mobi)

Cover Image by Mara Blom Schantz
www.artisticimpressionsbymara.com

This book is dedicated to:

Trinity

(for once, you get your name mentioned first)

Tabitha

And

Louie

You are my everything.

Table of Contents

A NOTE TO THE READER

This book is my version of what transpired during a specific period in my life. I'm sure some of my family members, doctors, or teachers may remember it differently, but this is how I remember it. My memory is flawed, so I often had to refer to medical records, school records, and photographs to remember specifics. I have not included every hospital admission, procedure, or condition endured by Tiara. *Loving Tiara* is an accurate representation of our lives, but it does not include everything that transpired.

I created a dialogue between characters that closely resembled the tone and relationship between the parties, even though the words aren't direct quotes. This is especially true of my conversations between myself and numerous doctors. The information conveyed is based on my lay understanding of Tiara's health, and therefore some inaccuracies may exist. A physician has not reviewed any medical procedures, conditions, references, or descriptions written about in this book. I want to thank every doctor mentioned in this book. If I used your name, it's because I am forever grateful for the care you provided to Tiara during her life. I am also eternally thankful to the nurses at CHOC and UCLA for always taking excellent care of Tiara. The nurses were often my lifeline to the outside world, and I miss so many of them. I also want to thank every teacher, therapist, aide, caretaker, and support person mentioned in *Loving Tiara*. If I included your name, it's because you were wonderful with Tiara.

Many friends and loved ones who were a big part of our lives during this period are not mentioned in *Loving Tiara*, simply because they didn't fit in the storyline. I wish I could have included everyone who was a part of our lives during this time, but it wasn't possible. I did not ask anyone's permission to be included in the book, and the following names are pseudonyms: Mrs. Earl, Ms.Clay, Ray, Sarah, and Shelly.

I want to thank my incredible editing team, a collaboration of professionals and friends who helped me find all my mistakes: Jean Ardell, Noelle Cablay, Tom Hunter, Liz Mckibbin, Lynn Post, and Candi Sary. And thank you to my family and amazing friends (you know who you are) I couldn't do this life without you.

PROLOGUE

I can never find the quiet. I know that someday this will end and I will have plenty of quiet time, but right now I can't imagine that being my reality. Someone always needs me.

Most days I just hope to survive until she falls asleep. I constantly ask God, the universe, whoever can hear my thoughts, to give me the strength to carry on. It's the mantra that plays in my head all day long until she falls asleep at night, and then I say, "Thank you, thank you, thank you" with a huge sigh of relief. I survived another day.

I always wonder how I find the strength to keep going. Everyone in my family and inner circle are shocked that I keep doing what I'm doing. Some have begged me to stop, find another way, or have her placed outside the home, for they fear she will eventually kill me. I refuse to listen to them or entertain their suggestions, because I know in my heart, being her caretaker won't last forever. I'm meant to be her caretaker for her entire life, and no one can stop me from doing otherwise.

I often wonder how I can love, more than life itself, the person who abuses me daily. Why do I crave her kisses, her bear hugs, and her contagious smiles, when I know she will suddenly lash out at me without any warning?

Loving Tiara

I would rather die taking care of her than give up on her. I am her mother, her voice, her strength, her advocate, and her biggest fan. I am also a wife and a mother to my two other beautiful girls. They all need me to be strong, so they can pretend our lives are "normal." Even when I feel like dying inside, I carry on, because that is who I am. This is the story of loving Tiara.

CHAPTER 1

Playing Grown-up

Like most major decisions in my life, the decision to have a second child was made on a whim. One December morning in 1997, my four-year-old daughter, Tabitha, walked into the bathroom while I was getting ready for work and asked, "Mom, am I ever going to have a sister or a brother?"

"Well, I don't know. I haven't really ever thought about it. Do you want a little brother or sister?" I asked.

"Yes, yes! I want a little sister to play with," Tabitha proclaimed with excitement.

"Hmm, let me talk to Dad and think about it, sweetie," I said.

This was a shocker. I was twenty-seven years old, had been married for five years, and was working as a legal secretary while attending law school at night. My plate was full, and having another child right then wasn't even a blip on my radar. I barely saw my husband, Lou, because we were both working full-time, trying to figure out how to make enough money so we could live in the community I grew up in, Newport Beach, California. Lou was working six days a week selling cars at Huntington Beach Jeep Eagle Hummer, and my mom was watching Tabitha when she wasn't at preschool, which was a considerable chunk of time. We were just starting to recover emotionally and financially from the trauma we endured during the first two years of our marriage, and having another child didn't seem like the wisest choice at the moment.

Lou and I had a storybook wedding, but the fairy tale had ended once we started our married life together. We both came from affluent families and assumed money was something we would always have. I had first spotted Lou standing next to his white convertible BMW, which was a few years newer than the white BMW I was driving at the time. Lou is six foot two, with dark curly hair; but he kept it short, so the curls weren't evident until he needed a trim. His small nose, full lips, and large hooded hazel eyes contrasted his broad shoulders, bulging biceps, and long legs, which served him well as a defensive tackle football player in high school. Because his ears stuck out too far and his fitted Levi's 501 jeans were out of style, his handsome features weren't overly intimidating.

We met during a Friday afternoon party in September of 1989, in front of the Sigma Alpha Epsilon (SAE) house, where he was a pledge. I lived next door in the Pi Beta Phi house, so when I wasn't home, on campus, or at the gym, I was usually hanging out at the SAE house. All my male friends, past boyfriends, and current boyfriend were SAEs, so it was easy for me to insert myself into the conversation he was having with several people. He noticed me right away and introduced himself.

I was tall and thin like my mom but had fair skin and gray-blue eyes like my dad. I had naturally blonde hair, which I wore long, and an hourglass figure, with a butt my mom and I deemed too big. My physical features gave my mom a sense of pride because she didn't consider herself pretty, despite always being dressed fabulously and put together from head to toe.

My parents gave me love, family vacations around the world, and new clothes and shoes every week. Often I came home from school to find a new outfit waiting for me on my bed. My mom didn't like me wearing the same outfit more than a few times. I needed to be the best dressed and prettiest girl in school, or she would be disappointed. I feared failing her by not being pretty enough. At eleven years old, I had quit the swim team, the year after I had won "most valuable swimmer," because my shoulders were becoming too broad. In elementary school, I didn't allow myself to run during recess or PE, after discovering my face turned beet red when I overexerted myself. I took diet pills at thirteen, when my body started changing during puberty, but my mom found them and forbade me from ever taking them again. Being overweight wasn't an option, so every day, my goal was to make it without food; but I always got too hungry and failed.

After being bullied by eighth graders because my clothes were too nice, during my first week of junior high, I knew something had to change.

My mom's advice was to "ignore them all; they are just jealous."

She had been giving me this advice my entire life, and it no longer felt right. After thinking about my predicament, I decided I would push aside my shy tendencies, which everyone interpreted as being stuck-up, and become the nicest person in the school. At twelve years old, I realized I wanted to be more than pretty; I wanted to be liked for my personality, not admired or hated for how I looked.

The next day I started using my smile to greet every person I encountered, and my life changed immediately. Being overly friendly and outgoing felt comfortable, like who I was meant to be. From that day on, I started on my quest to becoming the person I was meant to be, and I have never stopped striving to be the best possible human. Sophomore year in high school, a boy I was dating introduced me to Leo Buscaglia's books, and my world opened further. Leo's words in *Living, Loving and Learning* taught me I was worthy of love, even if I wasn't perfect. I didn't understand being perfect was impossible and only an attribute given to God, but at fifteen, my mind was expanding beyond what I had been taught at home or in school.

While talking to Lou for the first time, I learned he was from Northern California and a new pledge at twenty-two years old. He appeared to be shy or had difficulty making conversation—I wasn't sure which. I could feel the immediate attraction between us as we stood talking together, long after everyone else in the group had walked away. He later confessed that he thought I was so pretty, he was overcome with nerves and couldn't figure out what to say. An hour passed and then he said, "I'm so sorry, but I have to leave. I need to go pick up my mom at the airport, and I'm already late. She's visiting for the weekend."

"Oh my gosh, go. I don't want you to be late for your mom," I said.

He paused, took a breath, and then hesitantly said, "Come with me."

"To pick up your mom at the airport?" I questioned.

"Yes."

"I'm pretty sure your mom wouldn't appreciate that."

"She won't care, I promise. Come with me," Lou urged.

"Hmmm, I don't think it's a good idea. But you should hurry; you don't want to keep your mom waiting."

"She doesn't mind if I'm late. I'll leave in a minute."

"I'm going to go find Mara. It was great meeting you. Have a fun weekend with your mom. I'll see you around," I said as I walked away with my trademark big smile. I didn't see him for a week.

When I finally saw him again, I was waiting in line at the SAE house, where we were to get our pictures taken for the composite. I was with one of my best friends, Mara, when I spotted him a few spaces in line ahead of us. I quietly pointed him out to her, and then she thought it would be a good idea to say in her loudest voice, "Tiffani, this line is taking forever!"

Everyone in front of us turned around, including Lou. He saw me, and his face flushed into a beaming smile. He gave me a slight wave and then turned back around. I was expecting a little more than just a wave and a smile from someone who had invited me to pick up his mom from the airport, but whatever. I started doubting my assessment of him. He had seemed so sweet and sincere, but maybe he was your standard frat boy, and I had misinterpreted his shyness. I decided I needed to find out the truth about this guy.

The next week we were picking SAE little brothers, and I told Mara I was going to put Lou down as my pick. Each big sister put down her first three choices, and the pledges did the same. My good friend Grant was in charge of matching up the pairs. A few days after we had made our picks, I asked Grant if he assigned Lou as my little brother.

He looked at me a little nervously and said, "Umm, he didn't put you down as a choice, Tiff."

"Well, that doesn't matter, just give him to me anyways. He will be happy when he finds out it's me," I declared.

"Well, I can't do that. It's not fair, honey."

Grant was one of my very best male friends, and he grew up in the same town as Lou, so he felt an obligation to us both.

I sweetly smiled at Grant and said, "I promise he will love having me as his big sister. I will give him the best presents during reveal week. Please," I begged.

"This is what I'll do. I'll talk to Lou about it and see what he says when I mention your name."

"Okay, fine."

The next day, I went in search of Grant.

"Did you talk to him yet?" I asked.

"I did, and when I asked him if he wanted you as his big sister, he flat out said, 'No! I don't want Tiffani. She has a boyfriend.' I'm sorry Tiff, but I can't give him to you."

I was super annoyed and decided to play hardball with Grant.

"Grant, you have to give him to me. You owe me," I said threateningly. He didn't owe me anything; I just said that.

He looked at me and saw I wasn't going to back down. I could see him weighing who was more important to him. Lou, his friend from high school and a pledge in his fraternity or me, one of his best friends.

He sighed. "Fine, you win. I'll give him to you, but if he is mad, it's your fault."

"Thank you, Grant! You won't regret this, I promise." I hugged him and ran off to prepare for little brother Reveal Week.

The short version: Lou received the best gifts of any pledge during Reveal Week, and when I revealed my identity to him, he picked me up, swung me around, and planted a big kiss on my lips. The next day he called to thank me for all the gifts and invited me to dinner as a thank-you. I immediately broke up with his pledge brother, who I had only been dating for about six weeks, just in case the night turned into a date; I refused to be a cheater. We fell in love on that date. When I came home from our date, I told Mara: "Oh my gosh, BF, he is totally into me!"

"How do you know he is so into you?

"Because I could tell. It's obvious. He showed up with a bottle of champagne and took me to the beach."

"Well, I'm worried he is a player. I know you like him, but you need to take it slow."

"I'm not going to get hurt, don't worry!"

"You know I worry. I just don't want to see you sad when he breaks your heart."

"He won't! I'm leaving for Paris in four months, so it's not like anything can really happen. I'm just having fun for once and not overthinking it," I reassured her.

The landline started ringing and interrupted our conversation. I picked up the receiver and heard Lou's voice. "Tiffani?"

"Hi, it's me. You're calling already?"

"I just got home—I miss you already. I needed to call and hear your voice," Lou said.

"Really? You miss me?"

"I do."

"Hmmm, I had so much fun tonight. Thank you," I said swooningly as Mara stared at me.

"What are you doing tomorrow? I need to see you."

"I have class all morning, and then I need to study."

"I'll pick you up after class."

"Okay. I guess I can study later," I said, then asked, "Do you have class tomorrow?"

"I only have water ski class, and then I'm free for the day. What time should I pick you up?"

"Come get me at two p.m., that should work."

"I'm not sure I can wait until then—but I guess I have to. Sleep good," he said.

"Bye."

I hung up and started jumping up and down in excitement as I said to Mara, "I told you he was into me!"

"Fine, you're right, but I still don't trust him. You need to be careful!" she warned.

Lou and I started spending all our free time together but decided to keep our relationship a secret from everyone, except our best friends. We didn't want to hurt anyone's feelings by being together. Lou had a girlfriend who lived in Santa Barbara, but they had agreed to date other people while away at college. They had dated for years, and she wasn't worried about him falling in love with someone else; so he didn't want to tell her unless we had a future together. I had my own baggage with several SAE boys, and we knew everyone would think our relationship was another fling for us both. We didn't think it was a fling, but because I was leaving to study abroad in Paris the next semester, we didn't know what would happen.

After Christmas, I left for Paris, he stayed in San Diego, and we desperately missed each other. We didn't make any promises to each other, but we ended up talking on the phone so frequently, Lou's phone was disconnected at the end of the semester because he couldn't afford to pay the exorbitant bill. When the semester ended, Lou came with my parents to pick me up from the airport. A few days later, we drove up north together so I could finally meet his family, and he broke the news to me: he wouldn't be returning to school next semester. His dad was refusing to pay for school because he thought college was a waste. He wanted Lou back in Danville, working for the family business.

Despite being devastated, I returned to school and moved into a house on Baja Street with my four best friends, Mara, Laura, Beth, and Jen, and we dated long-distance for a year. At the end of the year, I moved up north for the summer to see if we would still get along while living under the same roof for two months. I was initially supposed to have my own room in his mom's house, but plans changed, and we ended up moving into an apartment with a roommate. My parents were livid we were living together for the summer and made it clear it better not ever happen again until we were married, or else.

We loved being together all the time, and I needed to plan my future, so I gave him an ultimatum one morning at the end of the summer, while drinking coffee in our underwear: "I'm going back to college and graduating in four months. We need to be engaged before I graduate because my parents won't tolerate us living together, and I'm not moving up north without a ring."

"You know I want to get engaged, but I don't have the money for a ring right now," he said.

"I can wait for a ring. I just want to have a plan in place, so I will know we are getting married after I graduate in December," I declared.

"Well, if you want to get engaged so bad, why don't you just ask me to marry you then," he challenged.

"Really? You want me to ask you?"

"Sure, why not?" he said.

"Fine!" I said as I bent down on one knee, with a pair of floral satin underwear as my only clothing. "Will you marry me?"

His eyes became the size of saucers as he looked at me and said: "Yes, I will marry you."

"So, it's official; we're engaged?" I asked.

"Yes, we are engaged," he said as he ran off to the bathroom and started dry heaving into the toilet.

I picked up the phone and called my mom. "Mom, we are engaged."

"Well, it's about time. Did you get a ring yet?" she asked.

"No, he doesn't have money for one yet, but we can set the date," I said.

"What month do you want to get married?" she asked.

"We thought February would be a good month. Next month is my twenty-second birthday, so I'll be married at twenty-two, just like Dad. It's perfect! We can plan the wedding during my last semester of college, and then I'll only have two months at home with you guys before I move up north with Lou. I'm so excited!"

"I'll call the church right now and call you back," Mom said.

The phone rang five minutes later.

"Okay, the church has February 15 or February 29, 1992. We need to lock in one of those dates because it's only six months away."

I yelled into the bathroom, "Lou, come here, we need to pick a date. Do you want to get married on February 15th or 29th?" I asked him.

"Well, February 29 is a leap year, so we'll only have an anniversary every four years, so I like that one." He laughed, "I'll only have to buy you a present every four years." He laughed again, thinking he was funny.

"I like that date too. February 15 is too close to Valentine's Day. I don't care if it's a leap year," I said as he returned to the bathroom.

"Okay, Mom, reserve the church for February 29. We can figure out the reception location when I come home next weekend to start planning," I said into the phone.

"Great, I'll bring the check down to the church today. Love you. This is going to be so much fun to plan. I've needed a big project! I better tell Dad to make more money," she said laughingly before hanging up the phone.

Lou disappeared for the rest of the day and kept avoiding my calls. I was so excited, and he seemed depressed. Lou finally came home later that night and told me why he was so sad. He had already started planning with my sister and Mara how he was going to ask me to marry him over Labor Day weekend before my birthday, and now he lost the chance.

"I'll only ever have one chance to ask you to marry me, and I fucked it up. I missed my chance, and it's my own fault. I dared you into asking me; I didn't realize you would actually do it," he said.

"I'm sorry, but you dared me. You want to marry me, right?"

"Yes! That's why I have been making a plan. I love you more than life itself; you know that."

"I thought so, but I got scared when you wouldn't talk to me today," I said.

"I'll start working on getting you the best ring ever, and I'll surprise you with that, so don't ask when you are getting your ring. It will be a surprise," he declared.

"Okay, deal. You know I want marquise- or emerald-cut diamond and not a round, right?" I said while smiling and laughing.

"I know what you want, Tiffani, now leave it alone."

"Fine. Don't get bossy with me, babe," I said teasingly.

Four months later, he surprised me with a two-and-a-half-carat marquise diamond on his twenty-fifth birthday, December 6, 1991. I was shocked the diamond was so huge since he barely had enough money for a plane ticket to visit me in San Diego, but I wasn't complaining. It was gorgeous!

"Lou, how much was this ring?"

"It's none of your business."

"I know, but you can't afford a ring like this. You don't have any money."

"I hate when you say I don't have any money."

"I'm sorry, but you are always worried about money, and now you bought me this huge diamond ring. It doesn't make sense."

"Do you like it?"

"Yes, I love it! It's absolutely gorgeous," I responded.

"Well, then leave it alone. Be happy you got the ring you wanted."

"You know I can't leave it alone. Just tell me how you paid for it, and I'll stop talking about it."

"Fine, I'll tell you the story if you promise to stop talking about it."

"I promise."

"I went to the Jewelry Mart in San Francisco with my dad, and he helped me pick this out for you. He said to buy the biggest diamond I could afford now, so I wouldn't have to upgrade it later. Your diamond looks like a three-carat, but it is only two and a half. It has a tiny flaw, but you can't see it. Because of the flaw, it wasn't as expensive."

"But how did you pay for it?"

"I'm getting to that part."

"Okay, I'm listening."

"Well, after we picked this one out for you, we negotiated a deal with the guy."

"And, you paid him with cash, a credit card, you financed it, what?"

"Be patient. I gave the jeweler two checks from the car wash and told him to hold the second one for a week."

"Please tell me the check isn't going to bounce."

"I'll make sure it doesn't bounce."

"This ring must have been almost ten thousand dollars. How can you afford that?"

"I'm not telling you how much it was, but it wasn't that much. You promised to stop talking about it if I told you how I paid for it."

"One last thing and I'll stop talking about it. You need to promise me my ring will be paid for. I can't walk around with this huge diamond and not own it. Promise."

"I promise I won't let that happen. Now stop. I love you, and I will make sure I get your ring paid for."

We were married two months after my graduation, in my childhood Catholic church, Our Lady of Mount Carmel, on the Balboa Peninsula in Newport Beach. Our reception was at the Surf & Sand Resort hotel, overlooking the ocean in Laguna Beach, and was an elaborate sorority/fraternity party with family. After the wedding, there was no honeymoon. We didn't have the money to pay for one, and his dad wasn't offering to pay. So the day after our wedding we drove a

Ryder truck filled with my stuff, from Newport Beach to Alamo, a small town in Northern California, located a few miles from Danville.

We didn't have money for a honeymoon, but we were moving into a six-thousand-square-foot home, situated on a hilltop with views of the town below. The house was too big, with dark wood floors, oak cabinets, and dark granite countertops, much like my childhood home. I liked everything white because I was never allowed to have it as a child. Mom deemed white furniture and cabinets cheap looking, and they accumulated dirt, so they weren't allowed in my childhood home. Lou and I didn't have enough furniture to fill the monstrosity, except a hand-me-down sectional couch and coffee table from his mom; a beautiful dining room set my parents gifted us for our wedding; and bedroom furniture. Lou loved watching TV, and luckily we were able to get a large television for the family room, on credit from Circuit City. I loved to read and didn't enjoy watching much TV, but Lou never read books or magazines, so a big TV was practically a necessity. Lou worked with his dad in their family business, and this house was part of a business deal. I had no idea how we would pay the rent on a house valued over a million dollars, but Lou told me not to worry; it would all work out.

I was so in love with Lou and excited to start our life together, I just ignored the warning bells ringing in my ears about our finances and Lou's job. I was raised to pay bills on time, never use credit cards unless it's an emergency, and save plenty of money. Lou's financial beliefs, learned from his dad, were the exact opposite of mine, which created friction. Lou's job was to run the family business, a car wash and gas station. The once-flourishing business, which used to consist of numerous gas stations and a car wash, was failing. After Lou's parents went through a nasty divorce that lasted for years, the family business did not provide enough money to support his dad and his new wife in their extravagant lifestyle, the employees, Lou's mom, and us. There wasn't enough money to go around, and before I totally realized the gravity of our situation, Lou and I thought it would be a great idea to get pregnant. We had been married for one month, and I didn't know what to do with all my free time. Lou didn't want me to get a job, so having a baby sounded like a great idea. Forget the fact that we didn't have health insurance and lived off our credit card—but hey, let's do it. I'm sure everyone reading this is cringing at our stupidity right about now. I'm embarrassed of myself as I write this, so I can only imagine what you are thinking.

I stopped taking my birth control pills and became pregnant the next month. We were into our third month of marriage, I was pregnant, and we only had one car because we sold mine to pay bills. Lou was gone all day chasing money to keep the business afloat while I sit at home bored out of my mind, with morning sickness. It was an El Niño winter, which means it never stops raining, so the car wash was continuously closed. We couldn't pay the rent on the ridiculously large home, and after Lou gave the owners his coveted gold Rolex as payment for several months of past-due rent, we moved to a more reasonable home in San Ramon, two towns away from Alamo. I was happy about the move and liked our new home on the man-made lake overlooking the golf course. I was hoping we would be able to afford the rent. Of course, this house was also part of a business deal. Lou had horrible credit, which was the norm in his family because everyone overextended themselves on credit cards and always paid them late, if at all. My credit rating was in the process of being destroyed as well, so we lived at the mercy of business deals for our housing options.

We became so poor that I worried about buying food. I was always starving and often ate at McDonald's, which wasn't healthy for my unborn child, but it was all I could afford. One day I went to the grocery store and had to leave my overflowing cart at the check stand because they wouldn't accept my check or any of my credit cards. I held back the tears and tried to hold my head up as I walked out of Safeway without any food. That was the final straw for me. The next day, I made Lou drive me to the mall, and I walked into the maternity store and asked for a job, despite being seven months pregnant. My aunt owned a very successful women's boutique in Newport, and I had worked for her after school and during the summers, so I had lots of retail experience and knew I could get a job. The manager offered me the job on the spot, and I started right away. Lou was not happy I took a job, but after repeatedly begging him, he refused to leave his family business and get a real job, so I didn't feel like I had a choice. He insisted things would get better.

Our credit cards were maxed out, and my once-perfect credit was destroyed because they used my credit to buy his dad a car, which was repossessed several times. We had fallen behind on our payments to the doctor, our rent was late, and the only car we had left was on the repossession list. My life was pathetic. Lou would drive me to and from work and do the vacuuming for me when I had to close the store at night. He felt guilty that I was lugging clothes for women who weren't as pregnant as me, but he refused to get a real job with a paycheck. The stress was starting to form a severe wedge in our relationship. We were always fighting about money—or the lack of money—but Lou refused to make a change. He didn't graduate college and had been told by his father his entire life, "Only losers have jobs and work for other people." Have you ever heard anything so crazy?

His dad was the original entrepreneurial, white-collar criminal. The weird thing was his dad was always offering positive, inspirational advice to everyone, was very caring, and genuinely believed he wasn't doing anything wrong. He had a way of talking people into using their credit to purchase cars, houses, businesses, and lines of credit for him and then never repaid the loans, even though he honestly acted as if he had every intention of always repaying them. He eventually went to prison for his business dealings, where he passed away from a heart attack when Lou was forty-eight years old. When I finally realized his sweet dad was an actual criminal, I knew I didn't want that life for my family. We needed to make some serious changes. It was during this time that I had a vision that changed my life.

Tabitha was six months old, and we were driving home from the car wash in an old BMW given to my dad by a drug dealer, as payment for my dad's criminal-defense attorney fee. It didn't have air conditioning, it was ninety degrees outside, and my sweet baby was sweating in her car seat. Her blonde, curly Shirley Temple hair was stuck to her overheated forehead and red cheeks. A blinding ray of light suddenly shot through the windshield, and I heard a voice say everything I had been thinking for months:

"This is not how your life was meant to be, Tiffani. People hate you at the bank, your credit cards are maxed out, you are fearful the car will be repossessed, you haven't paid your rent, and everyone thinks you are a scumbag because your payments are always late. Your perfect credit score is ruined, you don't have a reliable car, and your life is a mess at twenty-three. You need to be a good role model for Tabitha, and you aren't doing that right now. You need to change your life before it's too late."

It seemed as if God had spoken directly to me, and I heard him. I suddenly felt different and knew I had just received the strength I needed to change my life. The rest of the drive home, I formulated my plan. As I have already mentioned, I make major life decisions on a whim, and I wasn't kidding. As soon as I got into the house, I called my mom. We spoke every day, and I knew both of my parents were worried about what had become of my life. As soon as she picked up the phone, I asked her: "Will you babysit Tabitha if I move home and get a job?"

Without a moment's hesitation, she said, "Of course, I would love nothing better."

Mom was only forty-three years old and had always wanted a third child. Sarah, my younger sister by four years, was a freshman at the junior college near our house and had been living with Lou and me but had recently moved out to her own apartment. Even though she was like my first child and Lou's sister, the constant calls from creditors and fights about money caused her too much anxiety, so she needed to find her own place. From the moment Sarah was born, I had treated her like my baby, even though I was only four at the time. As she grew up, I brushed her hair each morning, helped her get dressed for school, and checked on her at recess when we were in elementary school. We slept in my double bed together each night until I was in junior high, when I decided I needed my own space, so Sarah started sleeping in her room for the first time since leaving her crib. She was devastated when Lou and I had moved away, so we invited her to come live with us after her high school graduation.

Because my sister was away at school and my mom didn't work, except for one day a week in her sister's store, she had plenty of free time on her hands and now could spend all of that time with Tabitha. She then asked, "Is Lou moving home with you?"

"I don't know. I haven't told him I'm leaving. I'll let you know after I talk to him tonight." I hung up and immediately started making a list of what needed to be done.

When Lou came home from work, I told him about the voice and the vision I had experienced earlier that day. Then I said, "I am leaving this weekend, and you are welcome to join us, but I can't do this life anymore. I'm done with all this craziness; I am moving back to Newport. I need to be the person I was meant to be. I want to be a good person, a role model to our daughter, a person who pays her bills."

Lou looked devastated but immediately said, "I am coming with you. I would never let you leave without me. You and Tabitha are my life."

My parents arrived that weekend, helped us pack up the U-Haul they had rented, and off we went to start our lives over. Lou's dad was furious with him for abandoning his family, but his mom was thrilled I was getting Lou out of the family business. I immediately got a job working as a secretary to the personal injury attorney who shared office space with my dad. I later started writing motions and filling in for my dad's secretary until she quit, and then I worked for them both. Lou also got a job right away, selling Jeeps, and was successful right from the start. He was a born salesperson, and the customers loved him.

We moved in with my parents initially, but after three weeks, we had saved enough money to get an apartment in Westside Costa Mesa. It wasn't the prettiest area and not a place I would have ever seen myself living, but it was our own. Westside Costa Mesa was considered dangerous and not a place someone from Newport would ever consider living, but it seemed safe enough to us. Most people who grow up in Newport either love it and never leave, or they can't wait to get out because they hate the pressure of living in such a superficial community. The beautiful beaches and gorgeous bay, lined with multimillion-dollar homes, are irresistible to even the biggest critics but always trying to keep up with the Joneses in a community filled with trust-fund babies can be daunting. You never quite realize how much pressure it is to live in Newport until you move away and see how the rest of the world lives.

One day while helping my boss prepare for trial, I became frustrated because I did not think he was taking the right approach to the case. I walked out of his office thinking, "Why is he preparing his opening statement like that? Hmm, maybe I should be a lawyer, instead of working for one." You can guess how the rest went. I immediately called Western State University law school in Fullerton, asked about the qualifications to get in, and found out that since I had graduated with over a 3.0 from college, I could be accepted immediately for the following semester, which started in two weeks.

I enrolled in the part-time law school program, which included taking one morning class and two evening classes while continuing to work full-time. It was a massive juggle for all of us, and I'm going to tell you Lou wasn't thrilled with my choice. But like always, he gave me his full support. He truly is one of the kindest human beings I have ever known. When I told Lou my plan to become a lawyer, he grimaced, as if sucking on a lemon. He wasn't a fan of lawyers, but he didn't let that stop him from supporting me. So, for the next four years, we worked and raised Tabitha, with the constant help of my family, as I studied to become a lawyer in my free time.

It was at this point in our lives, when I was starting my final semester of law school, that Tabitha asked me about having another baby.

Wow, I had been so busy trying to survive, I never once thought about having another baby. I barely had time to sleep, study, or spend time with my only child, why would I want to add more chaos to my life? "But, on second thought, it would be nice for Tabitha to have a sibling, and I am getting older," I thought to myself. Not that twenty-seven is old, but according to our biological clocks, I had already passed my prime baby-making age, and my eggs weren't getting any younger.

I thought about having a baby the whole next day, and by the end of the day, my decision was made.

"Let's do it! Let's have another baby and give Tabitha a brother or sister," I told Lou that night after work. He was thrilled! I stopped taking my birth control pills and was planning on waiting three months to get pregnant so that they would be out of my system, but I didn't last that long. I was pregnant by the second month, despite trying to be careful.

I finished my last semester of law school while working and enduring severe morning sickness. Luckily, my professors were extremely understanding of my morning sickness—or they didn't want me vomiting during their lectures—so they let me miss more classes than allowed. I graduated and immediately started studying for the bar exam. It was a tough time in our lives because I couldn't be the mother, the wife, the daughter, the granddaughter, or the student I needed to be. I felt like I was mediocre at everything. On top of it all, Popie, my mom's mother, and one of my favorite people in the world, had a serious health problem.

On the first day of the bar exam review, I remember rushing to the pay phone before the review started to find out if she had gotten the results from her doctor yet. She had, and it was the worst possible news: pancreatic cancer. We buried her six months later on the exact day I found out I hadn't passed the bar exam. I missed it by ten points, but looking back, I was never meant to be a lawyer. God had other plans for me. Two weeks before Popie passed away, Tiara made her entrance into this world on October 27, 1998. I had a textbook delivery, without any complications, and Tiara appeared to be a perfectly healthy baby. I took her to see Popie immediately after she was born. Popie was in the end stages of cancer, and when I placed Tiara in her arms as she lay in her hospital bed at home, she kept saying, "Who is the angel with the dark hair?"

At the time, I thought Popie was hallucinating from the morphine, but in retrospect, I believe Popie knew Tiara was an angel and different from other babies. Popie was very special, and people often considered her an angel because she never said a bad word about anyone. She was always kind, patient, and just plain lovely, despite enduring so many struggles throughout her life. I came to believe that as one angel was departing the universe, another had arrived to take her place and would continue to teach us all lessons.

After I found out I hadn't passed the bar, everyone started urging me to retake it, but there was a problem. I had promised Tabitha that I would never retake the bar exam when she was a child if I didn't pass the first time. It was a big promise, but I meant it!

Why would I make a promise of this magnitude to a six-year-old child when 50 percent of California bar applicants fail the first time? To find the time to study for the bar, I had to enroll Tabitha in multiple summer day camps. One such camp was a theatre, art, and singing program. Each week was a different theme, and we had signed Tabitha up for the *Phantom of the Opera* week. All week the kids worked on props, practiced a song from the musical, and acted out a scene. On the last day of camp, there was a performance during the last hour. Tabitha had participated in this camp before, so I knew what to expect. All week she was stressing out about her song because she chose to do a solo. We kept practicing at home after camp, but she was very nervous about singing her favorite *Phantom of the Opera* song. I dropped her off at camp on Friday morning and said I would be back at three o'clock for the show. I then rushed off to the library to study and returned to the camp at two forty-five and saw my dad waiting in the parking lot. Both of my parents and Lou were coming to watch her performance. We started talking about how weird it was that the parking lot was already full. As we waited for Lou and Mom to arrive, it was oddly quiet. All of a sudden, people were filing out of the camp front doors. What was going on? Why was everyone leaving instead of going in? Then I saw Tabitha emerge from the door with tears in her eyes.

"You missed my performance. I was looking for you, and no one was there. I was so scared, Mom, and you weren't there!"

"I'm so sorry, honey! I'm not sure what happened. I thought it started in fifteen minutes." I immediately turned into a hormonal sobbing mess and started begging her forgiveness. Then I got mad. I went in search of the director and demanded to know why they had changed the time of the performance without notice. She explained there was notice. She had written it on the huge sandwich-board sign that was at the entrance of the studio, two days before. I walked to the sign and saw the big words, alerting all parents to the change in schedule. In my haste that morning, I had failed to notice the sign indicating the performance had been moved up to two o'clock. I was the only loser parent who had screwed up the time. And why? Because I was so busy being pregnant and studying for the bar exam that I didn't see it. After spending the rest of the day in a state of self-loathing, I came up with a plan. As I tucked Tabitha into bed that night, I said something like:

"Sweetie, I know how hard me going to law school has been on you. It was my choice to work full-time and go to school at night, and you didn't have any say in the matter. I want to be a lawyer, but more than anything, I want to be the best mom in the world. If I don't pass the bar exam, I won't retake it, while you are a child. Your sister will be born by the time I receive the results, and I am going to figure out how to be a better mom."

And now what? I had a law degree, but wasn't a lawyer and had two girls to raise. What was I going to do? Go back on my promise to Tabitha or make a new plan? Lou and I decided to create a new plan.

Lou had succeeded as a car salesman and was close to reaching his goal of becoming a manager. His income had increased as mine had decreased because I couldn't work as a law assistant and study for the bar exam. At this point, I was working part-time from home, writing motions for my dad, and we were still able to pay our bills. How could I break my promise to Tabitha and then expect my mom to watch both my children after her mother had just passed away? It didn't seem fair to anyone, so I decided that was the end of my law career. It might seem insane to throw it all away after spending the last four years studying, but no education is ever a waste.

After thinking about my decision for a few days, I got up the nerve to talk to my dad.

"Dad, I need to talk to you."

"Okay, I hope I'm not in trouble for something?" he responded jokingly.

"Of course not. I'm not going to retake the bar exam."

"Why? Are you worried you won't pass again?"

"No, I've just realized, I don't want to be a lawyer, I want to be a mom." I said.

"Well, if you don't want to be a lawyer anymore, then don't take it. It's your life and I want you to be happy," he said.

"I don't think I could defend your clients. I have gotten so conservative, I know I wouldn't feel good doing your job. Plus, to be a great lawyer, it's a full-time job. I can't work part-time and be an amazing lawyer like you."

"I'm not that great," he said.

"Yes, you are! Everyone knows you are a great lawyer, and all your clients love you.

The whole reason I went to law school was so Lou and I would have enough money to survive. Lou is making good money selling cars, and mom can't watch my kids forever, so it feels like I need to make a decision," I declared.

"I'm a little disappointed, but I will support you whatever you decide. Of course, I wish your future was working with me and someday taking over my business, but you should do what is best for your family. I love you no matter what you do, as long as you continue to write my motions," he said laughingly.

"Of course I'll still write your motions."

"I'm just kidding, but not really. I still need you to help with my motions," he said.

"Don't worry; I can still write them from home. Thanks for understanding. I love you."

The more time I spent away from home, working and studying, I realized my priorities had gone astray. Society was always telling women to be smart, have a career, your children will be proud of your accomplishments, but in reality, it didn't feel like that. I felt like I had been a crappy mom to Tabitha for the past four years, and it was time for a change. I knew in my gut my girls would be happier having me at home, hugging them and taking them to the park, rather than bragging to their friends that their mommy was a lawyer. Kids don't care what we do for a living; they just want to feel loved and secure. I can thank Dr. Laura Schlessinger for this opinion. I used to listen to her on talk radio while driving, and the more I heard, the more I realized I had made some significant errors in judgment. So, with a law degree under my belt and $45,000 in student loan debt, I decided to become a full-time stay-at-home mom to Tabitha and Tiara. Are you wondering how Louie took the news? As in his typical fashion, he supported my decision and was thrilled I would be staying home to raise our kids. Despite the debt, my law school education would prove to benefit us all in ways we had yet to discover.

Tabitha (5 ¾) and Tiara (2 weeks)

CHAPTER 2

Finding Answers

At Tiara's one-month checkup, her pediatrician, Dr. Krumins, noticed a large white patch on her neckline. He thought it was a typical ash-leaf birthmark but said we should keep our eye on it. Sometimes these types of birthmarks are indicators of something more. He didn't tell me what "something more" was, nor did he show much concern, so I wasn't concerned. She was on target for her milestones but, considering that all one-month-old babies do is eat, sleep, and poop, she was doing a great job. At her three-month checkup, she was starting to fall behind developmentally. She didn't follow or track with her eyes, she wasn't moving like a regular three-month-old, and her neck control wasn't great. We weren't super worried, since all kids progress at their own rate, but we were now on alert. When she was four months old, it became apparent Tiara was not like other babies. There was definitely something medically wrong with her.

Tiara would cry endlessly, but not like other babies. She didn't seem to have gas; she didn't appear colicky. It was a different cry, and I could feel it. None of the usual tricks worked, like driving her in the car, putting the car seat on the dryer with it on, loud music, lullabies, rocking her, etc. One day I discovered she would stop crying if I held her tightly in my arms, against my chest, and jumped up and down while singing some weird tribal mantra I made up. It was a great workout, and I looked like a freak, but she was happy and would stop crying. But relatives who witnessed my jumping and singing dance were shocked. It seemed as if I had gone insane, but I would have done anything to stop the constant crying. I was grateful that my tribal dance, as we labeled it, stopped her crying, but I worried the jumping would hurt her, or rather shake her brain. When I was an intern in the public defender's office, I spent a whole semester working on a "shaken baby syndrome" case. The child had died from head trauma as a result of being shaken by either the babysitter or the parents. I would replay the facts of the case in my mind every day while I jumped up and down with her in my arms, but instinctively I knew I wouldn't hurt her, and she needed the jarring movements to feel calm. I later learned in one of her therapy sessions that children with neurological issues crave that type of stimulation, such as jumping on a trampoline, as it calms their brains. Now that the family was getting a reprieve from the chronic crying, it was perfect timing, because we had just bought our first house and were going to be moving.

Lou and I had worked hard to clean up our credit and were able to qualify for a loan. Popie had left me a small inheritance, which we used for the down payment. Tabitha was in first grade at Carden Hall, Tiara was five months old, and we were moving into our new home, so for the first time in a long while we were feeling hopeful for our future.

It was during the moving process that Tiara started having what appeared to be stomach problems. She would repeatedly crunch her body forward and simultaneously scream out in pain, over and over again. Each incident would last approximately five to ten minutes and happened many times throughout the day. I immediately took her to the doctor, and she was seen by Dr. Conrad, who thought Tiara could be having problems digesting my breast milk. I had some issues with my milk when I was breastfeeding Tabitha, so we agreed I would start supplementing Tiara's diet with formula. We put her on soy formula because we had lots of allergies in our family, so soy seemed the safest option. Much to my dismay, the screaming and pain episodes only worsened. We then tried a regular formula, and when that didn't work, we switched her to Nutramigen. It smelled so disgusting and had a gray tinge, I felt guilty feeding it to her, but I would have done anything to help her. The tribal dance was no longer working, and worst of all, she looked like she was in pain and suffering. It was devastating to watch her repeatedly lunge forward in pain, and I was in a constant state of panic. I also had Tabitha to care for and a new house to put together.

Tiara continued to suffer daily from these episodes. She then developed a series of ear infections, which only confounded the puzzle of trying to figure out what was going on. Dr. Conrad considered the possibility that she was constipated. After all the changes in formula, her bowel movements were no longer regular. She suggested I stick my finger up Tiara's rectum when she was crying, to see if she had a hard stool stuck. As you can imagine, it was terrifying the first time I had to do it, but like all things, with practice, I became an expert at probing her rectum. After a few days of torturing Tiara with my exams, we determined constipation was not the problem. I was still panicky because I didn't know how to help my baby. I took her to the doctor's office every other day because I knew something was very wrong, but I didn't know what it was. And neither did they. I felt so helpless.

At this point, her pediatrician asked me, "Do you think she could be having seizures?"

"I don't know. She isn't shaking or anything," I said.

"I'm wondering if I should write a referral for an EEG, instead of focusing on her stomach," she declared.

"Why don't you write a referral for the gastroenterologist consult and the EEG. I can take her for both."

"Let's do that to be safe," said Dr. Conrad.

A few days later, we attended a dinner party at friend's house. I refused to leave Tiara with anyone, so we brought her along. Soon after we arrived, she started having a screaming episode. One of our friends at the party was a nurse who worked in the recovery ward at Hoag Hospital. I asked her, "Is this a seizure?"

"No, that's not a seizure, something is wrong with her stomach," she said.

I called Dr. Conrad the next morning and confirmed we should continue exploring the problem as a stomach issue because they were not seizures. She expedited the authorization for the gastroenterologist, and we saw a specialist within the week.

At this point, Tiara slept for most of the day. When she sat in her highchair or bouncy seat, she would stare at nothing. She was listless and dazed, as if she wasn't truly present. She was fading away from me, and I didn't know why. The gastroenterologist prescribed two different medicines, which only made her worse. He also ordered an emergency upper GI. I got her an appointment at the Hoag Center in Huntington Beach because they had a cancellation for the next day. I was afraid she wouldn't be able to drink the barium, and then they wouldn't be able to perform the test. Surprisingly, she was able to drink enough of the barium to get the X-rays. As I tried to hold her still for the X-rays, I kept laser eyes on the technician for any change in his demeanor that might indicate he had found something wrong.

He finished the test and said, "There is nothing wrong with her intestinal tract. You will have to wait for the report from the doctor, but I can tell you he won't find anything."

I was stunned. How could there be nothing wrong with her stomach? This was a mistake; somebody needs to help us; something was wrong with my baby! Why can't anyone figure it out?

A few days later, Lou came up with a brilliant plan. "Let's video an episode so we can show it to the doctor."

I don't know why nobody had thought of it sooner, but it was 1999, and we didn't have video or cameras on our cell phones. We charged the video camera, and the very next morning, she had an episode while driving to Tabitha's school for a performance. We pulled the car over and started recording.

After Tabitha's performance, Lou left for work and said, "Take her straight to see Dr. Conrad and show her the video."

Usually, I tell Lou what to do, not the other way around, but he knew I was stalling. "But, I don't have an appointment," I said.

"That's never stopped you before, Tiffani. Go there now."

I knew in my heart something terrible was about to happen, and there was nothing I could do to stop it. At the pediatrician's office, I told the receptionist I needed to see Dr. Conrad right away. She saw me nearly every day, so without hesitation or mentioning the fact that we had no appointment, she showed us to a room. I had the video ready to show Dr. Conrad when she walked in.

She watched the video intently and with pursed lips, looked at me and said, "I need to show this to Dr. Krumins. I'll be right back."

A few minutes later, she returned with Dr. Krumins and two other pediatricians. All four of them watched Tiara intently as she sat, staring out into space from her car seat. They looked back and forth from one another as if secretly communicating, and then Dr. Conrad said, "Based on this video and how she looks, we want you to drive her straight to Children's Hospital of Orange County [CHOC]. I am concerned with her pallor and how dazed she looks; she has changed in the last few days and not for the better. I think she is having seizures. I will call ahead and let them know you are on your way."

"Seizures?"

"Yes, I'm sorry. She needs to be admitted right away."

I called my mom and asked her to pick up Tabitha from school and then called Lou. We agreed he would meet us at CHOC since it was close to his work. He was working as a Mercedes-Benz salesperson at the House of Imports in Anaheim. It was Friday of Memorial Day weekend, and for once, Lou was going to have the whole weekend off. But now we were on our way to the hospital. As soon as we got to the hospital, she was admitted and taken to a room—they didn't even send us through the emergency room. Tiara had an episode while the nurse was doing her intake assessment. Within minutes an EEG tech rolled in his equipment and started putting the electrodes on Tiara's head.

Once he turned on the machine and started recording her brain waves, I immediately saw his face change.

"Is something wrong?" I asked.

"You will have to speak with the doctor. I am not allowed to give you results; I am only a technician," he said.

The test lasted about ten minutes, but soon after he left, the on-call neurologist, Dr. Stein, came into the room. He explained that Tiara was having infantile spasm seizures, which are extremely rare and the worst possible type of epilepsy. They were causing Tiara to have abnormal brain activity every second of every day. He then examined her with a special light, looking for depigmented lesions on her skin. He found more than six, the largest one being the one on her neck that Dr. Krumins had seen at her one-month checkup. He told us he suspected what was causing the seizures but needed to confirm his suspicions with a CT scan of the brain and an ultrasound of the heart. If you have ever been in a hospital, you know that their procedures can take forever unless it is an emergency. Clearly, everyone was as concerned as Lou and I, because all the tests were completed within a few hours.

That afternoon Dr. Stein gave us the diagnosis: "Tiara has tuberous sclerosis."

I can't remember much of what Dr. Stein told us that Friday afternoon in May of 1999 because I fell into a state of shock. He said something about our daughter having brain tumors, abnormal brain function, a genetic condition, tumors in her heart, epilepsy, possible tumors in other organs—and no cure . . . .

He followed that news with something to the effect of: "I am sure you have a lot of questions, so I have arranged a meeting for tomorrow morning with the team. We can develop a care plan at that time and answer all your questions. But most importantly, we must start her on phenobarbital right away. Most likely, it will not stop the seizures, but it is our best option right now. The medicine that works best at stopping infantile spasms in children with tuberous sclerosis is called vigabatrin, but it is not FDA approved, so I cannot get it for Tiara. We will talk tomorrow about enrolling her in a drug study at UCLA so she can get the vigabatrin. Stopping the seizures is extremely critical. A correlation exists between how seriously delayed and how much brain damage she will suffer in relation to when the infantile spasms become controlled."

After Dr. Stein left, Lou and I sat staring at each other. What are you supposed to do when someone tells you your baby is sick, and everything you knew in life to be true, no longer was?

My child's life was in jeopardy, and there was no cure. If that same scenario happened today, I would jump on the Internet on my phone and start researching, but twenty years ago, that was not an option. Smartphones didn't exist, and the hospital didn't have laptops to loan you, so there was no way to research her condition without leaving her bedside. As I was pondering how to get more information, Lou left to call our family and tell them the devastating news.

I found a nurse and asked, "Do you know what tuberous sclerosis is?"

Her response is what I most remember about those conversations that afternoon: "Well, I know it is very rare, and I have never actually seen a patient with tuberous sclerosis, but I just looked it up in a medical book because I was curious. It says that your child will probably be severely mentally disabled, she may never walk or talk, and her life expectancy is three years."

"What?"

I shook my head in despair, trying to process what the nurse had just told me. Lou came back into the room, and I told him what the nurse said.

I began to sob and shake. I wailed to Lou, "Everything is different now—our life is not the same. Tiara is going to die."

Lou just kept saying, "Everything is going to be okay, honey. She will be okay. We will figure it out."

Lou and I process reality at different speeds, so it hadn't quite sunk in for him. But he knew he had to take care of me right then. Through the years, we have learned to take turns "losing it." If one of us is crying, the other one is required to be strong for that moment, and then we trade. I think I cried for about an hour.

Then I stopped. I had to make a plan—how was I going to survive this new reality?

I made a promise to God right then:

Just keep her alive. I don't care if she can't walk or talk and is mentally delayed. Please, just keep her alive, and I will do everything I can to care for her. I need her to live. I will never forget that moment. I can see myself sitting in that blue vinyl chair next to Tiara's metal crib as she quietly slept. I never forgot the promise I made to God in that moment.

That promise paved the way for how I would deal with Tiara's illness.

First, keep her alive; second, give her a life of love; and third, hope she can be happy. Those were my goals, and I never wavered from them. I vaguely remember the next two days at the hospital. Our family came to visit, cry, and try to figure out what to say to us. It is an awkward moment when you find out your grandchild or niece has a rare condition and is continually having seizures. Do you say that it's going to be okay? Well, it's not, so why pretend? There are no words to make it better. Everyone was so confused and shocked; it didn't feel like my life.

Saturday morning, we met with Dr. Stein and Tiara's new team of doctors at a large conference table—a group that hadn't existed the day before. Dr. Stein went through Tiara's condition more thoroughly. He explained to us that tuberous sclerosis complex (TSC) was a rare genetic disorder, which causes benign tumors to form in the major organs of the body. Tiara had tumors in her brain and heart and could eventually develop them in her eyes, kidneys, thyroid, and even her lungs. TSC was genetic, but about 60 percent of the time, started spontaneously. Researchers didn't know what caused it to begin in a child spontaneously. (Current research and information on TSC can be found at tsalliance.org.) His biggest concern for Tiara was the tumors in her brain because they were causing the seizures. He told us that patients with TSC have three different possible types of brain tumors: (1) cortical tubers, which are small areas in the outer layer of the brain that do not develop normally and usually disrupt the typical wiring of the brain—like a birth defect on the brain—and are the tumors generally responsible for the seizures; (2) subependymal nodules, which typically develop near the walls of the cerebral ventricles; and (3) subependymal giant cell astrocytomas (SEGA), which, if large enough, can block fluid in the brain.

Dr. Stein told us that, unfortunately, Tiara had all three types. He was concerned about the SEGA, so she needed to have a consult with neurosurgery right away. I wanted to know how many tumors she had in her brain. I needed a number, for some reason, but he wouldn't give me one. He said the number wasn't significant. He said she had more than twelve malformations in her brain, but what was important was how they affected Tiara.

The cardiologist then told us Tiara had three rhabdomyomas in her heart, but he did not believe they were causing any problems with heart function. Usually, the tumors in the heart shrink as the child gets older, so we would have to monitor them yearly. Finally, a speck of good news: Dr. Stein explained that there was a spectrum for tuberous sclerosis. Some people go through life with TSC and never know it until they have brain or kidney imaging for another condition, and it is discovered. They can be doctors, lawyers, and teachers. At the other end of the spectrum, they are severely developmentally delayed, autistic, and have intractable epilepsy. He did not know Tiara's future, but the fact that she was having infantile spasms was grave and suggested she would most likely fall at the latter end of the spectrum. He told us about the drug study at UCLA for vigabatrin and urged us to take Tiara there as soon as she was released from CHOC. He explained that the reason vigabatrin was not FDA approved was because loss of peripheral vision was a known side effect.

So our precious daughter had just been diagnosed with a rare disorder, tumors in her brain, tumors in her heart, a rare type of seizure, and the only drug known to help can cause blindness. That was a lot to process, but I knew she had to get in the drug study. It felt like her only hope of stopping the infantile spasms and, as Dr. Stein explained, if we didn't get the infantile spasms under control, her future was bleak.

At nine months, Tiara was sleeping away most of her days. She could no longer sit up on her own, which she had previously learned to do at six months. She was regressing developmentally, and it was devastating to watch. Tiara was discharged from the hospital on Monday, and we had an appointment at UCLA the following week, which was the soonest possible. The criteria for admission to the study was stringent and required me to complete buckets of paperwork. In addition to UCLA reviewing all her current medical records, they needed to perform their own exam and EEG on Tiara, which took time to coordinate and schedule. Once all that was completed, she had to be approved by the director of the study, Dr. Donald Shields.

Six weeks after being diagnosed with infantile spasms, Tiara was accepted into the research study at UCLA. She took her first dose of vigabatrin on July 19, 1999, and the infantile spasms stopped! They literally stopped—a real miracle. Within days, it was as if Tiara had awoken from a deep slumber and joined the world again. Now she was sitting up, smiling, and trying to crawl. My baby was back, and we were all so relieved. Maybe she would beat the odds. Perhaps she would catch up developmentally and be like any other child. I had no idea, but I was secretly starting to hope for her future. After the diagnosis of TSC, CHOC had referred her to the Regional Center of Orange County, where Tiara was immediately granted status as a consumer, which was a good thing. It meant the county was going to provide her with early intervention services such as speech, occupational, and physical therapy to help her catch up developmentally. She was referred to a place called SKY Pediatrics, where she started to receive speech, occupational, and physical therapy. Our life was suddenly a sea of appointments.

I drove her to UCLA once a week for the first month of the study, then twice a month, and then once a month. In addition to the vigabatrin study, UCLA requested to also have Tiara participate in a related behavior/developmental psychological study. Of course, since they were committed to saving my child's life, I agreed to put her in the additional study, but it was a lot! Before or after each neurology appointment, I had to take Tiara to the other study, and it made for a very long day.

Over the months before Tiara's first birthday, I started to understand how unpredictable our lives would become while raising a child with TSC. One moment I could be pushing her in a swing at the park, and the next hour, we could be headed to the hospital.

CHAPTER 3

Learning the Signs

Several weeks after being on vigabatrin and numerous visits to UCLA Medical Center, Tiara started to feel unwell again. Signs of a typical virus displayed as a fever, runny nose, or congestion could also be construed as a bigger problem, or so thought everyone on her team. Her cardiologist told us she could start having heart problems at any time, so we had to be vigilant about any changes in her health. During this time, her pediatrician was on hyperdrive, as was her cardiologist, neurologist, and myself. Each little thing was deemed a possible life-threatening situation for Tiara.

One Saturday in August, Tiara was highly agitated and crying incessantly. The pediatrician office was closed, so I took her to a walk-in clinic. I gave the doctor Tiara's medical history, and he refused to treat her. He'd never seen a patient with tuberous sclerosis and told me to take her to Hoag Hospital. Once there, the waiting room was overflowing with sick people, and I knew I shouldn't wait with her for hours in that germ-infested place. I called my nurse friend for help, and luckily she got us in the back door. The Hoag ER physician came in and introduced himself. I explained Tiara's history, and he immediately got an attitude with me and became super defensive. I was puzzled by his behavior but kept talking and requested he test Tiara's heart. He finally admitted he had never seen or treated a patient with tuberous sclerosis and wasn't sure what tests to perform. His lack of experience with tuberous sclerosis explained his initial superior attitude. He hated not knowing something but redeemed himself with me by offering to perform any test I wanted on Tiara.

"I think if you do an echocardiogram, that's all we need. If the results come back normal, I think Tiara is fine," I said.

"Sounds good, I'll order it right now," he said.

The echocardiogram results confirmed her heart was working correctly, and I asked to have Tiara discharged. He complied, and I took Tiara home, even though I still didn't understand why she was crying. Maybe she was getting a tooth or had a stomachache. Only Tiara knew what was wrong, and she couldn't tell me.

My fear and panic continued to follow each virus, fever, and infection until I learned how to decipher Tiara's symptoms better than any doctor.

I was required to chart any seizures or changes in her health for the vigabatrin study, and once I started charting, I never stopped. Tracking her development, her health, her progress, her appointments, her doctors, and her therapies became my life, along with caring for Tabitha and being a wife to Lou.

Weeks after our quick ER visit to Hoag, Tiara appeared to have picked up another virus, as she was running a fever of 101 degrees. Suddenly her whole body became mottled and purple. I rushed her to the pediatrician, and by the time we arrived, her temperature had risen to 105. The fever had escalated so quickly that her body couldn't adjust, but we didn't know that then. All we knew was that she had a temperature of 105 and her skin was mottled, which could be a sign that her heart wasn't working correctly. We also did not know that Tiara was unable to sweat and release body heat. Years later we learned her inability to sweat was caused by one of her brain tumors. Tiara's body couldn't regulate its internal temperature, so her skin would turn purple and become mottled. Because we didn't know any of this information at the time, her pediatrician told us to drive straight to CHOC.

At CHOC, they assumed the worst, believing she might have an infection in her heart. After a three-day visit filled with numerous tests, specialists, and interns, she was discharged as merely having a virus. Really? There had to be a better way, and it was my job to figure it out. Tiara was a medical anomaly, and every physician, nurse, and student wanted to examine her and order more tests. It was horrible for her to endure and for me to watch. I was always giving her medical history from pregnancy until the present for each new physician.

Because Tiara was a baby, she was required to sleep in a crib at the hospital but refused. At home, she slept in bed with me, and when I tried laying her down in the crib, she threw a fit and wouldn't stop crying. I let her sleep in my arms all day, but when it was time for me to sleep, I needed a plan. So, it was during her first visit after the diagnosis that I struck a deal with the nurses. If we could have a twin bed instead of a crib for Tiara, I would stay in bed with her at all times. I had to sign special paperwork, but I got us the twin bed. The only problem was that when I had to go to the bathroom in the middle of the night, I had to call a nurse to stand guard over her bed while I went. I didn't mind because what mattered most was that Tiara felt safe and comforted.

And so Tiara made it to her first birthday, having experienced more medical tests and probing than most people experience in a lifetime.

Because she appeared to be seizure-free, Dr. Stein thought it was a good time to wean her off phenobarbital, since it can have serious side effects. Learning difficulties are a known phenobarbital side effect. Tiara was spending so much time in therapy trying to catch up developmentally, the last thing she needed was a medication that could hinder her progress.

While weaning her off the phenobarb, I got to learn about titration schedules, which is a weaning schedule that tells how much to decrease a medication by each day, week, or month. If an anti-epileptic medication is decreased too quickly, it can cause an increase in seizures or rebound seizures. Often, one medication needs to be increased as another is decreased so that another can be added to the regimen. It can get complicated, which is why I always typed and printed out the schedule and taped it to the kitchen cabinet, so there would be no mistakes. This first schedule was very straightforward, and Tiara seemed to be doing great with the weaning process—until one day, I noticed her making funny grimaces.

At the time, I didn't know seizures could appear as gestures, head tilts, eye blinks, laughs, or vomiting episodes. A seizure can present itself in countless ways. Tiara rarely had a stereotypical tonic-clonic or grand mal type of seizure that we have all seen on television. Her seizures always looked different than what you might imagine, which is why I didn't immediately know the funny face was a seizure.

It was Christmas morning 1999, and once again, Tiara wasn't feeling well. While Tabitha was excitedly opening her presents, Tiara was sitting in Lou's arms across the room from me. I looked over at Tiara, and she gave me the strangest look, without really looking at me at all. *Why does she look like that?* I wondered.

Something was wrong; I could feel the fear and dread spread through my body. For days, I watched Tiara make the same weird expression repeatedly, and then she started lunging her chest forward just like before. I knew the seizures were back. I immediately called UCLA and told them I thought she was having infantile spasms again, and they had to do something right away. They increased her vigabatrin dose and scheduled an EEG. The EEG showed she was not having infantile spasms but complex partial seizures, even though they looked similar.

With the infantile spasms under control, another type of seizure had developed. From this moment on, Tiara would endure at least one complex partial seizure every day of her life, despite all the different combinations of drugs we eventually tried. I can't remember Tiara ever having a seizure-free day once the complex partial seizures appeared in 1999.

Dr. Stein put her on Lamictal to help control these new seizures. He suspected the phenobarbital had been controlling this type of seizure, and when we weaned her off, they appeared again. Despite being on two anti-epileptic medications, she continued to have an average of three seizures a day.

CHAPTER 4

Noticing Everything

April 6, 2000, I had been holding Tiara in my arms all day, as she was once again sick. She seemed so weak, and yet her fever was only 101.5 degrees. My intuition was telling me something was really wrong. Was it her heart? Seizures? Had she developed a problem with her kidneys, or was it just another virus? I didn't know, and neither did her pediatrician. I took her to see Dr. Krumins, and he thought it was another virus, but something felt different. Once again, I was terrified.

Sarah brought dinner over to Tabitha and me, since I couldn't put Tiara down for even a moment to cook, and Lou was at work. I was holding Tiara in the crook of my left arm, staring at her face and eating with my right hand when suddenly her legs started twitching. She flung her arms up over her head, and I knew instantly she was having a seizure. I figured it was just one of her typical seizures, but it didn't stop.

After fifteen minutes, I called the nurse's line, and as I was talking to the nurse, Tiara started foaming at the mouth and throwing up white bile. Her body became limp, and her lips turned blue. The nurse told me to hang up and dial 911. I had never dialed 911 before, so it was very intimidating that first time. I would eventually learn to call 911 without thinking twice, and when they arrived, I would usually recognize a least one paramedic or firefighter, as they frequented our house and Tiara's school regularly.

Once the paramedics arrived, they said it was a code red and immediately put her on oxygen and placed her into the ambulance on a gurney. While driving to Hoag, the paramedics wanted to give her medicine to stop the seizure. I insisted they wait until we got to the hospital. Not trusting they knew what they were doing, I feared it would be too much. I now know that it would have been fine, but status seizures were new for me at that point, and I didn't want my seventeen-month-old toddler overdosed.

Despite pumping her full of Ativan once at the hospital, the seizure wouldn't stop. She was becoming too sedated to breathe on her own, so they needed to intubate Tiara and put her on a respirator. Sitting in silence at the foot of her bed, I watched them try to place the tube down her throat numerous times without success. They needed a smaller breathing tube, but they couldn't find one. Hoag is not a pediatric hospital. The nurse was frantically calling other departments, looking for a doctor that could intubate Tiara with the larger tube or find a smaller tube.

In their stress, they forgot to ask me to leave the room. Parents aren't allowed to watch something as serious as intubating a child. I knew that if I remained silent, they would forget about me, and I couldn't pry myself away from her side. In the future, when doctors asked me to leave during a procedure, I would tell them: "I have seen my child intubated; I think I can handle it." They were always shocked to hear that, but they then knew I wasn't squeamish and let me stay with Tiara.

After they finally intubated Tiara, they continued to pump her full of drugs for two hours, until the seizure stopped. When she stabilized enough for transport, we took an ambulance ride to CHOC.

Once the seizure stopped, my thoughts turned to Tabitha. I knew she was probably traumatized as she had watched Tiara turn blue, foam at the mouth, and be taken out of our home on a stretcher and put into an ambulance. Tabitha was seven years old and understood Tiara was not well, but this whole experience must have been terrifying. I have never believed in keeping vital information from my children, so Tabitha knew everything about Tiara's condition, to the degree she could comprehend. But the complexity of TSC was hard enough for Lou and me to understand, so I knew Tabitha didn't get it. What I did know was that this was the first time, but not the last time, Tabitha would worry about her sister dying.

Through the years, and all the hospital stays, I would sometimes find myself worrying more about Tabitha and Trinity, our third daughter, than Tiara. Before Tiara's diagnosis, Tabitha enjoyed a life filled with soccer games, piano lessons, playdates, and being the only grandchild. Once Tiara was diagnosed, Tabitha's life changed as well. I tried to overcompensate for this by being what I deemed "the perfect" mom. A mom who loved unconditionally, enjoyed volunteering to be the team mom, watched every athletic event with enthusiasm, hosted fabulous birthday parties, sewed Halloween costumes, and above all else, focused on raising her girls to be good people. I didn't want to follow in my mom's footsteps.

Tabitha was born an old soul and living with Tiara only enhanced her inner beauty. Tabitha had an extraordinary sense of compassion for others, which many people will never understand. Every time I think about Tabitha and her kindness to others, I am reminded of a specific incident.

Lou, Tabitha, Tiara, and I were at my parents' mountain house in Lake Arrowhead for the weekend. We went to the village for a little diversion, and Tabitha wanted to feed the ducks. We bought the duck food in the sporting goods store, and as soon as she started throwing the food, the ducks all swarmed. There was this ugly white duck that kept missing all the food because she wasn't fast enough. All the other ducks kept stealing her food just as she was about to grab it with her beak.

Tabitha kept moving around to different spots on the walkway, trying to feed the ugly, slow duck and keep the other ducks away. She even went so far as to walk out on the public dock and started yelling to the unattractive duck to try to coax it over to her so she could feed it. No matter what she did, the other ducks kept taking all the food. She finally got so frustrated, she said, "I'm done!"

"Honey, you didn't use all the food we bought," I said.

"I can't take it, Mom. Those other ducks won't let the white duck have any food. It is not fair, and I won't give them any more food if they can't share with the white duck!"

To this day, Tabitha has always had a special bond with the less fortunate, the underdog, the disabled, or anyone not being treated fairly. I believe she was born this way, but I also know having Tiara as a sister has made this characteristic prominent in her personality.

Tiara remained in the intensive care unit (ICU) at CHOC for two days until they transferred her to the general ward. Tabitha wasn't old enough to visit Tiara in the ICU, so Lou stayed home with Tabitha, while Sarah sat with Tiara and me at the hospital. At SKY pediatrics, I learned Tiara responded to music. Music calmed her, brought her joy, and helped her learn, which is why Sarah and I took turns singing to Tiara nonstop, the entire visit.

While Tiara lay motionless, I noticed a rash on her legs and feet. Lamictal had the possible side effect of causing Stevens-Johnson syndrome, which starts with a rash and can be deadly. Even though

Stevens-Johnson syndrome is rare, Sarah had it as a teenager and was seriously ill for months. When I showed the neurologist Tiara's rash, he said we couldn't take a chance and needed to get her off Lamictal and on a different anti-epileptic as soon as possible. During this stay, they did a spinal tap and another CT scan, along with X-rays and zillions of blood tests. The doctors were always fearful she had some crazy infection, like meningitis, causing the prolonged status seizure.

She arrived at the hospital for a status seizure, but after their repeated attempts to intubate her, she ended up with fluid in her lungs—her first pneumonia. Having pneumonia would become a common occurrence in Tiara's future, but we didn't know that then. On the fifth day of her stay, they tried to start her on IV antibiotics, but they had blown every vein in her body after all the blood tests and numerous IVs, and she had nothing left to use. They wouldn't be able to get blood from her or put in an IV without performing a small operation to put in "a line" for access. I did not think a surgical procedure to insert a permanent line was necessary, so they decided to release her and send her home on oral antibiotics.

Two weeks later, Dr. Stein became concerned with the escalation of her seizures and decided she needed more testing. He had put her on a new medication called Topamax, but since taking her off the Lamictal, she was averaging six seizures a day. She was also throwing up often. He wasn't sure why she was vomiting. He wanted her hooked up to an EEG for several days and ordered another MRI.

By this time, our family had developed a hospital routine. My mom knew what clothes and products to pack in my overnight bag and was in charge of picking up Tabitha from school and keeping her on schedule until Lou got home from work. While living in the hospital, I only wore dark-colored sweats or comfortable pants and a tank top. I also brought a supply of knit cardigans to keep me warm at night. After Tiara went to bed at night, I would take a shower and put on a clean pair of clothes for bed. I would wash my face, brush my teeth, and try to make my hair look decent. When I woke up in the morning, I was already dressed and ready for the day. All I needed was coffee, and I could start talking to nurses and doctors. Lou usually got up at five thirty and drove up my morning Starbucks coffee, along with some breakfast. Then he would rush back and get Tabitha off to school. Depending on his schedule, Lou would come back to visit us either before or after work. Every day, my dad would call the hospital and either bring me lunch or dinner, depending on where he had court that day. His office was reasonably close to CHOC, so he was in charge of my main meals. Sarah would visit as much as possible, despite living in Los Angeles and working full-time in the music industry. Whenever possible, Grandma Cindy would fly down from Northern California and fill in with taking care of Tabitha or visiting with Tiara and me.

After reviewing Tiara's MRI and EEG results, Dr. Stein and Dr. Muhonen, her neurosurgeon, said more needed to be done to stop Tiara's seizures. They wanted Tiara to try a vagus nerve stimulator

(VNS), a device sometimes referred to as a "pacemaker for the brain." Dr. Muhonen would place the small device under the skin on her chest wall and thread the thin wires from the device to the vagus nerve in her neck. Then using a laptop, he would program the VNS to transmit stimulation to the vagus nerve throughout the day. When Tiara had a seizure, I would hold the magnet provided on her chest, over the device. This would activate the VNS to deliver additional stimulation, and, hopefully, stop the seizure. Dr. Muhonen had implanted the VNS in only one other child as young as Tiara, but because Tiara was running out of medication options, they believed the VNS was something we needed to try. But the VNS was not FDA approved for children less than five years of age, so I started my war with the insurance company to get approval.

While working on the VNS approval, Dr. Stein vanished. Without warning any of his patients, he picked up and moved out of the area, so I had to find Tiara a new neurologist fast. Tiara was still in the vigabatrin study at UCLA, but it was ending soon. She was going to remain on vigabatrin for a while longer, but she had to have a local neurologist. Thankfully, the UCLA team put us in contact with Dr. Rho, who worked out of University of California, Irvine (UCI). Even though he was a fantastic neurologist, he didn't have privileges at CHOC, which made everything more complicated.

As Tiara's seizures continued to worsen, Dr. Rho continued to add, increase, and change her seizure medications regularly, but by the age of two, she had gone through almost every viable option. I still hadn't gotten approval for the VNS, and I had been working on it for months. During this phase of her life, I was in contact with Dr. Rho or his nurse, weekly, if not daily. If you have ever had a subspecialty doctor, you know this is uncommon, unless you have some serious medical problems. There were days Tiara would seize all day. I would call him, explain what I was seeing, and he would direct me to drive straight to his clinic at UCI or sometimes, if he was booked in the clinic, to his private office, where he did all his paperwork.

Once we arrived, he would examine Tiara, sometimes get her hooked up to an EEG over at the lab, give us a new prescription, or tell me to drive her straight to CHOC. I lived in a constant state of panic during this time in her life. I was always trying to diagnose, determine, and assess her condition all day. I felt as if her life depended on it.

One of the most fascinating and primitive issues a parent faces when they have a child with epilepsy is how the seizures are diagnosed. Of course, EEG readings help, but your child can't live hooked up to this machine. So, as a parent, you are expected to remember every detail about every seizure. The doctors want you to describe each seizure: Which way was her head turned? Which arm flew up? Which way were her eyes looking? How long did her body stay rigid? How long did the episode last? Was she postictal? So while you are panicked over your child's safety during a seizure, you are also expected to catalog every detail. The sad part is, if you fail to do this, you are failing your child and their potential to receive the proper medication. You see, the doctors determine what part of the brain the seizure started and traveled to by knowing what the body was doing during the seizure. If you can't tell them, they don't know exactly what type of seizure your child had and from what area of the brain it developed, so they can't give the proper medication. On more than one occasion, a neurologist has asked me, "Of the three seizure medications Tiara is on, which one do you think is the least effective?" Once I decide, we drop that medication and change it for a new one. What if I am wrong? Will my kid have more seizures? But that is how it worked, and it sucked. Which is why I had to chart every seizure by detailing how she looked, how long it lasted, whether she was sick at the time, how it started, how she was when it ended, etc.

Dr. Shields always said, "There is so much we don't know about the brain, and patients like Tiara remind us of this truth."

So much of neurology is a guessing game with a patient like Tiara. She always lived outside the norm, and what worked for most never worked for her. Luckily, I learned to give myself a pass if I made a mistake. I knew I was only human, and I also knew I had done everything in my power to care for her; so if I picked wrong, I picked wrong. As I am sure you can imagine, because of my constant need to assess her seizures, I never liked for Tiara to be out of my sight. As a result, we were both extremely attached. She wanted me and only me to hold her all day, every day. She was practically never out of my arms during this phase of her life. That is why it was so shocking when I woke up one morning and felt odd, different—like how I feel when I'm pregnant. *Hmm. Not possible*, I thought, *since Lou had a vasectomy last year.* But I always know the moment I'm pregnant.

I looked at Lou and said, "I think I am pregnant."

He responded, "Well, that seems impossible, but you do have that look. You better go buy a test."

I want to explain why Lou and I had decided on a vasectomy, even though we were practicing Catholics. It was a difficult decision for us, but we didn't think we could care for another child. I was already going against our faith by using birth control pills and didn't want to stay on them forever, so having a vasectomy seemed like the best option. After Tiara was born, we had grown in our faith as a family, so permanent birth control felt worse than temporary birth control. So, we were conflicted. After lots of discussion and prayer, we decided it was what we needed to do. Lou moved forward with the procedure and had his vas deferens snipped. Two or three weeks after the vasectomy, the patient is supposed to return to his urologist and provide a semen sample to confirm the procedure was effective. The urologist told us many men skip this last step, and sometimes their wives end up pregnant because the procedure wasn't a success. No one knows until the wife gets pregnant. I wasn't taking any chances, which is why I forced Lou to go back to the doctor's office several weeks after the vasectomy to confirm he no longer had any sperm. The sample came back with a zero sperm count.

With that in mind, and because I had never cheated on Lou, how could I be pregnant? I had no idea how it was possible, but I rushed out and bought a pregnancy test. I peed on the stick and waited. A very faint plus sign appeared in the window after five minutes. I freaked out and started yelling at Lou.

"How is this possible? Did you really go back and get your semen tested?"

"Of course I did! I didn't lie to you."

"So, then how can I be pregnant? It's impossible! You need to call his office right now and tell them I'm pregnant! You need to give them another sample! This is horrible!"

"Calm down, babe, it's going to be okay. I'll call his office right now. This isn't the worst thing in the world. We will figure it out, we always do."

"I'm really scared, Louie. What if this baby has TSC too?" I asked.

"It won't. Let's just take it one step at a time. I love you."

Lou provided his urologist with a semen sample, and this time the result showed he had live sperm. The doctor was baffled and later consulted with other doctors and said he had never seen anything like it. Wow, the story of our lives! He said the chances of this happening were .02 percent. He offered to do another vasectomy for free in the hospital, with Lou under sedation so he could take a really long section of each vas deferens, but Lou did not think that sounded like a good idea. We now had nine months to figure out another method of birth control.

As you can imagine, telling our family and friends was a little awkward because at this time, we didn't even know if Tiara's tuberous sclerosis was genetic or not. My mom was so mad at me for being pregnant, she refused to speak to me for weeks, which didn't help. The odds were 60 percent the TSC spontaneously started with Tiara, but believe me, Lou and I got right on completing the genetic testing. Not that I would have ever considered an abortion if I was pregnant with another disabled child, but I needed to mentally prepare myself. Gratefully, the genetic testing confirmed the TSC had spontaneously started with Tiara, so the odds of having another baby with TSC were rare.

Nevertheless, it was a pregnancy fraught with worry for many reasons. Once it was confirmed Lou's sperm had returned, I knew it was a miracle from God. Why would God give us another child when we were already so overwhelmed? Because Tiara wasn't going to live a long life, and we would all need another child in our lives to help us get through whatever the future held? The answer was obvious, and it terrified me.

During this time, I was still at war with the insurance company because they refused to approve the VNS device Tiara so desperately needed. Dr. Rho said it was her only hope of stopping the seizures, and yet the insurance company kept denying the claim. We had added and taken away several seizure medications, and nothing was working. Tiara was still seizing daily and not progressing developmentally. Because we weren't getting the VNS approval, Dr. Rho said we needed to explore brain surgery. You may think that sounds scary, and yes, it is, but several of the other children in our TSC support network had gone through brain surgery at UCLA, with miraculous results. Her UCLA team and Dr. Rho hadn't considered surgery a viable option because, based on her seizure types, it appeared as if her seizures originated from both sides of her brain. Now, because her situation was so dire, they decided to complete formal testing.

Tiara was admitted to UCLA for Phase I telemetry in May of 2001 to see if she was a candidate for brain surgery. We spent four days in a hospital bed, with Tiara hooked up to an EEG monitoring her seizures. The only time she left the hospital room was for an MRI and a PET scan, both of which required sedation to keep her still. As you can imagine, she hated every moment of it. She wanted out of bed, and her frustration resulted in me getting hit and scratched repeatedly. After all that, the doctors determined she was not a candidate because she had multiple tumors on both sides of her brain, and they couldn't operate on both sides. Besides, in patients with TSC, once a tumor is removed, another inactive tumor may then start causing seizures. Since she had so many tumors, it was very likely another would start causing seizures after they took one out. Because of these reasons, the team at UCLA told me: "Sorry, we can't help her." Why was it that so many times in Tiara's life, doctors have told me they are unable to help?

I returned to my obsession with getting approval for the VNS. Because Tiara was only two and a half at this point, they were still automatically denying the claim. I needed letters and documentation from both Dr. Muhonen and Dr. Rho to verify her desperate medical situation, but no one was doing enough to help me. I sat at my kitchen table on the computer, with Tiara in one arm and typing with the other hand, writing letters to anyone and everyone. I finally decided I was done with following the proper channels of communication and would go to the press for help. I contacted the *Daily Pilot*, our local paper, and they agreed to profile Tiara and tuberous sclerosis for an issue in May because it was National TSC Awareness Month. I then called and wrote to our insurance company to let them know I had an article lined up with a local paper and would go to every news media possible if they did not approve the VNS for my daughter. Guess what—I got the approval. It took over a year to accomplish, but I did it! I felt such triumph and relief in knowing that my baby was going to be saved.

But life wasn't getting easier: I was pregnant with a child I never planned for, dealing with Tiara's daily seizures, and preparing for the VNS surgery under general anesthesia.

Then, Tabitha was diagnosed with asthma. Tabitha had chronic ear infections as a baby and toddler. She then started having regular bouts with the croup cough, and now at eight years old was experiencing case after case of strep throat. With each instance of strep throat came extreme sickness and problems breathing. The doctors finally realized she had asthma, which made every virus and infection that much worse. I mean, couldn't anyone give me a break and give me a healthy child? Is it so much to ask for? I prayed my third baby would be healthy. Lou and I weren't prepared to handle a third child financially, emotionally, or physically, yet we were having one, whether or not we were ready. As for Tabitha and her asthma, it was just another medical condition that needed constant monitoring as she played soccer, softball, and later, volleyball.

CHAPTER 5

Knowing

One month shy of her third birthday, in September 2001, Tiara was implanted with the VNS at CHOC, by Dr. Muhonen. The surgery went smoothly, and Dr. Muhonen started the VNS on the lowest setting. We were hoping for a miracle and prayed her seizures would decline. But during the first two weeks, we saw no change in her seizure activity; she still averaged six seizures a day.

And in the third week, Tiara's seizures increased, and she began to decline developmentally. Her speech, which consisted of babbling, completely stopped, and she grew withdrawn. And then I saw the dreaded familiar movement—Tiara lunged her chest forward as if her stomach hurt, while crying out, over and over, just as she had as a baby. I watched in horror as I realized the infantile spasms were back, and I knew it the VNS causing this to happen. I called Dr. Rho, who assured me it was impossible for the VNS to cause a relapse of infantile spasms but told me to bring her in immediately so he could perform an EEG.

Sadly, I was right, and he was wrong. The EEG showed she was having hypsarrhythmia again, the brain pattern associated with infantile spasm seizures. Dr. Rho explained that it was impossible to have infantile spasms at her age because she was no longer an infant, and he had never seen this before. The story of our life—something a doctor had never seen before, and yet it was happening to Tiara. I knew the VNS was causing this to happen, but Dr. Rho refused to believe me and didn't want to turn it off. I had fought so hard for the freaking device, and now it was destroying my child, but I wasn't going to let it.

I told him: "You need to turn it off right now. I know in my heart, the VNS is causing the spasms."

"It's impossible," he claimed.

"I know it doesn't seem possible, but it's the VNS. Tiara is always the patient that responds differently than everyone else. You know this about her. We can't take a chance. I need you to turn it off immediately, and I want her put back on vigabatrin right away," I demanded. He wasn't happy with me but offered to strike me a deal.

"I will turn off the VNS right now, if you let me try her on Lamictal first, before putting her back on vigabatrin," he offered.

"You know I don't like Lamictal for her, and I don't think it will work, but I will give you one week if you turn off the VNS now. If the spasms haven't stopped in a week, she goes back on vigabatrin," I declared.

"Agreed. Let's turn it off, and then I'll put together a titration schedule for the Lamictal. I'm going to be as aggressive as possible, and I'm hopeful it will stop the spasms," he stated.

I shook my head in compliance, even though I knew he was wrong. I was willing to give it a try, but I was terrified for her to endure a whole week of spasms because I knew in my gut, the Lamictal would fail her.

You may be wondering why I would argue with her neurologist when I had no facts except my intuition to back me up. Because I was her advocate, and if I didn't put aside my fears and insecurities and fight for what I knew was right, no one would. As her mother, and constant companion, I could sense things about her medical state that couldn't be measured or verified; I just knew how she was feeling or responding to a treatment even though she couldn't verbally tell me. Growing up in a home with a mom prone to lashing out, I learned to become an astute observer early in life. Even though I always tried to avoid my mom's triggers, other people could set her off, so I studied everyone around me. This skill of reading a person's movements, tone of voice, energy, facial expressions, and overall demeanor, along with my constant quest for knowledge about TSC and epilepsy, gave me the confidence to argue with physicians when I knew they were wrong. And my biggest motivator, which allowed me to set aside my fears of appearing stupid in their eyes, was keeping Tiara alive. What if I listened to the doctor and allowed her to endure substantially more infantile spasms and she suffered irreversible brain damage because I was too afraid to speak up? Then, I would fail my child, and we both would suffer. If her condition worsened because of my fear of challenging a highly educated person, I'd never forgive myself. So, I learned to speak up when my gut told me something wasn't right. Every doctor in the room might have thought I was crazy, but I didn't care.

Unfortunately, I was right about the Lamictal, and after a week, she still had infantile spasms daily. I called Dr. Rho and asked him for a prescription for vigabatrin and a titration schedule. He tried to convince me to give the Lamictal more time, but I refused. She needed the vigabatrin; it would stop the spasms completely. He gave me a prescription, but I had to obtain the drug myself. I could get it in Mexico or through a Canadian pharmacy. I didn't have time to wait for it to arrive from Canada, and I wasn't sure how I could get to Mexico right away and pick up a bottle, so I reached out to my friend Tricia.

I had met Tricia through my connection with the Tuberous Sclerosis Alliance, or TS Alliance. Soon after Tiara was diagnosed, I had learned about the TS Alliance through the UCLA vigabatrin study. I called the TS Alliance, and they put me in contact with a local mom, Lee Ann, whose son Timmy also had TSC. Lee Ann was the Southern California representative for newly diagnosed families and was in contact with several local families who had very young children with TSC. She planned a potluck lunch at her home, for all the families to get acquainted with one another. During lunch, several of us decided we wanted to get more involved by helping raise awareness and funds for TSC. April, a mom of identical twin girls, both with TSC, worked for a commercial real estate company at the time and was able to get us free office space to start a meeting each month. Our original group consisted of Lee Ann, April, Sheri, and me, but it quickly grew. We were planning on starting our own local nonprofit for those affected by TSC, but the TS Alliance urged us to join forces with them. We worked together, and with their support, our little Orange County group of moms became the first official TS Alliance community chapter. We went on to raise money through an annual golf tournament, educate physicians about TSC, and bring families together at our annual picnic.

It was through this group that I had met Tricia. Her daughter was also on vigabatrin, so I called her up and asked if I could "borrow" some.

"Of course! Come over right now, and I'll give you some. It's perfect timing because my husband is making a run to Mexico in a few days to pick up a supply. If you want him to pick up a few bottles for you, he can," she said.

"Oh my gosh, that would be wonderful! How much does a few bottles cost?"

"Last time he went, I think it was $110 a bottle, so bring me $220 cash," Tricia said.

"I can't thank you enough! I'll come right now," I said. And just like that, Tiara was back on vigabatrin within hours. I remember thinking, *What if we couldn't afford $220 for the medicine? What if I didn't know other families who could help out? Then what? She turns into* *a vegetable?* I was grateful for my need to always be involved because, without my involvement in the local alliance, Tiara would not have gotten her medication that day. Once again, the miracle drug stopped the spasms within two days.

At this point, Tiara was supposed to start at Harper Preschool, the school for all special needs children in our district. When you have a child with special needs, they are given therapy through the Regional Center of Orange County up until their third birthday. After that, the child's educational needs become the responsibility of the school district. As Tiara transitioned from SKY Pediatrics into the school district, she was undergoing testing at both ends. SKY's therapists measured her progress in their program and current levels of development in speech, physical, and occupational skills. Knowing my child is developmentally delayed was one thing but seeing the test results in writing was another. At almost three years of age, she was developmentally between that of a six-month-old and thirteen-month-old child. Her speech and occupational skills were both below that of a one-year-old; she was only progressing in her physical abilities.

I tried not to focus on her delays and hated her SKY speech therapist when she told me, "Tiara will most likely never speak." I thought she was insane and extremely negative, but now I was wondering if she might be right. Was it possible Tiara might never learn to talk?

Loving Tiara

The school district's results of Tiara's abilities were similar to SKY's, but luckily, the school district's speech therapist had a more positive outlook for Tiara's future. She believed Tiara would learn to speak one day, so I chose to believe her and try to forget what the other speech therapist had told me. Tiara's first Individualized Education Program meeting was extraordinarily depressing but a success. I had heard horror stories of the school district not offering children the services they needed and the parents enduring months, if not years of legal battles to get the services they felt their child deserved. I came prepared for the school district to offer Tiara individual speech, occupational, and physical therapy along with a one-on-one aide, who would remain by her side at all times. Because she was functioning at such a low level and was a fall risk, due to her daily seizures, they offered everything I wanted, except the therapy would be in a group, not individualized. I didn't want her working with a group because I considered it to be less effective, but I listened to their reasoning with an open mind. I still wasn't entirely convinced modeling her peers in a group setting might be more beneficial than a therapist working with her one on one, but I agreed to give it a try. The most important thing to me was knowing she would be safe at school, and I had already told myself I would never allow her to attend without her own aide. Because I didn't have to fight for this service, I was more flexible with the therapy.

The whole system didn't make sense to me. The district wanted my kid, who couldn't even talk, was on a ton of meds, having seizures, and always off-balance, to get on a bus and go to school for four hours without me. I said, "no, thank you" to the bus; I would drive her myself. As the first day of school neared, the school district told me they hadn't yet been able to hire an aide for Tiara. The options were: Tiara could get passed around to available aides, she could stay home from school and not receive any of her therapies, or I could fill in as her one-on-one aide until they hired a full-time aide. I'm sure you can guess what I chose to do. I volunteered to be her aide.

I was excited about working with her teachers and classroom aides while also seeing what she would be doing all day. We were walking hand in hand into her classroom, when a smiling young teacher, Miss Aimee, greeted us at the door.

"Welcome! I'm Miss Aimee, and I will be Tiara's teacher," she said happily.

"Hi, I'm Tiffani, and this is Tiara," I said.

"It's nice to meet you both. Before you go in, I need you to take out Tiara's pacifier. We don't allow them in the classroom."

"Why?" I asked anxiously.

"The children can't work on improving their speech while sucking on a pacifier."

"But Tiara needs her pacifier. She has seizures all day, and her pacifier is a huge comfort to her. I can't take it away from her," I said with tears in my eyes.

"I understand this is upsetting, and I'm so sorry, but she'll get used to it. I promise. Plus, it's against school policy for sanitary reasons. I really can't allow it; I wish I could."

"Well, she needs her pacifier," I demanded.

"I'm sorry, Mrs. Goff, but that isn't an option. I promise she will be fine without it." said Miss Aimee.

I looked down at Tiara frantically sucking on her pacifier and said: "We need to take out your pacifier before we go into class, sweetie. I'm going to put it in my purse, and you can have it after school." I pulled the pacifier out of Tiara's mouth, and she immediately grabbed for it and started crying. I looked at Miss Aimee and put the pacifier back in Tiara's mouth.

"I'm sorry, but I can't do this to her. If she can't have her pacifier, then we are leaving."

"You can't leave."

"Yes, we can," said my tearfully pregnant self.

"How about if I let her have it for today because it's the first day, and then we slowly wean her off?"

"That works for us, thank you. Let's go see your classroom, Tiara," I said while walking her inside the cute room.

After a month, they finally had an aide for Tiara, and I was so scared to leave her. Kelly, her aide, looked very similar to me, which made the transition easier for Tiara, but not me. Each time I left her at school, I felt physically sick to my stomach and tearful. Despite how I felt, I needed the free time to get the nursery ready for Trinity, scheduled to arrive in late April.

When I'm pregnant, I tend to have a lot of pre-labor pains for weeks before the baby's arrival. This time, it was worse. After Christmas my pain increased, and I started bleeding. After an ultrasound and an exam, my obstetrician put me on bed rest and said I couldn't carry Tiara anymore.

What? How could I not carry Tiara?

It was only the first week of January, and the baby wasn't supposed to come until mid- to late April. What was I going to do for the next three and a half months if I couldn't get out of bed? Who was going to take care of Tabitha and Tiara? I thought it must be a joke.

Of course, you know by now that I do whatever the heck I want, regardless of what anyone says, but Lou was adamant about following the doctor's orders. Before she put me on bed rest, he was always getting mad at me for doing too much.

"Slow down, take a rest, stop painting by yourself. Why do you always have to be doing something?" he would say.

"Because somebody has to do it and you are always working. If I don't get the baby's room done, who will?"

"Getting the baby's room ready is fine, but you always have to overdo it. You didn't need to make all the crib bedding yourself. You could have bought bedding like a normal person, Tiffani."

"I couldn't find any bedding I liked, so I needed to make everything. I want the girls to have matching bedding, since they are sharing a room. I mean, how adorable does it look so far?" I asked him while flashing a big smile.

"It's beautiful, but that's not the point. You need to take care of yourself. I'm worried about you."

"Thanks, babe, but I'm okay. I promise," I said while thinking, *Blah, blah, blah, leave me alone, I have stuff to do.*

After the doctor put me on bed rest, Lou and I sat down and made a plan. That was right after Tabitha's birthday party at Girl Mania in Fashion Island. The day I was rushed in to see the doctor was the day of Tabitha's birthday party. Of course, Lou wanted me to stay at home in bed, but I walked very slowly through the mall, and then stayed seated the whole party. That was very hard for me, but I knew Lou would send me home if I pushed it. We decided it was time to hire a nanny to help with Tiara after school and do laundry and household chores. Ugh, I hate relying on other people for help, especially paid help. That sucks. He wanted me to get help every day, but I agreed to three times a week. My mom and Sarah offered to help the rest of the time. The good news was that the doctor said once the bleeding stopped, I didn't have to stay in bed, I just couldn't do too much. Mom rented me a wheelchair so she could push me around the mall and fabric stores. I also learned to use the motorized wheelchairs at Target and Costco. I felt like a loser at first, but then I figured, *Who cares? I need to get the shopping done and get out of the house.* Lou allowed me to drive Tabitha and Tiara to and from school, so I was able to accomplish everything I needed during my bed-rest phase.

At this point, Tiara was attending school most days, but she also had hundreds of seizures every day. Going to school was practically pointless because she was unable to learn anything when she was always seizing. Dr. Rho wanted to turn the VNS back on, and I let him because she had no other options at this point.

CHAPTER 6

Giving Birth

I wasn't expecting to have a baby the day Trinity was born, but like all babies, they never seem to follow the plan. It was April 4, 2002, and I was rushing around doing a million things, even though I was allegedly still on bed rest. I can't remember what I was doing all day, but by five p.m., I was exhausted. I sat down at the kitchen table and hoped the stabbing pain searing through my pelvis up to my abdomen and then radiating to my lower back would subside. Trinity wasn't due for two weeks, so I figured it was just more pre-labor. A side note: I find it fascinating that during Lamaze class and every book you ever read about childbirth, they always say that you will know when you are in labor. That is such a bunch of crock; I never knew. I had three kids and could never tell when I was in real labor until my water broke. Even then, I was like, "Did my water break, or did I just pee my pants?" God knows, when you are pregnant, it could be either.

I had spoken to Mara earlier in the week, and she told me to drink half a glass of wine when the pains got intense. So that you know, I am a freak about not drinking alcohol during my pregnancies. I refuse even to drink one sip. She told me this theory that if you were in real labor, the pain would continue, but if it were pre-labor, the wine would relax you and the pain would go away. So, for two days, I had been contemplating the wine. I kept asking Lou what he thought, and I think he was so sick of me asking, he finally poured me half a glass.

"Here, drink it and see what happens," he said.

"I feel so guilty. Are you sure?"

"A half a glass won't hurt the baby. Just do it and stop talking about it," he begged.

"Okay." I slowly lifted the glass to my mouth and sipped as if I was ingesting poison. I was waiting to be struck down by lightning and sent directly to hell, when I suddenly felt so much better.

"I feel better; I guess it was more pre-labor?" I said to him. An hour later, the pains returned with a vengeance, and I was even more confused. Was I in labor, or not? I kept feeling drips of dampness between my legs, but no gushing water, so I assumed it was my normal loss of bladder control. It was time for bed, but once I got in bed, I couldn't even think of sleeping because the pain was so bad. Finally, at around two a.m., a burst of water came gushing through my legs. It was time to go to the hospital. My ob-gyn was on vacation; just my luck. We called the office anyway, and they said the doctor on call would meet us at Hoag.

Sarah, who had moved back to the area and was pregnant with her first child, came over with her husband, Ray, to watch Tabitha and

Tiara. I was worried about leaving Tiara but didn't have a choice unless I wanted to give birth at home, which wasn't my vibe. I'm a fan of epidurals and sterile hospitals. Once we arrived at the hospital, I got my epidural, and everything was great until the doctor I had never met before came in to deliver our baby. Once she positioned herself at the base of the table and I was in that lovely position with my feet in the stirrups, I suddenly panicked when she said to push. I thought, *Oh my God, what if something is wrong with this baby? How am I going to take care of a new baby and Tabitha and Tiara? What if God gave me this baby because Tiara is going to die soon, and he doesn't want Tabitha to be an only child? What if this baby has TSC?* Every fear I had been suppressing my whole pregnancy came pouring out with the doctor's directive to push, and I started sobbing hysterically. Lou understood because he, too, was panicked.

The confused doctor looked at me and asked, "Are you okay? Are you having pain?"

"I'm afraid. We have a daughter with tuberous sclerosis—she has seizures, so many medical problems—I'm so scared," I cried.

She looked at me, somewhat stunned and said, "Well, I hope you did the genetic testing for this baby. Is this baby okay?"

"She should be healthy, but you never know! Tiara's TSC spontaneously started with her, and I didn't do any extra testing on this baby," I said.

She looked at me in horror, and the room fell silent. Suddenly, I hated this woman and wished anyone but her was about to deliver my child. Clearly, she hadn't won any awards for her bedside manner. I was in desperate need of a compassionate doctor, but there wasn't one around. She tensed, realizing she could be delivering an unhealthy baby any minute. Lou could see I was about to spin out of control, so he tried calming me down. After only a few minutes of pushing, Trinity appeared. Visually, she looked healthy and weighed in at a whopping nine pounds.

Of course, I couldn't keep my mouth shut about the half glass of wine I had drunk the night before. I was still feeling guilty, so I told every nurse who checked on me during the delivery about Mara's theory, which in retrospect, wasn't a great idea. If only I would have shut up about the wine, no one would have known. So, I shouldn't have been surprised when the head nurse told me they would need extra blood work on Trinity to measure her blood alcohol level, since I had drunk every day during pregnancy. What?

"I didn't drink wine every day! I only drank a half glass my entire pregnancy, I promise," I declared.

"Oh, it was our understanding that you drank wine daily during your pregnancy."

"No, I never drank alcohol, only last night. I swear!"

"I believe you, but since Trinity is nine pounds, I'm required to perform additional blood tests, regardless. Any baby weighing nine pounds or over needs to be tested for diabetes, so you will need to stay in the hospital an extra day."

"An extra day? I guess that will be fine," I said.

When Tabitha and Tiara were born, we were out of the hospital in twenty-four hours, and now I had to stay three days. I was secretly so happy. I couldn't believe how tired I was and staying in the hospital seemed like a vacation. They kept bringing me those fabulous cranberry spritzers and offering to take Trinity to the nursery. I had never let the nurses take Tabitha or Tiara away from my bedside, but now with Trinity, I said, "Sure, go ahead, I'm going to sleep." My life with Tiara had caught up with me, and I was enjoying my rest.

When we arrived home, we were all nervous to see how Tiara was going to react to her baby sister. We thought she might get jealous of Trinity and try to hurt her in response. Funny enough, Tiara just pretended Trinity didn't exist for the first two weeks. Tiara would cover her eyes with her hand each time Trinity came into her view, pretending she couldn't see her. After the second week, Tiara started acknowledging Trinity during nursing. If Trinity nursed on my right breast, Tiara would climb up onto the couch and position herself next to my left side. She'd reach down into my shirt, place her hand on my left breast, rest her head on my shoulder, and relax in my arm as she watched Trinity feed. When it was time for Trinity to switch sides,

Tiara would move to the other side of my chest with some gentle prodding. Within a few weeks, Tiara was fascinated with Trinity and kept saying, "Baby, baby," which were some of her first words.

Tiara was okay with having a baby in the house, as long as I continued to carry her everywhere. At first, it seemed impossible to carry them both at the same time, so I spent the first month on the couch or in bed with both of them. Once I felt strong enough to move from a stationary position, I carried Trinity in a Baby Bjorn on my chest and Tiara on my hip as I walked around the house. Tiara was always trying to touch Trinity on the head, so I started carrying Tiara in a backpack carrier, generally used for hikes and long walks. As Trinity outgrew the chest carrier, she moved to the backpack, and Tiara latched herself onto the front of my body, with her legs wrapped around my waist for support. I was rarely without a child draped on my body, but I had terrific arm muscles, which would require hours of daily exercise to replicate. I'm always trying to look at the positive.

Unfortunately, Tiara's intractable epilepsy didn't leave room for the fact that I had just given birth to Trinity and needed a break. She was seizing more times a day than I could count or keep track of. I hoped for a reprieve. She was heading down a bad path, where she kept having status seizures lasting over ten minutes, so Dr. Rho prescribed Diastat, a rectal sedative that can be administered for seizures that last more than ten minutes. Dr. Rho explained that once a seizure lasts ten minutes, it becomes harder to stop without medical intervention. So, unless I wanted to drive her to the hospital every time she had a ten-minute seizure, I needed to learn how to use Diastat. He trained me how to turn her on her side, pull down her pants, take the childproof lid off the applicator, pull apart her butt cheeks, position the tip of the applicator far enough into her rectum so the medication wouldn't leak out, and then slowly push the medicine into her rectum. Once I pushed in all the Diastat, I needed to immediately remove the applicator and squeeze her butt cheeks together for several minutes while monitoring her breathing. Really? Could it get any worse?

The first time I had to give her Diastat, it was terrifying. She was seizing, and I was watching the minutes pass on the clock. I could tell this seizure wasn't going to stop, so I put Trinity in her crib, got everything prepared, and then, crying, called Lou and said, "I don't think I can do it."

"You can do it, honey, it will be okay," he promised.

"I can do it. I can do it," I repeated to Lou and myself.

"I love you," I said as I hung up the phone and then gave Tiara a dose of Diastat. It's hard to explain why giving Diastat was so scary for me. It isn't that it grossed me out. I guess it was the fact that I had to drug my child with a sedative to stop this horrible seizure, and if I gave her too much, she might have trouble breathing, from being too sedated. Of course, the doctor prescribed a specific dosage, but like with everything else, the doctor gave me the discretion to use a second vial, "if needed." So, I was making medical decisions for Tiara, then executing them myself. That's a lot of pressure. Tiara and I both survived the first time I gave her Diastat, and unfortunately, I got used to giving it to her, as she needed it every other day.

Tabitha (9), Tiara (4) and Trinity (7 months)

CHAPTER 7

Praying it Stops

Before getting pregnant with Trinity, I had committed to be a bridesmaid in one of my best friend's wedding. She lived in Hawaii, so once I found out I was pregnant, I contemplated backing out. But Beth had been my friend since third grade, and I wanted to be a part of her wedding. Lou and I brainstormed and realized Trinity would almost be three months in July. We decided if his mom came with us to Hawaii, we could probably pull it off.

What we hadn't anticipated was that during the time we were in Hawaii, Tiara would not be medically stable. We should have realized it was a possibility, but we were still trying to lead somewhat normal lives. We were excited and terrified for the trip because we had never flown nor taken Tiara much of anywhere. What if she had a status seizure on the plane and the Diastat didn't work? I had so many "What if" questions, but everything was prepaid, and Tabitha was thrilled to be going on vacation, so we went.

Imagine the amount of luggage we had for a three-year-old special-needs child, a nine-year-old, and a newborn. Two strollers, two car seats, books, diapers, medicine up the wazoo, videos, DVD player, toys, and clothes for six people. Plus, I had to carry both Tiara and Trinity, because one of them would cry if I didn't. My mother-in-law, Grandma Cindy, was eager to help with the girls in any way we needed, but Tiara was so attached to me, she made it difficult for Grandma Cindy to help with her.

Grandma Cindy lived by herself in an apartment in Northern California, worked in a doctor's office, and came to visit us every four to six weeks and all major holidays. Despite having a son who was over six feet tall, Grandma Cindy was petite. She had blonde curly hair like my girls, Lou's perfect nose, and fair skin like mine. Each of the girls was taller than her by their tenth birthday. When she was in town, her only goal was to play with her granddaughters and make them happy. She would take them to the park, change diapers, play dress up, and always offered to babysit at night, so Lou and I could go on a date. Babysitting Tiara required learning how to give her evening medications and how to administer Diastat. Grandma Cindy was the only family member who willingly learned both. While she spoiled the girls with her time and attention, my mom spoiled them with new clothes and any material possession they needed or wanted. It was the best of both worlds for the girls.

While waiting to check our six bags, and later get through security at LAX, someone in our group had to sing at all times to keep Tiara calm. Being embarrassed wasn't an option. You either sang, or she screamed bloody murder, which would result in a higher level of embarrassment; so someone sang, and it was usually me. Tiara was in her "Wheels on the Bus," "I'm a Little Teapot," "Itsy Bitsy Spider," and "Twinkle, Twinkle, Little Star" stage. Grandma Cindy only knew all the verses to "Wheels on the Bus," so she sang that song at least a hundred times before we boarded the plane.

Once on the plane, I remember thinking, *We made it. Everything is going to be okay.* Right then, Tiara coughed and made a gagging sound. I knew she was about to throw up, so I quickly looked through the front seat pocket for a barf bag. I found the bag and put it in front of her mouth just in time to catch the vomit. Motion sickness? Soon after Tiara's diagnosis, I had developed a unique skill for blocking unfavorable memories, so all I remember from that flight is her vomiting on the way up and her vomiting on the way back down.

Once in Honolulu, I do remember that we had a beautiful condo with a kitchen, several bedrooms, a working DVD player, and a fantastic view. The second day after we arrived, Tiara had a status seizure, and I had to give her the Diastat, but she recovered quickly.

On the day of the wedding, I took Trinity with me, so I could nurse her as we all got our hair and makeup done. With all my girls, I have never been able to pump breast milk, which meant I had to have my babies with me at all times, or they didn't get to eat. Once it was time for the wedding pictures, Lou showed up with Tabitha and took over caring for Trinity. They followed us to the wedding and watched as we took pictures. A few minutes before the wedding party lined up to enter the church, Lou handed Trinity over for a quick feeding, and she slept through the ceremony. Grandma Cindy stayed with Tiara at the condo until the reception. Immediately following the wedding vows, Lou, Tabitha, and Trinity headed back to the condo to pick up Grandma Cindy and Tiara. Once at the reception, Tiara was in Heaven because of the music and dancing. She loved dancing so much, we had to drag her off the dance floor to go home. The planning paid off, and the night was fun for everyone.

The day after the wedding, we went sightseeing and Tiara had another status seizure. The Diastat worked once again. We went to this super-cool cultural center, which was Tabitha's favorite part of the trip. It was hot, humid, and miserable for Tiara and me, but Tabitha didn't want to leave. We still hadn't discovered that Tiara was unable to sweat, to release her body heat. Her face was beet red, so I just kept dousing her with water. Trinity seemed fine in her infant carrier, and Tabitha was having so much fun, we stayed as long as possible. The next day we flew home, and the trip was deemed a success. It wasn't perfect, but everyone was still alive, and everyone had a good time.

A week after returning from Hawaii, Lou started a new job at Irvine BMW as the general sales manager. He had been a new car sales manager at Mercedes-Benz of Anaheim for eight years and now was changing brands and job position. It was a significant increase in pay and an increase in responsibility, so we were both excited but nervous because he would be working longer hours. Eighteen days after starting his new job, Tiara had a status seizure, but this time the Diastat didn't work.

Tiara plopped down on our hand-me-down leather sofa with a broken spring, and a high-pitched squeak emitted from the couch. The piercing sound jarred Tiara's brain into her first tonic-clonic seizure. While Tiara was rigid and shaking violently, I administered the first dose of Diastat after ten minutes. I paged Dr. Rho but realized twenty minutes had already passed. I had to call 911 again. While waiting for the ambulance, I called Mom and Lou, and sent Tabitha across the street to Leslie's to ask for help. I knew Leslie would take care of my girls if I left before Mom arrived.

They drove her to Hoag because she wasn't stable enough for the longer drive to CHOC. As usual, they started pumping Tiara with drugs, but two hours later, she was still seizing as if she hadn't received any drugs. They intubated her, without a problem this time, but no amount of medication was slowing the seizure. The ER physician was visibly stressed. Each time he ordered the nurse to give her another dose of Ativan, he would say, "Come on, Tiara, stop seizing."

Finally, he said to his nurse, "Get her neurologist on the phone."

It only took a few minutes to locate Dr. Rho, who instructed him to give her a bolus of Dilantin, a large quantity of a strong seizure medication that can be quickly administered via IV. Dr. Rho instructed him to alternate Dilantin and Valium until the seizure stopped. The first dose of Dilantin made a visible difference, but it only lightened the shaking and twitching.

Three hours into the seizure, everyone was starting to lose hope, and the tension in the small space was palpable. Lou and I were both quietly sobbing while holding her hands and begging her to stop seizing. My memory returned to the nurse who had told me Tiara might only live to be three years old. Was Tiara going to die in this ER?

I begged God to give her more time. Dr. Rho kept calling to check on her, and I could hear the despair in the ER doctor's voice as he spoke about Tiara. As more time crept by, the ER doctor stood staring at Tiara from the end of her bed. He then placed his hands together in prayer and said aloud, "Please, God, stop this seizure!"

This was the first but not the last time I saw a doctor pray over Tiara.

After four hours it appeared as if the seizure had stopped, but I wasn't convinced. I could feel that it wasn't entirely over. The doctor declared that she was no longer seizing, but I thought he was wrong. I stared at every inch of her body to look for the slightest twitch. And there it was: her eyelids flickered. Did I imagine the movement?

"Lou, watch her eyelids, I think they are moving!"

"I don't see anything."

"I saw something . . . See, there it is! Look at her eyeballs—they are moving side to side under her lids!"

"Oh my God, you're right, I see them moving," Lou said.

"Lou, hurry, go get the doctor, he needs to see this."

The doctor appeared seconds later.

"Tiara is still having a seizure; look at her eyelids," I told the doctor.

"I don't see it," he said.

"Wait for it. Look—her upper lip just twitched. There—there, see her eyeballs—they are moving!"

"I see it now; I can't believe this. We need to give her another dose," he said despondently. We were all wondering—would she ever wake up after being pumped with drugs for four hours straight? Two more doses later, and she finally lay utterly still. As we rode in the ambulance to CHOC, it dawned on me that my chest was in severe pain. To be more honest, my boobs were as hard as rocks because I hadn't breastfed Trinity in over eight hours. At four months old, she usually fed every few hours. What was I going to do? I had formula and baby bottles at the house for emergencies, so I knew that Trinity would survive without me, but what about my engorged breasts? Maybe Mom could bring Trinity to CHOC, every four hours, to feed? She would never do that; she hates the drive to CHOC. Plus, Trinity isn't allowed in the ICU, so I would have to feed her in the lobby and leave Tiara alone. I guess we were both weaning ourselves from breastfeeding cold turkey.

My poor Trinity; it wasn't fair. I asked Mom to post a feeding schedule on the refrigerator, so whoever is caring for Trinity would know when to feed her. I needed to figure out who was going to take care of Trinity full-time while I was at the hospital. Usually, I could depend on Lou and Sarah to fill in when Mom needed a break, but Lou was so stressed with his new job, I couldn't ask him to take time off work. Sarah had just had her first child two weeks earlier, by cesarean section, so she couldn't help, and Grandma Cindy couldn't afford to take time off work after we just got home from Hawaii. I decided to call Aunt Connie to see if she could fly down and help.

Aunt Connie, who I like to call the safety marshal, had helped to raise Lou and is more dependable than 99 percent of people in the world. She was always offering to help and was the perfect person to care for Trinity. She flew in from Oakland the next morning and took over caring for Trinity.

Tabitha and Trinity were being taken care of—now I needed Tiara to wake up. For three days, I sat staring at her, with my only companions the swooshing of the ventilator and my chest pain. A nurse noticed I was in pain and offered to bring me a breast pump, but I declined. I had already made my decision to quit breastfeeding; there was no going back now. She then showed me how to bind my chest with blankets, to help ease the pain. She asked Tiara's doctor if he could prescribe me medication to stop my milk from coming in, but he said no. I would have to see my physician, which meant I was forced to endure the pain. Binding my chest helped, but the doctors looked at me oddly when discussing Tiara's condition. I explained my predicament to a few, but I kept the rest of them guessing.

I didn't care about how ridiculous I appeared—I just wanted to know when Tiara was going to wake up, but no one could give me an answer. By the sixth day, Tiara started to move a little—she was waking up! This good news was dampened because I had just learned she had developed pneumonia. They put her on antibiotics, and we focused on her waking up. As she became more alert, the breathing tube attached to the ventilator was causing her pain. She needed to cough out phlegm produced by the pneumonia, but she couldn't with a tube in her mouth. When her oxygen level declined, we knew she needed suctioning. Each time they suctioned her, tears would drip from the corners of her eyes, and she would make a loud gagging sound like she couldn't get her breath. I could hardly endure hearing it.

Thankfully, the doctor decided it was time to take her off the ventilator, even though she wasn't completely awake. I was so scared that once they removed the breathing tube, she wouldn't be able to breathe on her own. They warned that this was a real possibility, and if it happened, they would immediately have to reinsert the tube. They were pushing for[?] the removal of the ventilator because they were worried she would develop additional secondary infections. The respiratory therapist, who was supposed to remove her tube, rushed into the room and seemed put off by having to complete this job. I instantly didn't trust him, for some reason, and was terrified he was somehow going to screw it up. Luckily, my gut instinct was wrong this time, and the removal of the breathing tube went fine.

She was then transferred to the fourth floor to finish her recovery. The neurologist taking care of her during this visit, Dr. Phillips, was new to CHOC and seemed very knowledgeable. It was hard because I wanted Dr. Rho to treat her, because he knew her the best, but he wasn't a CHOC doctor. I called him every day to update him on her status, but it wasn't the same as him seeing her. Dr. Phillips decided to put Tiara on Depakote because he said it was the strongest anti-epileptic and very old-school, but very effective. The possible side effects were significant: weight gain, excess facial hair, damage to the liver, nausea, early puberty, and the list goes on. But we didn't have a choice. On her tenth day in the hospital, just before being discharged, Dr. Phillips came in to talk with us.

"So, are you ready to go home?" he asked us

"Yes, we are so ready to get out of here," I said.

"I need you both to understand Tiara's condition," Dr. Phillips said while looking at Lou and me.

"What do you mean?" I asked.

"What happened with Tiara this time is going to happen again. I've worked in the state mental hospital for years, and I had many patients with tuberous sclerosis."

"They lived in the institution?" I asked. Thinking of a child, like Tiara, living without the love of their parents daily, broke my heart. It must be so hard to have seizures every day and to be taken care of by people who didn't love you.

"Yes, most of them were on the severe end of the spectrum, like Tiara. Tiara will have another status seizure that requires her to be placed in a drug-induced coma. I have seen patients like Tiara, and this will happen again, but next time, she may not be so lucky."

"For sure, you know this will happen again?"

"Yes, it will. I have seen other patients like her, time and time again, and it always happens. I'll see you in my office in a few weeks."

"Thank you." I looked away from him and stared at Tiara, sleeping next to me. He was wrong; I couldn't let him be right. No doctor had ever given us a prognosis on Tiara's condition, because it was so unknown. Yet, this guy was telling me this was going to happen again, without doubt. Hating Dr. Phillips was more comfortable than facing Tiara's future, so that's what I did.

Unfortunately, I heard his words in my head, over and over again, each time she had a prolonged seizure. I wondered, is this the "next time"? Will this be the seizure that ends her life? Once we got home from the hospital, Tiara was still weak and wobbly on her feet, but like always, she recovered pretty quickly. Depakote worked miracles for her seizures, but caused a severe increase in her appetite, resulting in immediate weight gain. It wasn't a big deal at first, but as she continued gaining a pound a week, it became serious.

CHAPTER 8

Moving

Now home from the hospital, with my three girls, I was struggling to figure out our routine. Lou was always working, Tabitha had what seemed like endless amounts of club soccer all over the county, Tiara was off balance and falling all the time, and Trinity was only five months old and already trying to crawl. I couldn't trust Tiara to walk anywhere safely, so I needed to be by her side all the time. Trinity somehow understood this and learned from a very young age to keep up, or she could be left behind. The poor kid was always crawling after one of us or trying to get her fair share of time in my arms. During this time, we lived in a two-story house in Costa Mesa, in a gated community with fourteen other homes. Tabitha had her own room; Trinity and Tiara shared a room for their clothing and toys, but they both slept in bed with Lou and me.

One day, while doing laundry in the upstairs hallway closet, Tiara wandered into her bedroom. As I was turning on the dryer, I heard her squealing with delight. I looked into her bedroom and caught her jumping on the bed. Supernormal behavior for a kid and it would not have been a big deal, except her bed happened to be pushed up against a wall, under a window, which was open. She was jumping with so much force, she could have easily flown through the screen. I screamed for her to stop because I was terrified she would plummet to her death in front of my eyes. I scooped her up into my arms and scolded her by saying: "No jump on the bed, Tiara, no jump!"

Once Tiara found something she liked to do, she found a way to continue doing it no matter what anyone said. From that moment on, every time I left her unattended for even a second, I would find her jumping on the bed. I kept the window closed at all times, but Lou was freaking out about the situation. Then she started falling down the stairs almost every day.

Our staircase had glass supporting the handrail on the bottom level, instead of spindles, so she would miss a few steps at the top of the stairs and then come rolling down and hit the glass. We were worried the glass would shatter on her, or she would break her neck, as she fell down the stairs. We put baby gates at both the top and bottom of the staircase, to prevent her from walking down on her own or going up to jump on the bed. Good idea, right? Well, they worked for Trinity, but Tiara was tall enough to lunge her body over the gates, like a pole-vaulter. Tiara would then come flying down the stairs with even more momentum than before. The whole situation was just too dangerous. I couldn't watch three kids on my own in a two-story house and keep everyone safe. It was becoming impossible.

Lou was making more money than he had ever made, and for the first time in our lives together, we were not in debt. I had always wanted a one-story cottage-type house, but Lou liked the newer Mediterranean style, which we were currently living in at the time. We discussed it and decided even though we didn't want to overextend ourselves once again, we had to buy a new house and fast; otherwise, Tiara was going to get seriously hurt. Lou got us pre-approved for a loan and said: "You can find a house for $650,000 or less. The more you spend, the less you will have for fixing it up."

"Perfect! I can find us a house for that."

I called Mom, loaded the kids into my minivan, and started driving the streets of Costa Mesa and Newport looking for a house. It was in 2002, and finding a home in Dover Shores, my desired location, wasn't possible. My second choice, Eastside Costa Mesa, had more options, but most of the houses were too small for our family. We needed about two thousand square feet and a home with good bones that just needed some updating. We couldn't afford to tear down walls or do major remodeling. We could afford new flooring, kitchen countertops, and lighting, but not much more. I also have to mention that I refused to live anywhere but Eastside Costa Mesa or Newport Beach. I was a complete and total snob at this point in my life and couldn't imagine living outside a specific five-mile radius, which revolved around Seventeenth Street in Costa Mesa.

Lou would have been happy moving to Irvine or South Orange County, where we could find a more reasonably priced home, but I would have nothing to do with it. I had to live right next to my family, who all lived within the "designated area" we deemed an appropriate place to live.

I found a house within a week, in the Eastside Costa Mesa neighborhood with a Newport address because back then it was an unincorporated area. It incorporated into Newport Beach a year later, which was great for our property value. It had three good-sized bedrooms, three bathrooms, and both a living and family room, each with fireplaces. The large galley kitchen was perfect, except for the countertops, tiled in avocado green with brown grout. The bathrooms weren't much better. The whole house was really grandma looking, but I loved it instantly and saw the potential, plus it had big front and back yards. Land, I love it!

I called Lou at work and asked him when he could see the house.

He said, "I don't have time to look at the house, Tiffani, I am trying to work. If you like it, buy it."

"What? I need you to see the house, please, Lou. What if you don't like it, and then you are mad at me forever? It is older, and I know you like newer houses, so you have to see it, please. If you don't hurry, someone else will get it, and I want it."

This discussion went on and off for two hours. I kept calling and begging him to leave work to see the house, and he kept saying no. This wasn't like Lou. He usually would do anything to please me, but he was more stressed than I had ever seen him. I knew he wouldn't love the house, because it was old and ugly, but I needed him to see my vision and not hate the house. I knew I could transform it into something beautiful. Finally, I got him to see it the next day.

He walked in, looked around, and said, "I hate it, but if you want it, I will buy it for you." I told the agent we wanted it, and Lou negotiated the deal.

After the deal was done, Lou said, "You have two weeks before we move in and $20,000 to fix the house. I can't help you with anything, and I don't want to see any workmen in the house after we move in."

"I can do that. I'm so excited, thank you, Louie!"

Lou hates having anyone working in our home. Remember, I had a six-month-old, a four-year-old having seizures every day, and a ten-year-old, plus a considerable list to accomplish. I had to replace the kitchen countertops, put in a new stove and dishwasher, recessed lighting, carpet, flooring in the kitchen, baseboards, crown molding, switch out the mirrors in the bathrooms, add closet doors to Tabitha's closet, and paint every room in the house. That was just the inside, but the outside could wait until later. One of my good friend's husband, who was super handy and out of work at the time offered to help do all the electrical, plumbing, and baseboards for a great price. He then commissioned his brother-in-law to do all the painting. My uncle referred me to a great granite guy, who worked through the night for cash, and my friend from college had his company do the carpet. I drove around with my girls, at all hours, passing out money to workers to meet my deadline. The funny thing is that I didn't have one problem. Every contractor and friend who helped me did exactly what he promised, and everything came out the way I wanted. And so, two weeks later, Lou took half a day off from work, and with the help of movers, we moved into our safe, new one-story home, where we continued to live for twelve years.

I guess this would be a good time to explain how Lou and I operate as a couple. I run the house, the kids, their schooling, their medical issues, the bills, and insurance paperwork. Lou makes money and is in charge of home loans and purchasing our cars. He also washes our cars weekly and takes them for service. If I want to paint huge fuchsia stripes on our family room wall, which I have done, Lou doesn't care, just don't ask him to help. He doesn't go with me to any of Tiara's doctor appointments, parent-teacher conferences, or IEP meetings, but when he isn't working, he is spending time with our girls. He plays with them, takes them to the park, to the fair, and to the beach, where he digs enormous holes in the sand for them to play in. He reads them books, takes them for drives, teaches them softball, soccer, and basketball. While he hangs out with them, I'm always starting new projects, which drives him a bit insane. I'm either painting a new wall, gardening, hanging curtains, regrouting the shower, planning an elaborate birthday, volunteering for the school or the TS Alliance, or coming up with a new business idea, which I think I can do in my nonexistent free time. He wants me to stop doing so much, and I want him to do more. I spend more money than we have because I think everything is a necessity, but he doesn't get mad. He just refinances the house or tells me to get another credit card. If I say we can't afford something for the girls, he tells me that's ridiculous and to get them what they need. This is why we always have money problems. When I finally realized we needed to cut back on expenses severely, he thought I was overreacting. Once the recession hits, we will both be on the same page regarding our finances, but it will be too late.

CHAPTER 9

Defining a Seizure

By Spring 2003, Tiara's development was improving, as she only experienced a few short seizures every day. At four and a half years old, she could say her name, which sounded like: "TT," so that became her new nickname. When presented with cards of different animals, she could identify a dog, a cat, a cow, and a horse. She knew her colors but couldn't speak the words, so she tried using sign language to identify colors. But that was also difficult because her fine motor skills were lacking. She could make the signs for *hungry, thirsty, more, thank you, please*, and *sorry*. She always said "Hi" to everyone when entering a room and "Bye" when leaving. She learned best through music, which is why I sang everything she needed to learn. She had been attending music therapy since she was a baby, and I had learned all the teaching songs. We had a "clean up" song, a "colors" song, a "body-parts" song, an "animal" song. We sang all day long, which was hilarious because I have a terrible voice.

Despite Tiara's increased mental development, her behavior had started to escalate. It wasn't uncommon for her to bite, hit, or pinch when she didn't get her way. The therapists blamed her inability to speak, along with transition anxieties, for her bad behaviors. She loved to drive to school but refused to get out of the car. Once in school, she loved playtime but hated to sit for learning time. She would get in the bathtub but not get out. At school, they started using the Picture Exchange Communication System (PECS) to help her learn how to communicate more effectively and create smoother transitions.

PECS is a system that helps a person initiate communication, make choices, or prepare for transitions by seeing an image on a two-by-two-inch card. While at school, they would put three cards in front of her. One with a picture of a book, one with a ball, and one with an instrument.

Her aide would then ask: "Would you like to read a book with me, play ball, or play an instrument?" Tiara was then supposed to choose the picture which corresponded to the activity she desired to engage in.

Well, it didn't work like that for Tiara. Tiara would typically pick up the closest card and stick it in her mouth. Oh, I forgot to mention her obsession with putting everything in her mouth. Most babies go through an oral sensory phase, where they stick everything in their mouths to learn about textures, softness, firmness, and hardness. As they develop, they usually outgrow this phase and move on to picking up items and feeling them with their hands instead of their mouths. Tiara was still in the infant stage of putting everything and anything in her mouth to learn about the object. No matter how hard I tried to teach her not to put everything in her mouth, she still did.

Just because Tiara wasn't compliant with PECS at school, didn't mean we were giving up. Miss Susan thought Tiara needed more practice.

"I think it would be best for Tiara if you start using PECS at home," said Miss Susan.

"Okay. Do you want me to use PECS for everything we do at home?"

"That would be ideal, but I understand it's going to take some getting used to," said Miss Susan.

"I can do it if you think it will help her. Where do I get the cards?"

"You can download them free from the website. After you print them out, the pages need to be laminated. Once laminated, cut out the squares and place a piece of Velcro on the back. You'll need a big binder, organized by categories, to store all the cards. It's a big job, but I know it will help Tiara."

"Then, I'll do it!" I started on the massive project right away and immediately hated it but tried to keep a positive attitude. At home, the system was supposed to work like this: "Tiara, would you like oatmeal or pancakes?" I would show her a picture of oatmeal and one of pancakes, then I would wait for her to choose. She would stare at me like I was crazy, grab the closest card, and put it in her mouth. Then I would retrieve the card from her jaws while trying not to get bitten. It was a fun game and one that I only stuck with for several months until I admitted defeat. I did love PECS for helping with transitions. I would show her a card that said: "First this _____ and then _____. I would put a picture in each open spot and explain to her, "First, you will eat breakfast, and then we will drive in the car." I would repeat this statement not just once but many times, constantly reminding her what would happen next. This part of the PECS system worked great for her. She loved knowing what was going to happen next, which helped to reduce her anxiety with transitions, and she was not being asked to make a choice herself.

I continued to use this technique throughout her entire life. I can tell you that PECS is a wonderful system for many autistic children and their families, but not Tiara. The school district had not officially labeled Tiara autistic, but it was becoming clear she had obvious autistic tendencies, so the diagnosis seemed imminent. Yet, it didn't matter at this point.

Even though Tiara was considered severely delayed, she was sweet, loving, and a fighter, all in one.

Tiara was a Scorpio, born the Year of the Tiger, which meant she was a force to be reckoned with. She was stubborn and determined to always get her way, which could be a disaster for us, her therapists, and teachers, but was mostly a huge blessing. I knew her stubborn streak had kept her alive on more than one occasion. It allowed her to live with hundreds of seizures each day and keep putting one foot in front of the other. Or rather, lift her arms to me so that I would carry her everywhere. Yes, I still carried her, despite her increasing size and age.

The Depakote was helping to reduce her daily seizures, but she continued to gain weight at a rapid pace; so much weight that her cardiologist, pediatrician, and neurologist accused me of not taking control of the situation, as if it was my fault she was starving to death and had an insatiable appetite. Dr. Rho was concerned about the dangerous side effects of Depakote and wanted to explore other options. She had tried almost every combination of seizure medications that existed, had the VNS implanted, turned on, then turned off, and wasn't deemed a suitable candidate for brain surgery at UCLA.

So, what was next? He convinced me that we needed to relook at brain surgery, but at UCI, instead of UCLA. I dreaded enduring another extended inpatient ordeal, but Dr. Rho was convinced something in Tiara's brain might have changed. I wasn't as optimistic. I knew she wouldn't be a brain-surgery candidate—but what if I was wrong? I had to try.

Once we checked into UCI, I got a bad feeling. As you may or may not know, back then, UCLA had an old hospital, which was pretty dingy. Well, let me tell you that UCLA looked like a five-star hotel next to UCI Medical Center. It was beyond disgusting. They gave her a room with broken window glass, which you couldn't see out of because it had some weird, dark film over it. The hot water faucet that everyone was supposed to use to wash their hands before examining my child didn't work, and there was no sanitizer dispenser in the room. I was feeling so uncomfortable with the conditions, I was ready to discharge her before they even finished the intake procedure.

As we were sitting on the bed together, I looked at the wall and saw old boogers stuck to it. At first, I thought I imagined it, but upon closer inspection, they were boogers. I immediately called for the nurse, who apparently couldn't find our room, because we waited in that horrible room for an hour before anyone came in. Also, the EEG telemetry technician hadn't even started placing the leads on Tiara's head yet, which takes over an hour. I must have sung "Twinkle, Twinkle, Little Star" to Tiara over a hundred times before anyone even showed up. I could already tell this wasn't going to be a pleasant experience.

Once Lou arrived, I explained the situation.

"I'm freaking out! I don't think I can stay here. This place is horrible," I said.

"Honey, you just have to deal with it. You'll be fine," he promised.

"Really? I don't think so, and I can tell you right now, they won't find anything different than UCLA did two years ago."

"You agreed to give it a try, so you need to follow through."

"I'm so not happy!" I declared.

"You know I love you, right?" Lou said.

"Yes, but that doesn't help right now."

"You are so pretty—does that help?"

"Not even close. I'm about to punch you in the face, so stop saying nice things to me when I'm so mad." At this point, Tiara started laughing at us, and Lou reached over to give her a hug.

"I'm gonna go. Tiara, take care of Mommy, and make sure she doesn't hurt anyone," Lou said laughingly. He kissed us both goodbye.

After thirty-six hours in that disgusting room, she was hooked up to EEG telemetry but had yet to complete an MRI or a PET Scan. I couldn't take it anymore. I complained to Dr. Rho about the filthy conditions and lack of nursing support. He tried to convince us to stay another few days. He said they were planning to build a new hospital and that he had no control over the current room situation. He also said they hadn't captured any seizures yet.

"What? She's had at least two seizures that I witnessed with my own eyes."

"What did they look like?"

"It's the one she always has when she falls asleep. After falling asleep, her eyes suddenly pop open, she starts gagging and drooling, while making teeth grinding sounds. Sometimes she even vomits."

"I saw the events you marked, and those weren't seizures."

"Really? I find that hard to believe. What are they?"

"Probably just a reflex or a behavior."

"How can it be a behavior, when she is asleep? That doesn't make any sense. She's had this seizure her entire life, and I know it's a seizure."

"It may look like a seizure to you, but it's not."

"Well, now that you have confirmed you have nothing after thirty-six hours of torture, we are leaving. I'm sorry, but we can't do this anymore. Plus, to be honest, even if you did find something and thought you could do brain surgery on Tiara, I would never allow her to have brain surgery in this facility. We are out of here!"

Needless to say, Dr. Rho wasn't happy with me, and I wasn't pleased with him.

In his defense, the definition of a seizure had significantly changed in Tiara's lifetime. For the first nine years of Tiara's life, a neurologist would only qualify something as a seizure if the EEG findings correlated with physical manifestations. If you saw physical signs of a seizure, as I did with Tiara described above, it wasn't deemed a seizure unless these actions correlated with abnormal brain activity. So, Dr. Rho was correct based on this theory, but guess what, he should have stepped outside the box and looked at the obvious. Later in life, while meeting with her UCLA team and talking about this exact seizure in question, they admitted that not all seizures could be captured on an EEG. As research developed, they learned a seizure originating from a tumor deep in the brain might not be able to be picked up by telemetry. So, I wasn't crazy!

Luckily, neurologists now consider a seizure to be "real" based on either the physical signs or telemetry; it doesn't have to appear on both. Thank God for medical progress and doctors finally admitting they don't know everything about seizures and how the brain works. Soon after this admission, Dr. Rho left UCI to work at another hospital out of state, so we didn't have to break up. He moved on, and we tried a new neurologist at CHOC.

As for my other children: Yes, they still existed, and I struggled to care for them as best as I could. Trinity had just turned one and was walking and running by her first birthday. She moved from crawling to walking at ten months old, after Tiara accidentally sat on her.

Trinity was crawling around the family room, and Tiara walked by, lost her balance, and plopped on top of Trinity's back. Trinity screamed and I ran to her and pulled Tiara off of her. The next day,

Trinity started pulling herself up to a standing position with the aid of the coffee table, bar stools, and couch. Trinity also developed quite the vocabulary, which oddly enough started with the word "time." As soon as I heard her say it, I thought I had heard wrong. Why would she be saying "time"? What a weird first word for a child to express. And then it hit me. Of course, "time" would be her first word.

Why? Because when Tiara would have a seizure, I would yell, "get the time!" Not all of my watches had a second hand, and I needed to know precisely how long each seizure lasted, so I would yell to whoever was near.

"Time, what time is it?" What a sad first word. It nearly broke my heart when I realized why she had learned that word first. Soon after she began walking, she started packing bags for our departures. Each time we left the house, she would run to her room and grab a Disney purse filled with things. She refused to leave without her bag. That's weird. Well, actually, it's not, because I could never leave the house without being prepared. I needed snacks, pacifiers, Diastat in case of a status seizure, other seizure meds, diapers, wipes, and a change of clothes for both of them. A bag was continually being packed and reloaded. I had different bags for different excursions, based on the length of time we would be away from the house. Trinity was just modeling my behavior. As for Tabitha, she was ten years old, playing club soccer year-round, and was an amazing big sister to Trinity. She loved carrying Trinity and gave her the attention I couldn't always provide. Trinity had become both Tabitha and Tiara's favorite sister. God knew what he was doing when he gave us Trinity. On that note, I should fill you in on what ended up happening with Lou's vasectomy issues after Trinity was born.

When Lou decided not to have another vasectomy, he admitted to me that before I got pregnant with Trinity, he had wanted a third child. He had visualized getting me pregnant repeatedly until it actually happened. Once I was pregnant and he realized how terrified I was to have a third baby, he decided to change his thought process. He started visualizing himself no longer being able to get me pregnant. He did this technique for a few months, until he was convinced it had worked. I thought he was insane, but, guess what. He went back to the urologist right before Trinity was born, and his sperm count was once again zero. The urologist was baffled and said it was impossible. Yes, our family believes in miracles, mind over matter, angels, psychics, ghosts, mediums, and all things related to God intervening and helping us through life.

To be safe, I would periodically make Lou go back to the urologist and test his sperm. His sperm count has remained zero. We have never once used birth control since Trinity was born, and I have never conceived another child. She was a real miracle.

CHAPTER 10

Transitioning

B efore Tiara started Killybrooke Elementary, we had an IEP to review what services she would receive and how her day would be structured. Because of her seizures, the school district readily agreed to continue providing her with a one-on-one aide at all times. They also decided she would receive occupational therapy, speech therapy, and adaptive PE several times per week. They promised Tiara would be safe and taken care of wonderfully in Ms. Jesse's class. Despite their assurances, I was nervous about her first day of kindergarten. Because I was so worried, I decided it would be best if the teacher and aides in the class knew about Tiara in depth. I put together a mini book to present them on the first day of school. It was about thirty pages long, with tabbed sections. I included a summary of her medical condition, what her seizures looked like, her past speech and OT therapy reports, and descriptions of some of her behaviors. I explained what certain verbal mumblings meant, because even though she wasn't talking, each expression signified something different.

I drove Tiara to school, as I had done throughout preschool, instead of having her take the bus, like most of the other special-needs children. As we walked onto campus the first day, I wasn't sure what to expect, but I kept telling myself to be positive. As we walked into her classroom, Ms. Sheri, a classroom aide, greeted us. She seemed nice, and I gave her one of the books to review, but she placed it on the table without so much as even opening a page. She then took Tiara's hand and said: "Okay, bye, we will see you at the end of the day."

"Wait, where is her one-on-one aide?"

"She isn't here yet, but don't worry. I'll take care of Tiara," she said.

"Don't you need to ask me a few questions about her seizures, how she communicates? And what about her diapers, wipes and sippy cup, don't you want them?" I asked.

"You can put all her stuff in that cubby, over there." She pointed to a cubed shelf against the wall.

"Where is Ms. Jesse?"

"She went to the office to make some photocopies; she'll be right back. You can go now. I know how to take care of Tiara. This is what we do," she said.

I stood, staring at her, refusing to release Tiara's hand from my own. Luckily, Ms. Jesse arrived just as I was willing myself not to start crying on the spot. I introduced Tiara and myself to her and explained I needed to meet the one-on-one aide and brief her on Tiara before I left.

"Well, she hasn't arrived yet. I think she'll be here at nine o'clock. We will watch Tiara until she arrives," she said.

"That's not going to work for me. I need to meet her aide and explain everything in the book to her."

"I can give her the book when she arrives, and she can read it herself," said Ms. Jesse.

"You might have questions for me, and I'm not leaving Tiara with someone I have never met."

"Okay, then, you can take Tiara over to the play area and wait for her aide to arrive, if you'd like," said Ms. Jesse.

She showed us to the so-called play area. I was horrified. The carpet was filthy, the toys were basically nonexistent, everything was shoved into this little space that couldn't accommodate more than one child at a time, and there was already a child playing in the space. To top it off, the windowsill was filled with a stream of live ants, marching their way down to the play kitchen area. I was speechless. Was this a joke? This is where you want my immune-suppressed child to spend her days? I took a few deep breaths and said, "I need to speak with the principal immediately."

"Oh, is something wrong?"

"Actually, everything is wrong! I'm not trying to be rude—but— Tiara can't stay in a classroom this dirty. She's sick all the time, and I work hard to keep her well. When she gets sick, she ends up in the hospital. This carpet must be fifteen years old, and I don't want her sitting on it. No child should be playing on it. Even if I wanted her to sit and play in this area, there isn't any room for her. She falls easily and needs a clear path to accommodate herself and her aide. Ants are crawling all over. Do you see them?"

"I'm sorry, I didn't see them. I'll take care of the ants. Mrs. Goff, I've been teaching special ed for a long time—no other parents have complained. I promise Tiara will be safe in my class. My aides are wonderful and have worked with me for years," she said.

"Well, I don't feel safe leaving Tiara here. Plus, you don't know anything about Tiara. I need to explain her needs to you."

"I have a file on Tiara. I read it."

"Does the file explain what her seizures look like? Does it tell you to sing her songs if she isn't following directions? Does it say someone has to hold her hand while she walks anywhere? I made up this book describing everything about her, and no one has even bothered to look at it."

"I'm sorry, but I just walked in from the office—I haven't had time," she said.

"I handed it to Ms. Sheri when we arrived—she didn't even bother to flip through it. Then she told me to leave. I don't feel like anyone realizes how serious Tiara's medical condition is. I can't just drop her off somewhere and hope for the best."

"Like I said, Mrs. Goff—we know how to take care of children with special needs."

"Have you ever taken care of a child with tuberous sclerosis?"

"No, but I have taken care of lots of children with seizures," said Ms. Jesse.

"Either way, I'm not letting Tiara sit on that filthy carpet. I won't allow it. I need to talk to the principal right now."

"Would you like us to watch Tiara while you speak with the principal?" she asked.

"Ummmm—I guess. Can Tiara play at the table? I don't want her near the ants or on the carpet."

"Yes, we will play with her at the table. She will be fine, Mrs. Goff."

"Okay, thank you. Please watch her closely," I begged. I stormed off to the principal's office.

"Hi—I need to speak with the principal," I said to the front office secretary.

"I'm sorry, but she is busy right now, can I schedule you an appointment for later?"

"No, this is important. I need to talk to her now."

"Let me go in and ask her if she has a few free minutes. I'll be right back."

"Thank you."

"She has to be at flag deck in ten minutes, so you have seven minutes. You can go in; her office is over there." She pointed to the corner office.

"Thanks." I rushed in to meet the principal.

"Hi, I'm Ms. Sanchez, please sit down. How can I help you?"

"My daughter, Tiara Goff, is in Ms. Jesse's class. I'm sorry, but I'm freaking out—the classroom is a disaster. The carpet is filthy, ants are in the play area, and her aide doesn't arrive for another half hour. None of this is okay. Tiara has seizures—she is chronically sick; she can't spend her days in a room like that. Plus, I need to meet her aide and explain Tiara's history."

"It will be okay, Mrs. Goff. Tiara's aide can't arrive until nine a.m. each day because of funding."

"Then, I won't bring her to school until nine a.m. each day."

"That's not necessary. One of the classroom aides can watch Tiara for thirty minutes until her aide arrives. This is a common problem, and we can resolve it by all working together."

"I don't think any of you understand how complicated Tiara's medical history is and how often she has seizures. She cannot be left unattended in that classroom for even a minute! I can't trust that the classroom aide won't get pulled away to take care of another child. Plus, no one even bothered to look at the book I provided with Tiara's history. And what about the ants and the filthy carpet?"

"I will talk to Ms. Jesse and maintenance and see if we can get the room cleaned up."

"The carpet needs replacing, not just cleaning. It must be fifteen years old, at least."

"I doubt that, Mrs. Goff. New carpet was put in all the classrooms five years ago."

"Well, it wasn't put in Ms. Jesse's class; I can promise you that! Also, the arrangement of the play area is dangerous for Tiara. She easily falls and needs to have more space to move around."

"I can talk to Ms. Jesse about that too. I'm sorry, but I need to be at flag deck. I'll talk to Jesse this morning. Thank you for stopping in to speak with me," she said while standing to leave.

"Okay, thanks for meeting with me."

I was physically sick to my stomach by now. As I walked back to the classroom, I peeked into other rooms and looked at the carpet. None of them had the same blue carpet as was in Tiara's special education classroom; they all had newer carpet, in a completely different color. Figures, why bother putting new carpet in for the disabled kids? Once I got back to class, the teacher and aides had decided I was a threat and a crazy parent. They didn't realize I wasn't attacking them personally, just the situation. Once the aide arrived, I briefed her on Tiara but decided I still couldn't leave Tiara in that room—we left. I told Ms. Jesse we would return tomorrow, and if the room was cleaned up and in suitable condition, Tiara could stay. Once we reached the safety of our car and I had Tiara buckled safely into her car seat, I put my head down on the steering wheel and sobbed. I felt so defeated. How could my sweet angel spend the day in that disgusting room? Then, I got mad. Tiara would never attend that school unless they fixed that room!

We walked in the next day, and everything was the same except the ants were dead, but not cleaned up. I looked around, and we walked straight to the principal's office. "Tiara will not be coming to school until someone fixes the carpeting and rearranges the furniture!" I said to Ms. Sanchez.

That afternoon, Ms. Sanchez called me and said we would be having a meeting on Thursday to discuss the situation. "Okay, great. Tiara will remain at home with me until the situation is rectified." Thursday rolled around, and I walked into the meeting only to be greeted by twelve adults with bad attitudes and bad looks on their faces. Oh, crap, I guess this was war, and I didn't bring any weapons except my mouth. The speech teacher, Jennifer, who I hadn't met before, was leading the meeting and had an apparent dislike for me. Jennifer explained it was an IEP meeting and then instructed everyone in the room to go around the circle of chairs and introduce themselves to me. The principal hadn't said it was a formal IEP. There was the speech teacher, the adaptive PE teacher, the principal, the occupational therapist, the nurse, a regular education teacher, a district employee, Tiara's teacher, and all the classroom aides.

After everyone introduced themselves, Jennifer launched into a speech about my conduct. She started by saying I was overreacting, overprotective, too demanding, that I had unreasonable expectations, blah, blah, blah. Well, Kathy, the school nurse, who had known Tiara since she was thirty months old, sided with me and shut her down. Nurse Kathy explained that I was not overprotective, and the room was a health hazard to Tiara. She also agreed that the carpet was not acceptable for any child to be sitting, playing, or resting on. Huh, take that, people! She also told them that, unlike other children, the aide assigned to Tiara had to be within reaching distance of Tiara at all times because she was a fall risk. Tiara was never to be left unsupervised for even a second. If she was sitting in a chair, her aide needed to be sitting behind or next to her. Nurse Kathy then went on to describe the seriousness of Tiara's health issues and why the carpet wasn't acceptable, nor was the arrangement of the play area. The area where Tiara played needed enough room to allow her to walk safely with her aide by her side. The current set up didn't allow for this, which is why it needed to be changed.

Every adult in the room avoided eye contact with me, except Nurse Kathy, who had saved the day. After Kathy finished with Tiara's health history, the room was silent until Ms. Jesse spoke up.

"I used to have the play area over in the corner. If I move it back over there, it will open up the space and allow Tiara to have more room. Do you think that would work for you?" she asked, directing her question to me.

"That seems like it would work," I said.

The district employee then said, "I'll contact the district head of maintenance and ask him to assess whether the carpet should be cleaned or replaced. Until then, can we come up with a solution for the carpet?"

"We have carpet squares we can place on top of the carpet. Would you let Tiara sit on the carpet squares? I got them last year; they are clean. I can show them to you, if you like." said Ms. Jesse, while standing and walking toward a pile of carpet squares.

"Those look fine; that should work. Please make sure to put down several, so her hands don't touch the other carpet," I said.

Ms. Sanchez then spoke up. "Let me look at all the aides' schedules and see if I can play around with timing, so Tiara's aide could arrive earlier each day. I'll look into it today and call you this afternoon, Mrs. Goff. Jesse, can the staff come in early tomorrow and disinfect all the toys?"

"Yes. We will move all the furniture around and clean everything," she said.

"Did we address all your concerns, Mrs. Goff?" asked Ms. Sanchez.

"Yes, I feel better. Thank you."

"If no one has anything else to say, this meeting is over. Thank you all for attending," said Ms. Sanchez.

Within a week, the school district installed new carpeting, after realizing Ms. Jesse's room had somehow been overlooked when all the other classrooms had been updated with new carpeting years prior. Hum, how odd! Everything else we agreed upon was completed, and Tiara finally started kindergarten the next week.

CHAPTER 11

Gaining Weight

Over the next few years, Tiara entered into a new phase of her life where, for once, her biggest worry wasn't seizures, but chronic pneumonia, obesity, and eczema. She was eating more than a high school football player and continuously snacking. At first, I didn't think much of it. The doctors said Depakote could increase her appetite, but they never said she would become insatiable. Maybe it was a phase and her body would get used to the medicine, and she wouldn't be so hungry. But her eating just kept getting worse. I mean, overeating or seizures, which is worse? I would have taken overeating any day, until the day my child became obese and developed a whole host of new medical problems I had never contemplated before.

I needed to buy her new clothes often, as nothing fit for more than a month. It bothered Mom when Tiara's clothes were permanently stained or didn't fit correctly, so she often gave me money to purchase new clothes. Tiara drooled continuously, and only half of everything she tried putting in her mouth made it on the first attempt. The other half landed on her chest or pants, which didn't bother Tiara a bit. She would pick up whatever fell onto her body and try shoving it back in her mouth again. As a result, I changed her outfit several times a day.

Because I'm impatient, I never bothered sorting through each piece of clothing to look for stains to spray with stain remover, so all her clothes were permanently soiled. As long as I got them cleaned, who cared? Tiara didn't. She was only concerned with deciding which shirt she wanted to wear, as she was very picky. If I tried putting her in a shirt she didn't like, she would fight me or try running away. Those shirts remained at the bottom of her drawer. While clothes shopping, I would hold up each item for her review. I only purchased the articles which received a big smile, even if they weren't what I would choose. Once home, she modeled all her new clothes, usually with Grandma Cindy as the audience. She pranced and sauntered if she liked the outfit and scowled while saying, "No, no," if she deemed it a loser. I immediately returned these items.

Tiara was a born fashionista with more self-esteem than anyone I've ever met. Staring at her reflection in the mirror could captivate her attention longer than any other activity. She would sit on the ground in our bedroom, opposite the full-length mirror and pose. She'd inherited my smile and would smile at herself while flipping her hair and tilting her head, as she tried on headbands, sunglasses, and jewelry. She had her stash of accessories, but somehow, she always managed to get a hold of mine. If sad, she'd stare at herself in the mirror and fake cry. If angry, she'd repeatedly point her finger at the mirror, while glaring. Her face and body language were so incredibly expressive, she didn't need words to express her feelings. As her vocabulary increased,

I'd find her talking to herself in the mirror. Whether she was obese or desperately thin, she knew she was beautiful and loved herself. Gratefully, she didn't understand what other people thought of her fate in life.

Throughout her life, she was often jealous of Tabitha and Trinity when they had friends over, but aside from her sibling jealousy, she was happy with who she was. She seemed not to notice the stares from others while playing in the park sandbox, as a teenager. She sat on my lap in public, even when she outweighed me by a hundred pounds. As onlookers gaped and stared, she returned their looks of horror with a big smile while saying, "Hi." Tabitha often said, "I wish I had Tiara's confidence." We were all envious of her confidence.

Tiara didn't seem to notice that her hair was falling out and thinning while taking Depakote. Her biggest concern was finding enough food to satisfy her appetite while I tried controlling her intake to include only healthy options. We were in a constant battle, and I was losing. Her favorite foods were Brie cheese, avocados, french fries, and chicken fingers. She would cry and beg for them. I felt horrible denying her, but being overweight was causing her so many problems. Her cardiologist was continually getting mad at me because of her weight. "Absolutely no avocados, they are the most fattening food in the world," he said.

"But I thought they were healthy?"

"Not for Tiara, no more. If you have an avocado tree, pull it out of the ground," he declared.

Luckily, I didn't, even though it would have saved me hundreds on our food bill. He wasn't the only one after me. Her pediatrician and every other doctor, including her neurologist and pulmonologist were on me, because she now had asthma. The doctors didn't realize or didn't care that she was starving! She wasn't eating for comfort or out of boredom; the Depakote was making her hungry all the time, and she couldn't control herself. If you have ever been on steroids, you know how she felt.

It was frustrating because everyone was blaming me for her weight gain and telling me how bad it was for her health, but I didn't know what more to do. Everyone gave me unsolicited advice, but unless you lived with us, you couldn't understand how utterly impossible the situation was. I put a child safety lock on the pantry doors, but when she couldn't get the food out, she would lay on the ground and kick them until the wood was about to shatter. We couldn't afford to buy new kitchen cabinets, so I had to intervene. When I tried to stop her, she would turn on me, and I would be the recipient of the kicking and hitting. I would eventually cave and give her some crackers. We tried putting a baby lock on the refrigerator door, but she pulled on the handle so hard, it tore off, forcing us to buy a new refrigerator. After dinner each night, I announced, "the kitchen is closed," which meant no one was allowed to enter the kitchen for any reason. This was so

unfair to Tabitha and Trinity. Tabitha would come home from volleyball and want a snack, but if Tiara was still awake, she had to sneak because, once Tiara heard a cabinet door open, she would come running for food. I felt sorry for Tiara and helpless at the same time. She developed asthma, her blood pressure was creeping up, and she was covered in eczema.

Tiara wasn't the sole recipient of my worry that summer, as both Tabitha and Trinity became patients, for different reasons. Tabitha was eleven and still playing club soccer all over the universe, or what felt like all over the globe, since I was dragging Tiara and Trinity to all the games while Lou worked all weekend. The games were usually inland like Norco or Riverside, and the weather was sweltering. Tiara would sit under an umbrella while I doused her with water, trying to keep her cool, while Trinity, wearing her Belle costume, walked around, talking to all the other parents.

Trinity was two, and in the phase where she insisted on wearing a costume-type dress everywhere we went. If it wasn't Belle, it was a knee-length tutu or a Snow White outfit. She was a very stubborn child when it came to her wardrobe. If I asked her to wear something besides one of her tutus or princess dresses, she refused to leave the house. I quickly gave up the battle and made sure I had a clean princess dress for her to wear each day. The princess dresses helped her make lots of friends, as all the adults and other children would always comment on her beautiful dress. She was often socializing and entertaining herself, because sadly, she had no other option, as I was always looking after Tiara. If I took my eyes off Tiara for even a moment, she would run away. She was a serious flight risk and couldn't be trusted for even a second. Unlike other two-year-old children, Trinity never ran off or got into trouble. She always stayed close to me, without me having to ask.

During this time, Tabitha was struggling with her asthma. She had been diagnosed with asthma as a little girl but only had real issues when she was sick. Tabitha was an incredible goalkeeper and spent all her time waiting in the goalie box, which didn't require much running. Her team was exceptional, so she got bored waiting in the goalie box. When she asked her coach if she could try another position, he offered to let her try playing halfback and let the relief goalkeeper have a chance at goalie. Once she got out of the goalie box, we soon learned Tabitha could throw the soccer ball across the entire field, a huge advantage for her team. She wasn't a fast runner, but each time the ball went out of bounds, the coach instructed her to take the throw-in. Tabitha ran from end to end, throwing in every out-of-bounds ball. Everyone was always talking about how far she could throw the ball, and it wasn't uncommon for the other coaches to approach her after the game and ask how she learned to throw so far. She was born a strong girl and was also training for her black belt in Tae Kwon Do, so I'm sure her martial arts training was a big reason for her unusual throwing ability. Lou claims she inherited it from him, and most likely, he's right.

Nevertheless, this was the first time in her soccer career that she had to run up and down the field. Like everyone in our family, Tabitha had allergies to grass, individual trees, and dust, but she tolerated them without many problems. After running up and down the field during a particularly challenging game, she started to look sick and asked the coach to pull her out. Confirming something was wrong, she felt a tightening in her chest. The coach offered her an inhaler, but she didn't think she was having an asthma attack and didn't want to use an inhaler since she had never used one before. She sat on the sidelines for the rest of the game.

After the game, I took her and her two little sisters straight to the walk-in clinic. I told the doctor what had happened during the game. He listened to her breathing and didn't hear any wheezing but said he wanted to measure how much air she was able to take in and expel. He had her blow as hard as she could into a white plastic tube, called a peak flow meter, which had an arrow that moved up and down, measuring how much air was blown through the device. He had her repeat this several times, and then he declared she was in the red zone. *What the hell is the red zone?* I thought. Before I could even ask him what the red zone was, he went into an explanation of the different asthma levels. Green is good; yellow means caution, you need to get yourself back in the green zone with rescue medications; and red means danger, the lungs are struggling to move air in and out. He went on to explain that Tabitha could have died on the soccer field, and asthma was very serious and not to be taken lightly. Awesome, I felt so much better (me being facetious), and I continued to listen. He told us about his friend in medical school, whose fiancé had died from an asthma attack.

He said that if Tabitha was in the red zone, she had most likely started the day in the yellow zone and should not have been playing soccer. Loser Mom here, as I had no idea she was having an asthma attack. Of course, like Tiara, Tabitha didn't have typical symptoms. She wasn't wheezing or panting and didn't appear to be struggling to breathe. He wanted me to drive her to the hospital and have her admitted, but she was dead set against the idea, as I was. We had a nebulizer at home, which Tiara was using daily, so I knew I could take care of Tabitha at home. He agreed to give her a few breathing treatments in the clinic and then test her levels again and see if she had shown improvement. After a few treatments, she was in the yellow zone, and he sent us home with a prescription for an inhaler and instructions to follow up with her pediatrician the next day. From this point on, Tabitha continued to struggle with keeping her asthma under control and started taking Advair and Singulair daily, so she wouldn't need to use her rescue inhaler as often. As you can tell, our lives weren't getting any easier.

During this same summer, Trinity injured herself while playing bubbles with Tiara in the backyard. Bubbles were Tiara's current obsession, so I was standing next to her, trying to prevent her from dumping bubbles all over herself and the ground. Trinity was playing bubbles on her own because it drove her crazy when Tiara would dump the bubble dish onto the pavement. All of a sudden, Trinity screamed. As I turned around, she was running toward me with blood all over her foot. I quickly scooped her up into my arms. I could see she had sliced her foot on the dish, brittle from the sun, which caused it to break when she stepped on it. I knew she needed stitches and wasn't quite sure how to handle the matter since I was home alone with the three girls. I called my mom and dad. Luckily, they were home and agreed to rush over and watch the girls so I could take Trinity to the walk-in clinic. Tabitha was old enough to babysit a healthy sibling, but not Tiara. My parents lived three miles from our house, door to door.

Back then, Trinity was the toughest kid you have ever seen. The doctor at the walk-in clinic gave her a shot to numb the area, and she didn't even flinch. He stitched her up, and we were on our way home within an hour. Not a tear, a cry, or flinch. I felt like a horrible mom because my baby was only two years old and had just received five stitches. None of my girls had ever needed stitches, so apparently, this was the summer of being a loser mom.

A week later, Trinity started complaining about a spot on her hip. It looked like a mosquito or spider bite that had started to get infected. I put Neosporin on it, Lou's cure for every ailment in the world, but it kept hurting and seemed to be getting bigger. I attempted to pick at the large white head with pus oozing out. It hurt so much when I squeezed it that she started to cry, but it seemed like I needed to get the pus out. So, I kept at it whenever she would let me. Picking is one of my favorite pastimes; I love it. Pimples, ears, and belly buttons are all fair game.

Once Dr. Krumins saw it, he gave me a funny look and asked where or what she had been doing lately. I told him about the stitches on her foot, and he seemed suspicious of something. He pulled out a pair of gloves, which was weird, since they never wore gloves in the pediatrician's office. He squeezed the sore, and Trinity flew through the roof in pain as all this gross brown pus squirted out. It was fabulous to watch, even though Trinity was suffering. He then took a sample of the stuff for the lab and cut open the area with a scalpel to clean more out. Dr. Krumins circled the area with a red Sharpie. He told me to squeeze it twice a day to clean it out and if it got any bigger to call him right away. He suspected she had methicillin-resistant *Staphylococcus aureus* or, rather, MRSA, the dreaded staph infection. He thought she had picked it up at the walk-in clinic when I took her there for the stitches in her foot.

Like Tiara, Trinity had eczema all over, and the open sores on her skin made her more susceptible to picking up an infection. He told me it was highly contagious and to keep the wound covered at all times to protect ourselves, especially Tiara. He gave us a prescription for the only antibiotic that isn't resistant to the infection, and we went home. We returned for a follow-up two days later, and he confirmed it was

MRSA. Dr. Krumins was concerned. "She may need to have more of the area cleaned out." I had no idea what he was talking about and didn't realize he meant surgery. He said he would call an expert at CHOC and get back to me later in the day. Off we went. My mom offered to take Trinity to Fashion Island for pizza and a train ride, while I took Tiara to speech therapy, so we went our separate ways.

While at speech, the doctor called and said I needed to bring Trinity to CHOC by three p.m. for a five p.m. surgery. What? Surgery on my baby, today? I explained she was out to lunch with my mom, and once again, I was in trouble. "Out to lunch? She can't eat, she needs to be sedated for the surgery." I felt like one of those parents that live with their heads in the clouds, totally in denial. Did I miss all this information during the appointment that morning, or did he fail to give it to me? I am still not sure, but I am usually pretty on top of medical matters, so I was confused as to how I screwed this whole thing up and was clueless as to the severity of the situation.

He then said, "The surgery is scheduled for today; just don't let her eat anymore and see what the anesthesiologist says when you get there." I called my mom and explained the situation, and we decided to meet back at the house. Then she could take the other two kids.

At the hospital, the anesthesiologist read me the riot act and postponed the surgery until the next day but said we had to stay in the hospital until surgery. I was not ready for this. I can do Tiara in the hospital, but Trinity in the hospital, that was all new to me, and I didn't like it a bit. He then explained that the infection could be deadly, which is why she needed to be put under anesthesia and have the area cut out around the disease to make sure it was all gone. Oh great, glad I didn't know the severity of the situation before, or I wouldn't have slept for days.

Trinity made it through the surgery the next day without a hitch, and the surgeon was impressed with her bravery. Once again, she didn't cry, fuss, or scream. On the other hand, I was traumatized and wondering what God's plan was for me. I knew how to deal with Tiara's medical problems, but now with Trinity needing emergency surgery and Tabitha's asthma, I was feeling overwhelmed. I started to reflect on all the medical needs of my girls combined. I had three girls with severe environmental allergies, which required daily medication. Two of the three had asthma, which also required daily medication and breathing treatments. Two of the three had eczema all over their bodies, which required special creams, soaps, and laundry detergent, and as a result of the eczema, one had picked up a deadly MRSA infection. I also had a child with brain tumors, intractable epilepsy, tumors in her heart, tumors on her skin, developmental delay, speech delay, autistic tendencies, serious behavior issues, and was severely overweight from seizure medications and was now developing high blood pressure. That's a lot for one momma to handle, and I was feeling the pressure.

CHAPTER 12

Staying Close

At this point in our lives, Tabitha was a wonderfully hormonal twelve-year-old, who was starting seventh grade at Carden Hall. She decided she would be playing every school sport offered because she wanted to win the "best female athlete" upon graduating in eighth grade. She had already broken the school record for her ability to throw a softball farther than any other female in Carden Hall history and researched how to win the award for the best female athlete. She would need to make the volleyball, basketball, and soccer teams for both her seventh and eighth grade school years to be considered a candidate. Obviously, there were no real qualifications, but Tabitha was a serious athlete and determined to win this award. So, in addition to club soccer games, I was now attending volleyball games in the fall, basketball games in the winter, and soccer games in the spring, and I loved it! Watching Tabitha play sports brought me true happiness during this time in my life. As for the little ones, Trinity loved the action and was always up for watching Tabitha play sports, as long as I brought along plenty of snacks. Tiara wasn't quite as compliant, but with the help of my fellow moms, who took turns holding Tiara on their laps and singing to her, I managed to watch every game.

You are probably wondering why I didn't have help with Tiara. Why didn't I use the respite hours provided by the Regional Center? Well, I admit, I had issues with allowing anyone to watch Tiara except family members or teachers from her school. I did attempt to hire her aides from school, once in a while, to help, but good help was costly, and it was hard to justify the expense. I was also of the mentality that I was a stay-at-home mom, so I should have been able to handle taking care of my children, even though taking care of Tiara was an insane amount of work. I admit I'm an overachiever and think I should be able to do anything and everything, even when living in a state of constant sleep deprivation. I was often dizzy and finally went to the doctor to find out what was wrong with me. After examining me and listening to my daily routine, he declared, "You're exhausted and need sleep. You need to find a way to sleep more."

At that point in our lives, Tiara, Lou, and I all shared a bedroom because Trinity needed a safe space for her possessions. Both Trinity and Tabitha had safety locks on their bedroom doors, which protected their belongings from Tiara a decent portion of the time. Tiara didn't mean to destroy everything in her path, but somehow, she did. She loved to color on anything, including Trinity's artwork, the walls, toys, and furniture. She also liked to rip the pages out of books and magazines. When she realized Tabitha and Trinity's rooms were off-limits, she became obsessed with breaking into them. She often succeeded.

In Tabitha's teen years, it wasn't uncommon for one of Tabitha's friends to accidentally forget to close the bedroom door as they walked out. If Tiara was out of my sight and the house was quiet, I knew something was wrong. I would go in search of her right away. First, I checked to make sure she had not exited the house. Once I determined she was safely hiding inside, I knew she was either destroying Tabitha's bathroom, coloring at Trinity's desk, sitting on my shower floor playing with liquid hand soap, or tearing all my clothes off the hangers in the closet. The first time she snuck into Tabitha's bathroom, I found her balancing on top of the overturned trash can while admiring herself in the big mirror. All the lipstick caps were scattered around the room, and her face was a Picasso of lipstick. She was smiling ear to ear when I caught her. "I did it, I did it," she said. After she discovered the makeup and nail polish treasures in Tabitha's bathroom, it was her favorite place to break into. If Tabitha caught her, she would go ballistic, and a physical fight ensued between the two. It wasn't uncommon for me to pull Tabitha off Tiara when she got outraged. I was always worried Tabitha would hurt Tiara and get into trouble somehow. Tabitha was too powerful for her own good.

Lou and I tried our best to shield Tabitha and Trinity from Tiara's destruction and physical outbursts, which was why we shared a room with her. Luckily, the room was large enough to accommodate a California king bed, a twin bed, a dresser, a bookshelf, and a toy bin. Our master bedroom was anything but a retreat. As you entered, the first thing you might have noticed was that the box springs and mattresses for both beds sat directly on the floor. We had removed the bed frames after Tiara had fallen off the bed and chipped her front tooth during a seizure. The king bed was centered on the largest wall as you entered the room, with the twin bed at its foot, along the opposite wall. Tiara refused to sleep in the twin bed alone, so my six-foot-two hubby slept in it most nights, with his feet dangling off the end. Just past where Lou's feet dangled, Tiara's dresser resided, with a small TV placed on top. It wasn't uncommon to find the television lying on the bedroom floor, with toys and broken crayons strewn everywhere.

Next to Tiara's dresser was the door into our bathroom and walk-in closet. The closet was where Lou and I hid for our brief intimate encounters, several times a week. Without regular sex, Lou turns into a person I can't tolerate, so I scheduled sex for the days he worked the late shift. It wasn't romantic, or necessarily comfortable, but it kept us connected and married.

Most nights, we played musical beds, and it was rare for Lou and me to end up on the same mattress. Like so many children with neurological issues, Tiara had difficulty sleeping, often waking up many times throughout the night. I would often lie with Tiara and Trinity in the king bed and read books to them before they fell asleep. More often than not, I fell asleep with them. Lou would come into the room later, after consuming several bottles of chardonnay while watching TV, and try to squeeze in with us. When I saw him approach, I'd swat him away toward the twin bed. "Go sleep in the little bed," I'd whisper.

"I don't want to sleep in the little bed. I'm too big," he'd complain.

I motioned him to carry Trinity to her room so that he could sleep in her spot. Once in bed with Tiara and me, his snoring and flipping from side to side would start. Ugh, now I couldn't sleep. I'd carefully get up and move to the small bed, so as not to disturb Tiara. Sleeping in the twin bed myself was heaven. Suddenly, I'd hear the dreaded gagging noise, which meant Tiara was having a seizure. I'd jump up and quickly reposition her onto her side, so she wouldn't aspirate during the seizure, knowing Lou was passed out and wouldn't hear her.

Now awake, Tiara patted the mattress between her and Lou, indicating she wanted me to get in the middle and snuggle with her. Because I was desperate for her to get back to sleep as soon as possible, I'd comply with her request, even though I'm claustrophobic and hated sleeping between the two of them. She would fall back asleep, holding me hostage with her arm and leg draped across my body. I felt trapped and couldn't sleep like that. I'd try shaking Lou awake with my free arm, but he wouldn't wake up. I'd then try releasing my lower leg and kick him until he finally roused.

"Why are you kicking me?" he'd mutter.

"Shhhh, you'll wake Tiara. I can't sleep here, and if I move, she'll wake up. Please move," I'd beg.

"Fine, I'll move."

Finally, we would all sleep until she woke again. Because I was so exhausted, sometimes I wouldn't hear her wake up and get out of bed. She would head straight to the twin bed and find a way to get in with whoever was occupying that space. It was a tight squeeze, but if she fell back asleep, staying was worth it. Once Lou realized she was crammed in bed with him, he'd extricate himself and jump in bed with me. He'd immediately start grabbing my butt, which always woke me up. I'd repeatedly push his hand away until he finally gave up, and we'd fall back into a fitful sleep. Within an hour, Tiara might have another seizure, and the whole process would start over. Some nights were better than others, and some were horrible. I'm not sure how any of us were able to function the next day.

When I couldn't tolerate another minute of rotating beds, sometimes I'd decide to stay awake for the day, even if it was only three a.m. I'd work on the computer, do some crafting projects, or enjoy hours of quiet until it was time to wake Tabitha. Like me, Tabitha was a stickler for time and always wanted to be early, so we always allotted thirty minutes for the ten-minute drive to her school. I prided myself on never once bringing her late to school. Lou drove Tabitha to school whenever possible, but if he couldn't, it made for a hectic morning. I'd need to leave with all three girls by seven fifteen a.m. If Tiara had a tough night, I usually waited until the last minute to scoop her from the bed and put her in the car. Those hectic mornings often made for a stressful commute and unsafe driving conditions, such as the following scenario:

"It's seven fifteen, let's go girls. You two get in the car." I pointed to Tabitha and Trinity, sitting on the couch watching television together. "And I'll go get Tiara," I said.

"TT, time to wake up, sweetie," I said while placing a kiss on her cheek.

"Mommy's going to change your diaper, and then we will get in the car so that we can take Tabitha to school." I changed her before she was coherent, picked her up, laying her chest on mine, with her head on my shoulder, and carried her to the minivan.

In the car, Tiara was now awake and signaling she wanted something to eat. She knew the sign for "food" and was repeatedly signing, "Eat, eat, eat." I always packed a snack for the drive to Tabitha's school, but it usually wasn't enough for her. Because I wanted to feed her a decent breakfast when we got home, I didn't like her to fill up on crackers or granola bars. "Tabi, can you get Tiara's crackers out of my purse," I said. Tabitha reached into my oversized purse and got out the crackers, then turned to Tiara and handed her the Ziploc baggie, which she already had opened for her.

"Here you go, TT, here are your crackers." TT smiled while grabbing the bag and finished the snack before we arrived at school. She then frantically started signing, "More, more, more."

Trinity, who sat in the back seat with Tiara, started interpreting for her. "Mom, Tiara wants more food!"

"I know, but I don't have anything else. TT, please be a good girl and wait until we get home. Mommy will fix you some chicken fingers when we get home."

I heard the grunting and straining of Tiara trying to remove herself from the seat belt.

"Mom, she is getting out of her seat belt! Mom, stop the car!" Trinity screamed.

"Tabitha, try to stop her," I'd begged, to avoid stopping the car.

Tabitha leaned into the back-seat area and said, "Come on, TT, stay in your seat, please. We are almost to my school, and then Mom will look for more food." Tiara had already squirmed halfway out of her seat belt.

"Mom, she is almost out of her seat," Trinity yelled.

"Look through my purse and see if you can find anything else for her to eat," I forcefully said to Tabitha.

"Mom, pull over; she is out!" Trinity yelled. I pulled over the car, even though we were only blocks from Tabitha's school. Trinity thought that if someone was out of their seat belt, they would instantly implode and die. In an attempt to minimize Trinity's stress, I pulled over immediately to rectify the situation. I got out and opened the van door. TT was sitting on the floor of the car, where she was picking up old pieces of crackers and granola bars and shoving them in her mouth. She still didn't have good fine motor skills, so few crumbs were making it into her mouth. I picked her up and put her back into her seat. "Okay, girls, let's get Tabitha to school," I said. We finally made it to Carden Hall and dropped off Tabitha, with time to spare.

"Bye, babe, love you," I said to Tabitha.

"Bye mom, bye TT, bye, Trin Trin. Love you guys," she said as she got out of the car, swung her backpack over one shoulder, and took off toward the playground. As we exited the parking lot, Tiara was nearly finished with the granola bar I had found floating at the bottom of my purse. Now what?

I put in Tiara's favorite CD and started singing. She immediately started singing along, as did Trinity, and by some miracle, we made it home without another incident. That day had a good result; but that wasn't always the case. Most days, I was not so lucky and often had to pull over several more times before making it back home. Tiara's getting out of her car seat was extremely dangerous, so we eventually bought a car seat with a three-point harness that accommodated a child up to 125 pounds. Of course, it was close to a thousand dollars, but we didn't have a choice. Her continually getting out of her seat was a serious safety hazard for everyone in the car.

By the time we got home, it was already almost eight a.m., and Tiara was supposed to be at school by eight forty-five. But unlike Tabitha, she was usually late. I still needed to feed them both breakfast, give Tiara her medications, get her dressed, brush her teeth, fix her hair, change her diaper, and make sure Trinity was dressed or at least had on shoes and a coat over her pajamas.

"Breakfast! Go sit in your chairs," I said. They both rushed over to the table and sat. I brought over a plate of freshly microwaved chicken nuggets for each of them. None of my girls ate breakfast foods for breakfast, unless it was pancakes or donuts. Otherwise, they ate quesadillas, paninis, chicken nuggets, or pasta with butter. As they both started eating, I got each of them a sippy cup with juice. None of my girls drank milk because of allergies. I then started working on crushing Tiara's medications with my industrial medical crusher I had ordered online. She had three capsules of Depakote and three other tablets that needed grinding. Six pills was a small batch. In the future, she would be required to take twenty-five pills in the morning and at night. I scooped about a quarter cup of chocolate pudding onto a paper plate and mixed in the six pills. I went back to the table to see if they were done eating. Tiara would always be done and wanting more food, and Trinity would still be eating. I approached TT with the pudding.

"Let's take your medicine, and then I'll get you more food." I scooped up a teaspoon of the pudding and started directing the spoon toward her mouth. She opened her mouth and accepted the pudding. She then looked at me with disgust and shook her head in refusal.

"Okay, TT, another bite, sweetie," I said as I directed another teaspoon of the chalky pudding concoction toward her. Just as I got near her mouth, she quickly turned her head away. Then she climbed out of her chair and started running away.

"Wait, we need to wash your hands!" I yelled and she kept running. I grabbed a pack of baby wipes while in hot pursuit, with her plate of medication in my other hand.

"Come on, TT, please take your medicine for Mommy!" She shook her head side to side while grunting angrily and headed toward her room. Her hands were greasy from the chicken fingers, and she had ranch smeared all over her face. I set down the plate of pudding on the hallway counter outside our bedroom, caught her, and wiped up her hands and face with a baby wipe.

After I was done cleaning her up, I said, "TT, where are you?" I decided to take the hide-and-seek approach. She loved hide and seek, and if I could distract her, I could get the rest of the medication into her mouth.

"Oh, where, oh where, oh where is TT?" She started laughing as I approached her again. She was sitting on the edge of the bed and covering her eyes with her hands. This was her way of hiding.

"Tiara, where did you go? I can't find you, "I said in a sing-song voice. Then all of a sudden, I said, "There she is! I found you, TT." She removed her hands from her eyes and gave me a big smile. I quickly shoved in another bite. We played another round of hide and seek, and I got all her medicine done. Phew! It was already 8:25 a.m., and I was not even close to being ready to take her to school. I left her in the bedroom and checked on Trinity.

"Are you done eating, babe?" I asked Trinity.

"Yes, Mom."

"Let's wash your hands." I picked Trinity up and carried her to the kitchen sink. Turning on the water with my right hand, I balanced her little body against the sink with my left knee and hand and squirted liquid soap into her hands. As she rubbed them together, I scooped up a handful of water to clean off her mouth.

"Okay, sweetie, let's get dressed." I followed her into her room to help her pick out something to wear and left her to dress while I checked on TT.

I found Tiara with a red face and crouched in a squatting position in the corner. She saw me and started waving her hands at me to go away. This meant she was having a bowel movement in her diaper and wanted privacy.

"Okay, TT, I'm going to get ready while you go poopy," I said as she continued to wave me away. I walked into my bathroom to finish getting ready for the day. Five minutes later, I checked on Tiara. She was sitting on the floor in front of her bookshelf and coloring on a book.

"Let's change your diaper and get dressed for school." I laid her down and cleaned up her diaper while she fussed and tried to kick me in the face. I then sat her up and started putting on her clothes.

"Arms up, so I can take off your pajama top." As a part of her therapy, I was supposed to verbalize what we were doing so she could learn the words. She put up her arms.

"Good listener, TT! Keep your arms up; I'm going to put on your shirt."

After I got on her shirt, it was time for her pants/leggings. Everything she wore had to be easy to get on and off and accommodate a diaper. She usually wore black elastic-waist stretchy pants with a bright-colored shirt and Velcro tennis shoes. After I finished getting her dressed, I packed her backpack with a clean set of clothes, her lunch, extra diapers, and wipes. Taking her hand while slinging the bag over my shoulder, I grabbed my purse and called for Trinity.

"Let's go take Tiara to school." We all loaded into the van and head off to TT's school. If we were late, her aide wouldn't be waiting outside for us. She walked in with the other students after they got off the buses. Since we were late, I had to walk Tiara into her classroom, which was never fun.

Tiara still hated school, and every day was a fight to get her there. We pulled up to her school and had to find a parking spot. Eventually, she was given a handicap placard, which made dropping her off much easier, but at this point in her life, we had to park down the street, like everyone else. Once I found a spot, I had to coax her out of her seat.

"We're here. Let's go see your friends," I said happily. She wouldn't budge. When I wanted her out of her seat, she refused, but when I begged her to stay in her chair, she wiggled her way right out of the seat belt.

"Let's go, TT, let's go see Miss Donna!" said Trinity. Trinity had started preschool two mornings a week but loved visiting TT's classroom.

Time to distract and redirect Tiara again, so I started singing a fast, rambunctious version of "Itsy Bitsy Spider." As I sang, I'd pretended to play an electric guitar with such enthusiasm, I could have been mistaken for a member of AC/DC. I'm exaggerating, but she loved it when anyone pretended to play an over-the-top version of any instrument, especially a guitar. Tiara started laughing.

She signed, "More, more."

"I'll sing you more, but we need to walk into school. First, get out of your seat, and then I will sing."

I continued singing as we walked through the front office and to her classroom. Once we made it to her class, everyone greeted her happily, and she instantly started hanging onto my leg. Trinity dashed for the nearest toy, and now I had to try to get Tiara engaged in whatever activity they were doing until Trinity and I could sneak away. Initially, we used to say "Good-bye, TT," hug her, and then exit. This was the appropriate way to leave a child, and it was supposed to teach them that you will return and help reduce separation anxiety. After weeks of tantrums, her constant attempts to run after me, and her aide getting bitten, hit, and kicked as she tried to restrain Tiara, we all decided sneaking out was the safest option for everyone involved. Once we arrived in the classroom, her aide attempted to coerce, trick, or distract Tiara into a chair. She then started playing music on a CD player or brought out the crayons, which would hopefully entice Tiara to turn her attention away from me and toward the activity. Trinity and I waited until she was fully engaged and then bolted out of the room. Trinity and I were free as birds until one p.m., as long as the school didn't call me with an emergency before the school day was over.

Trinity had preschool from nine a.m. until noon on Tuesday and Thursday, so our next stop would be Westcliff Preschool if it were either of those days. The preschool only allowed potty-trained children, who were three years and older, but the director had made an exception for Trinity, even though she was only two and a half. After explaining our home life, she agreed to admit Trinity on a trial basis. Trinity loved preschool and was a model student, which meant she didn't wet her pants or throw sand in anyone's eye, so she was allowed to remain permanently. Once everyone was at their respective schools, I had two hours of freedom, as long as my phone had the ringer on and was on my body.

While Tiara was at school, I had to remain within a ten-minute driving radius of campus, in case she had a status seizure. Once a seizure hit the five-minute mark, both the nurse and I were called. I immediately drove to the school, as did the nurse, if she wasn't on campus. At the seven-minute mark, 911 was called, and the other children were cleared from the room. Once the law changed, only the nurse or I were allowed to administer Diastat at school. The nurse worked at five different schools because of funding issues, so she was only on campus once a week. That meant that if the nurse wasn't on campus and I couldn't get to the school quickly enough, the paramedics would give her medication to stop the seizure and then take her to the hospital. Well, the last thing I wanted was for her to be taken to the hospital without me, so I never strayed too far from her school. Even taking a class at the gym was stressful. I had to keep my phone out on vibrate and check it regularly. I had to explain to my Pilates teacher why my phone was always sitting out my mat and that I might have to run out of class suddenly if my child had an emergency. She understood when, on several occasions, I jumped up in the middle of class, grabbed my phone, bag, and yoga mat, and ran out the door. I lived in a constant state of anxiety, always waiting for the next emergency.

Tabitha (12), Tiara (7) and Trinity (3)

Original image by Mara Blom Schantz

www.artisticimpressionsbymara.com

CHAPTER 13

Ignoring Them

As the weather warmed, I knew that I had to work on teaching Trinity and Tiara how to swim. Tiara was now seven, and despite three summers of swimming lessons with different programs, she wasn't close to being water safe. Her teachers and therapists warned me to never put her in a life jacket or inflatable ring in the pool or ocean. They said Tiara wouldn't be able to differentiate between when she had her life jacket on or off, and would always think she could float, even if she wasn't wearing a life jacket. I wish now I had ignored their advice because she never learned to swim, and wearing a life jacket would have saved us all so much stress and worry.

Because Tiara was obsessed with Trinity, I wanted them to take swimming lessons together, so Tiara could model Trinity learning to swim. Tiara's therapists repeatedly told me that modeling the behaviors of other high-functioning children was an excellent way for Tiara to learn. I contacted the Michael Bryan Swim School. His company taught tons of local families and had a high success rate. It was a two-week program in which the children swam every day, except Saturdays and Sundays, for thirty minutes, in a small group. The lessons were held at one of the family's pools, and there were five or fewer children in each group. He guaranteed your child would be water safe at the end of the two weeks, as long as you followed all the program rules. I asked Michael if he would do a private lesson for Tiara before or after the group lesson Trinity would be participating in. He had never worked like that before, but because of Tiara's medical issues, he agreed to give it a try. He offered no guarantees, which was fine with me. I just needed someone willing to try.

We were assigned to a pool in the gated community of Bonita Canyon. Every day for two weeks, we drove the twenty minutes to the beautiful house with the gorgeous pool in the backyard. Trinity and the three other children took their lesson first while Tiara and I watched from a beach towel I spread out on the pool deck. Tiara was either eating a snack or lying down on the towel. When it was her turn to get into the pool, she usually decided it was time to fall asleep. Her lesson was only ten minutes, but it was plenty long. We had to fight to get her into the pool, but then she was pretty happy once she was in and, of course, didn't want to get out after ten minutes. She tried to follow the instructor's directions, but in true Tiara fashion, she ignored his rules and did what she wanted. She did learn to blow bubbles and was appearing to make progress, when she came down with another virus. Tiara sat out the last few days, but Trinity finished the whole two weeks and was practically water safe at the end.

At seven years old, Tiara now weighed over one hundred pounds and wore a size 16 in children's clothing. I seriously contemplated starting a clothing line for obese children because it was impossible to find clothes to fit her body that were cute, comfortable, and allowed for easy access to her diaper. Yes, she still wore a diaper and had not shown any indications of becoming potty trained any time soon. Lucky for us, there must be a large population of children who weigh over a hundred pounds and still wet the bed at night, because Huggies makes an overnight pull-up that fit her booty. I did have the option of having the Regional Center provide diapers for her, which would have been fantastic for our budget, but the diapers they provided were thin plastic diapers, which weren't good for her skin and required her to lie down for diaper changes. Changing a pull-up only takes seconds, and it is easier for her aide, who is expected to change diapers while Tiara is on campus. You probably didn't think about changing her diapers at school, did you? Allowing another adult, who isn't a family member, to change my child's diaper during the school day required a huge leap of trust and faith on my part. It placed Tiara in such a vulnerable position.

Tiara was now able to string together two words and continued to use sign language, but if someone touched her inappropriately, she couldn't tell me. She also couldn't tell me if she had to sit with a wet diaper or with poop in her pants at school. I never knew exactly what happened in her day, and prayed she was being treated with kindness and compassion when being cared for at school. Did her aide wipe away her drool and change her shirt when it became drenched? I assumed she did but don't know for sure. I knew what she looked like when I picked her up from school, but I never really knew what happened during the five hours she was away from me. I did spend a significant amount of time with the teacher and aides in the classroom, which is why I trusted she was safe there. They were good people and truly cared about the kids in their care, but it was also a huge undertaking and stressful, working in a special day class. As much as Tiara didn't love school, she liked her teachers, classmates, and of course, all the parties for every holiday!

With parties came treats, and Tiara was still gaining weight. She was now living in a problematic cycle of obesity. Walking farther than a few feet caused her to become overheated or have an asthma attack, so we bought her a wheelchair. Once we started using the wheelchair, she preferred being wheeled, rather than walking. She was getting less exercise, and her appetite hadn't diminished. Because of the weight, everything was a struggle, and she was becoming miserable. She couldn't do the stuff she did before, like play basketball, run, and play, so she ate more. Eating became an activity, a comfort.

People stared at us. They judged. I was a bad mother because she was obese, and she was deemed lazy. They didn't understand, and I knew it. So, I ignored their stares. From the time Tiara was little and acted different than other children, I learned to pretend; I didn't see their judging eyes. I trained myself to only look at Tiara or my other girls when I knew people were staring. I never allowed my vision to sway away from them. I pretended we were in our world, where no one judged us. Trinity, on the other hand, was embarrassed continuously by Tiara's actions. She often asked me if we could leave Tiara at home. When they played together in the sandbox at the park, Trinity noticed the other kids staring at Tiara. She saw them get up and run away when Tiara tried sitting next to them on the play equipment. As much as Trinity loved Tiara, sometimes she wished Tiara wasn't so different.

A few weeks after the swim lessons ended, Tiara got pneumonia as a result of the adenovirus. In healthy children, the adenovirus usually presents itself as pink eye and mild respiratory problems. It is common in the spring and spreads easily from person to person. Most children recover within a few days. But in Tiara's case, it wasn't so simple. One morning she woke up with extremely bloodshot, swollen eyes, which she could hardly open. She was struggling to breathe, so I rushed her to the doctor. He diagnosed her with another respiratory infection but was concerned and sent us straight to CHOC. As usual, once they saw Tiara's medical history, we were quickly called back and shown to an ER room. Her medical history spoke for itself, and she never had to wait, even if the entire ER was overflowing with people.

Once in a room, the doctor ordered the regular blood tests and cultures to check for specific types of pneumonia and a chest X-ray. She was immediately placed on oxygen and admitted to the hospital, once the results indicated she had severe pneumonia. They put her on IV antibiotics, and I assumed this pneumonia would progress like all the others. Oxygen, IV antibiotics, and breathing treatments every four hours for a few days, and then we would go home. Not this time. Tiara refused to wear the oxygen mask. Each time I placed the elastic around her head, she ripped it off and sent the mask flying across the room. As I got out of bed to retrieve the mask, her oxygen level immediately dropped, setting off the monitor alarm. By the time the nurse arrived, I had already been off and on the bed several more times, trying to keep the mask on her face. I sang, I danced, I read her books, I put on her favorite videos, I let her talk on the phone, but nothing worked. She was frustrated and angry during this admission and proved to us all she was in charge, which meant, no oxygen.

The nurses were mad, I felt defeated, and every new respiratory therapist that tried to help, failed until *he* showed up. *He* was a brilliant respiratory therapist who solved the problem. He built a tent around her bed with plastic sheeting, like in *The Boy in the Plastic Bubble*. He made an opening behind our heads, out of her reach, where he placed a tube, which blasted oxygen into the tent. Lou and I took shifts this admission because neither of us could tolerate caring for Tiara continuously because she was relentless in her quest to make our lives miserable. I felt sorry for her, but if she wasn't a compliant patient, she couldn't get better. It was always a struggle balancing her comfort while forcing her to endure things she didn't want to do, for the sake of her health.

On the second day, the doctor showed up and declared her pneumonia was viral, so he would be pulling the IV antibiotics and we would need to let the virus take its natural course. Logically, I know that antibiotics don't help with viral infections, but when my kid is sick in a hospital and fighting to breathe, just seeing them give her medication makes me feel better. I had to say something to the attending physician.

"Excuse me. I understand this pneumonia is viral, and I know antibiotics don't help viruses, but Tiara usually develops a secondary infection while in the hospital. It would make me feel so much better if we continued giving her antibiotics to be safe," I said pleadingly.

"I don't agree. It's viral, so I'm pulling the antibiotics. If she develops a bacterial infection later on, we will deal with it then," Doctor Smug Face, informed me.

I wanted to get out from under the tent and smack him in the face. How was I going to keep Tiara in bed long enough to let the virus run its course? I could see he was condemning me for Tiara's weight, and I was pissed.

I wanted to scream at every doctor, "It's not my fault Tiara is overweight; stop judging me."

Lou and I spent eight days under the oxygen tent while she got better. Unfortunately, we didn't get to leave the hospital for ten days because every time Tiara fell asleep, her oxygen saturation levels would drop, and the alarm would sound. Because of her weight, she had sleep apnea and was not getting enough oxygen during sleep. Let me tell you, by day ten, she was ready to murder me, and we had to get out of there before she went psychotic. Our saving grace was on the second to last day; they let me pull her in a wagon around the fourth floor. We spent hours and hours walking around and around the floor, saying hi to all the nurses and visitors. She loved to wave and blow kisses to everyone. Finally, on the tenth day, the doctor agreed to let us leave if she went home on oxygen for sleeping. Okay, just get us out of here! So, we returned home to a new life, which included sleeping with an oxygen mask and having a handicap placard. Whoop, Whoop, something good came out of all this: "princess parking" from here on out. Did you know that you don't have to pay for metered parking with a handicap placard and you get a discount at most parking structures? I was shocked but grateful to learn about this bonus. Unfortunately, finding an open handicap spot isn't always easy, and I soon became frustrated by the people who cheat the system.

A few weeks after being discharged, Tiara had a routine follow-up with Dr. E, who was new to the CHOC neurology team. Dr. E suggested Tiara try an anti-epileptic called felbamate.

"Is it new? No one has ever mentioned it before," I said.

"It's not a new medication, but I think it might be a great add-on for Tiara. One of the side effects is anorexia."

"How does it cause anorexia?" I asked.

"We don't know how the process works in the brain to induce anorexia, but we do know that a large percentage of patients lose weight and reduce their food consumption while taking felbamate," Dr. E explained.

"Let's go for it! Why hasn't anyone else suggested it?" I asked. I watched her demeanor change slightly and thought, here we go: now she is going to explain why no other neurologist had suggested this drug before.

"While taking this medication, Tiara could develop a condition called aplastic anemia. It's a rare but possible side effect. If Tiara did develop aplastic anemia, she most likely wouldn't survive. But, there are no reported cases of aplastic anemia in children, only adults," she quickly added.

"No cases have been reported in children, ever?" I asked.

"None—I think it's worth the risk," she said.

I took a deep breath and thought about the options. Once again, I was being asked to make a life-altering decision for Tiara, and I was scared, but I knew we had to try it.

"Okay, let's try it," I said reluctantly.

"Great. You will need to sign a waiver indicating that you are aware of the possible side effects," said Dr E.

So, with a heavy heart, I signed the waiver and prayed it was in her best interest.

Within days of adding felbamate to her regimen, Tiara started dropping weight, because she no longer ate. She went from always eating, to me begging her to eat. I couldn't feed her a fistful of crushed medicine twice a day on an empty stomach. I needed her to eat something, anything, but she wouldn't. As promised, felbamate induced anorexia, and Tiara lost forty-five pounds in five months. She no longer needed oxygen to sleep, but she wasn't running around or going to school very often. Instead, she lay on the family room couch and stared at the TV all day. She was too weak to do anything. It was one extreme to another.

I stared at her and wondered, *Did I make the right choice for you, Tiara?* Eventually, we reduced some of her other medications, her body finally adjusted to the felbamate, and she started eating again. I was so grateful. When she eventually returned to school, she was only having two to three small seizures a day and became very active. This was when her basketball obsession ramped up. She had always loved basketball, even though no one in our family played the sport nor watched it on TV. I think her basketball obsession started when she was a little girl, and we would drive through the Carden Hall parking lot. The area where you dropped off the students ran parallel to eight basketball hoops. She loved watching the kids run up and down the courts.

Whenever we walked onto campus, she would stop and stare up at the nets. Sometimes one of the students would give her a ball, so she could try to shoot a basket. Now that she had lost all the weight and had more energy, she spent her recesses shooting hoops with her one-on-one aide. She had a new aide, Tony, and he was perfect for her at this phase in her life. He ran cross-country in college, loved playing ball, and was kind, yet stern. He was so fabulous, I hired him to watch her after school and for a few hours on the weekends. We put a basketball hoop in the backyard, and she never wanted to come inside. Because she was still a flight risk, someone had to watch her at all times. We had both exterior side gates secured and a hotel lock placed on the front door, but somehow, she was still able to get loose once in a while.

The first time she eloped from our home was at four years old. It was a blazing summer day, and Sarah was at our house with her two young children. We were playing with the kids on Trinity's floor, when I realized Tiara wasn't with us. She must be hiding in one of the other rooms, I thought. My sister stayed with the little kids as I started searching every room and closet while calling her name.

As I walked by the front door, I noticed it was ajar. Oh no. I ran out the front door and headed straight across the lawn to our next-door neighbor's house. As I ran across the grass, I saw Tiara walking up their concrete path to the front door, totally naked.

"Stop, Tiara. Stop," I yelled.

She just kept trotting up to their front door with a determined gait. Just as I reached her, the front door swung open. I scooped my naked child into my arms and stood, staring at our new neighbor.

"Hi . . . Ummmm, I think she came in search of Spencer and his guitar. Sorry about this," I said with flushed cheeks and a look of horror written all over my face.

"Is everything okay?" asked the neighbor, awkwardly.

"Yeah—Tiara walked out the front door without me knowing. She scared me, but we're okay. When I realized she had gotten out of the house, I knew she must be coming over here to see Spencer," I said while holding back tears.

"Why would she want to see Spencer?" quizzed Spencer's stepmother.

"After you moved in last week, when we dropped off the cookies, Spencer played a song for Tiara on his guitar. Ever since that day, she keeps trying to come over here. She loves music, especially guitar playing. I'm so sorry; it won't happen again."

"Ohhhhh, that's right. Spencer mentioned it. Thanks again for the cookies," she said.

I ran back home with Tiara in my arms and started to cry. What if she had walked into the street and gotten hit by a car? What if she kept walking and someone abducted her? She had a few words in her vocabulary but couldn't say her name or where she lived. After this incident, Lou installed the hotel lock at the top of the front door, out of her reach. Making sure everyone secured the front door at all times was another challenge. I also purchased an emergency medical bracelet for her, but I couldn't get her to keep it on. Despite all these efforts to keep her inside the house, she still managed to escape a few other times.

For the first time in years, Tiara was attending school regularly and only having a few seizures each day, which gave me time to focus on items that generally got put on the back burner, like her teeth. Brushing them once a day was nearly impossible, and I will admit, they didn't always get cleaned. Every time I put the toothbrush in her mouth, she chomped down on the bristles and refused to let me move the brush around her mouth. She liked sucking on the toothbrush, but nothing else. So, her teeth weren't actually getting brushed much. As a young child, my uncle was her dentist, and my aunt was her hygienist. They had a difficult time cleaning her teeth, but they managed to get it done. During one appointment, my uncle found a cavity but wasn't able to fill it because we couldn't figure out a way to keep her mouth pried open long enough to deal with the issue. He referred us to a dentist who specialized in treating children with special needs.

When the specialist saw Tiara's cavity, he said she would most likely need a root canal. At this point, her teeth hurt while chewing, so it had become an emergency. Once the dentist learned about Tiara's medical history, he determined the procedure would need to be done in a hospital under anesthesia. This would require me to get clearance from her cardiologist and pediatrician before undergoing the procedure. I knew her heart was fine, and I felt like he performed unnecessary tests to bill the insurance, or because he wanted to flirt with me. He was a serious letch, and I had to be careful around him. During appointments, he found a way to position himself directly next to me, and several times tried sliding his arm around my waist. He once even offered me a job in his office, even though I wasn't looking for one. Doing what, I'm not sure, since I'm not a nurse, but I had the feeling my duties would have revolved around taking care of his personal needs. I should have changed doctors, and seriously considered it, but it didn't seem worth the effort. I can handle some slimy flirting as long as Tiara is getting the best care, so why go through the hassle of changing doctors?

Tiara was cleared for surgery, which was scheduled for two p.m. at St. Joseph's Medical Center. That was the worst time ever for surgery, since she can't eat for eight hours before being put to sleep. How was I going to keep her away from food the entire day? I was panicking. I needed to get her an earlier appointment and called the surgeon's office every day, requesting an earlier time.

"Hi, this is Tiffani Goff, Tiara's Mom. I was just wondering if you had any cancellations for the morning surgery time slots," I asked in my most charming tone.

"I'm sorry, Mrs. Goff, but I told you I would call if we had a cancellation, and we haven't. She is scheduled for two o'clock," she said with slight annoyance in her voice.

"Okay, so two o'clock. it is. Thank you." I said with fake enthusiasm.

The next morning, I woke Tiara at five thirty and fed her a light breakfast with her medications. She went back to sleep and stayed asleep for hours. Thank you, Lord! When she woke up, I distracted her by playing kitchen and dress up and coloring together. We needed to arrive at the hospital by noon. So, I got her ready, and we left at eleven a.m., even though it was only twenty minutes away. I could contain her in the car and keep her away from food and water. Upon arriving at St. Joe's, she started asking to eat. I was able to distract her during pre-op until one thirty, and then it got dicey. She tried getting off the gurney in search of food, and I knew I couldn't distract and contain her any longer. I rang the nurse for help and explained that if we didn't give her food or sedate her, she was going to beat me up. Seconds after I warned the nurse, Tiara started pulling my hair and dug her nails into my skin hard enough to draw blood. The nurse responded quickly, asking the anesthesiologist if we could give Tiara a light sedative until they took her back to surgery. He agreed, just as Tiara almost pulled out her IV.

They wheeled her off to surgery, and I sighed a breath of relief. I walked to the waiting room, where I was planning to zone out for the next two hours until the operation was complete. I wished I could go for a walk outside, but I was nervous about leaving the designated area, just in case. When I hadn't heard any news from the doctor after the two-hour mark, I asked the receptionist for an update. She called the operating room and learned Tiara was fine, but the procedure was taking longer than anticipated.

After three hours, the receptionist walked over to me and said, "I just heard from the doctor, and he is having a difficult time performing the root canal. Tiara will be in surgery for at least another thirty minutes."

"Okay, thanks for letting me know."

Feeling anxious, I kept calling Lou for support because I was sure Tiara was going to die having a routine root canal. Lou repeatedly tried calming me, until I saw the surgeon walking toward me and hung up quickly. His scrubs were drenched with sweat, and he looked angry when he announced, "That was horrible, but I was finally able to complete the root canal. It was nearly impossible for me because her tooth was tucked way into the back of her mouth, and her mouth is so small. If I had known it would be this difficult for me, I wouldn't have taken her on as a patient."

"Is she okay?" I asked hesitantly.

"She's fine, but it was a difficult surgery for me. You can go to recovery and see her, once they call for you," he stated as if this whole thing were my fault.

"Thank you," I said politely, even though I wanted to tell him he was a rude jerk and scared the crap out of me by keeping Tiara under anesthesia for four hours. Recovery called me back a few minutes later, so I could sit with Tiara as she woke from the anesthesia. Tiara never woke up happy from anesthesia. She either vomited or started hurting me; today was no exception. I heard her cough and knew she was going to start throwing up, so I quickly hoisted her into a sitting position and shoved a plastic tub under her mouth. I was grateful for the vomit, assuming I would be spared a violent outburst. She proved me wrong while grabbing a chunk of my hair as she finished throwing up. I called for help to avoid spilling the vomit over us both. Luckily, a nurse heard the rising panic in my voice and quickly responded. Tiara eventually calmed, and we were released to go home.

CHAPTER 14

Forgetting

I forgot most of 2006, which is why I had to pull out the photo albums and Tiara's school records so I could write this chapter. God gave me this wonderful gift of forgetting all the bad stuff, so I can keep moving forward.

I knew Tabitha turned thirteen, and we had a "spa day" with her friends. I took Tabitha and her five closest friends to lunch, to get their nails done, and back to our house for facials and a sleepover. I know that Trinity took tennis and ballet lessons and played soccer in the fall. I know that I volunteered to make her team's soccer banner because a mom told me she had done it in the past, and the girls loved it. After starting on it, I remember wanting to slap myself upside the head for listening to that woman. It was a total nightmare and took more time than I had, and Lou was not happy with the materials spread all over the living room. He didn't care about the mess, only the stress of keeping Tiara away from the project. By some miracle, I completed it, and the team loved it!

I found myself volunteering for Tabitha and Trinity's activities more than I should have. I was probably overcompensating for how much time and energy I spent on Tiara. I needed them to know they were just as important to me as Tiara, even if I didn't divide my time evenly.

As for Tiara, I know she took ballet lessons and played on a special-needs baseball and soccer team. I also learned from the pictures that we took a summer vacation to Alisal Ranch. In all the pictures, I look so exhausted I hardly recognize myself. In some photos, Tabitha and I are seen shooting targets, Lou is seen fishing with Tabitha and Trinity and my mother-in-law is pictured with Tiara creating art projects. There are also pictures of Trinity participating in the rodeo activities and riding a horse. There is one hilarious memory from that vacation, which I remembered without the aid of photos.

Trinity had a propensity for volunteering for anything anyone offered. Maybe she learned that from me? If a teacher asked a question, she raised her hand whether she had the answer or not. If a performer asked for audience participation, Trinity raised her hand. Well, Alisal offered lots of activities, and one of those activities was a talent show. One night after dinner, where Lou had consumed plenty of wine, our family went over to watch the talent show. We sat down in a row of chairs and waited for the show to begin. Tiara was obsessed with her pink child's guitar, and carried it with her everywhere, including dinner and the talent show.

An announcer started the show by asking for volunteers. The first volunteers were a father and son who had prepared a funny skit. After the second act finished, no one was volunteering, that is, until Trinity threw her arm up into the air. What the heck was she doing? We didn't prepare anything. The announcer called her up to the front. She looked directly at Lou and said, "Come on, Dad, let's sing a song and play the guitar." Lou looked horrified, and luckily, Tiara was on my lap, so I couldn't help. Lou tried to protest, but Trinity kept pulling on this hand to get up. Everyone was now staring at us. Tabitha was in a state of mortification because she was thirteen and already horrified to be seen with us, let alone have her father and sister participate in a talent show.

Trinity and Lou, with the pink guitar in his hand, went to the stage, even though Lou doesn't know how to play the guitar, nor did God give him a singing voice. He sat down on a chair with the guitar in his lap and asked Trinity, "What should we sing?"

She answered with lots of enthusiasm, "Let's sing 'Old MacDonald.'"

Lou nodded his approval and started strumming, with no idea how to play the song, and started singing loudly and out of tune, "Old MacDonald had a farm, E-I, E-I, O. And on this farm, he had a . . . *What?*" Lou asked this question while pointing to the audience for suggestions. Trinity started with a pig, then he did a cow, and then someone from the audience shouted out "dog." By this time, everyone was laughing, as they all seemed to realize Lou was drunk, because no sober person would endure such humiliation. And then it got worse.

"A goat," someone shouts from the audience. Lou started singing, "Old MacDonald had a farm, E-I, E-I, O. And on this farm, he has a goat, E-I, E-I, O. With a *baa, baa* here and a *baa, baa* there, here a *baa*, there *baa*, and everywhere a *baa*."

Oh my gosh, Lou just sang the sound for a sheep, not a goat! The audience immediately realized his mistake and became hysterical. At that point, Tabitha was mad at all of us because she was so humiliated by their performance; Tiara was pissed she wasn't the one playing the guitar on stage; and Trinity started to realize this wasn't going well. Once he finished the goat rendition, Trinity began pulling him off the stage. It has continued to be a great story to retell throughout the years.

Along with the Alisal pictures, I saw the photos of our parakeets perched on the curtain rods in our house. Yes, that wasn't a typo, we had parakeets that flew free around our home. Just call me the weird bird lady. This was the year I gave my nephew a parakeet for his birthday, but it didn't work out as planned. After it appeared, his bird, Jasper, was starving to death because my sister didn't know she needed to replace the hulled seeds daily, I brought Jasper to our house. I put him in with our parakeet, Harley. They were so happy together, and within days, Jasper looked healthier. I didn't know the sex of our birds, but we soon learned Harley was a female, and Jasper was a male after several eggs appeared in the bottom of the cage. Next thing we knew, we had three large bird cages and fourteen birds.

I decided I was going to train them and allow them to fly free for several hours each day. I know, I'm a legitimate freak. The plan started to go awry when one of Tabitha's friends, who was terrified of birds, was afraid to enter our house. Aside from this issue, the birds started pooping on my crown molding as they perched. Duh, Tiffani. Of course, they were going to poop everywhere. Well, that was the end of letting them fly free. I think it lasted for about three weeks, until I realized it was unsanitary, and they would have to live in cages from there on out. The three cages sat on top of one another on a rolling frame, so I would roll them in and out each day for fresh air. Once it was summer, I thought maybe I could leave the cages out all night and cover them with a sheet. Well, that was a great idea, and it saved me lots of clean up, until one night I heard the cage rattling in the middle of the night. I jumped out of bed and ran to look out the sliding glass door to see what was going on with the birds outside. An opossum was climbing up their cage. I started banging on the window and yelling and was just about to go outside and deal with the critter, when Lou finally got out of bed and came running. "What's wrong?"

"A freaking opossum is attacking my birds," I said as I pointed out the sliding glass door.

"I told you not to leave the birds out there," he said.

"Stop lecturing me, rude person. Are you going to help or not?" I questioned.

"Give me the broom; I'll do it," he said. I handed Lou the broom from my hand and watched as he hesitantly walked up to the cage. Lou is not a fan of opossums and seemed scared as he gently pushed the end of the broomstick at the marsupial. After several attempts and lots of loud yelling to encourage the opossum to leave, it finally figured out how to release its wedged claws that were stuck between the metal bars of the cage. I still tried to keep the birds outside overnight, until the same thing happened a few nights later. My bird-lady phase finally concluded when Harley and Jasper passed away. I didn't have enough time for breeding parakeets, so I sold the remaining birds to the Magnolia Bird Farm. I knew they would go to good homes, and I needed to live without birdseed on my floor every day.

This was also the year Lou turned forty. I threw him a party at our house and at least seventy-five people came. Whenever I offered to host a party for him, he wanted to invite everyone from work, high school friends he hasn't seen in years, and pretty much anyone he has ever known. I'm exaggerating a bit, but it was challenging to narrow down his list. I decorated the house, created photo collages with embarrassing pictures, and all his friends showed up. I do remember that I ordered Mexican food instead of making all the food myself, which was rare for me. It was one of those fabulous parties, where everyone is laughing and having fun, yet no one is too wild or drunk. Lou's birthday is December 6, so once his party was over, we moved into full Christmas mode.

I like to decorate the house for Christmas the day after Thanksgiving and take down the decorations the day after Christmas. A solid month of Christmas spirit. The problem is that once I married Lou, he informed me we couldn't decorate until after his birthday had passed. What the heck? I can't wait until December 7 to decorate for Christmas. The first two years of our marriage, I waited, in deference to his birthday, but after Tabitha was born and able to participate in picking out the tree, all promises were null and void.

The first weekend the Home Depot tree lot opened, we would go as a family to pick out our favorite six- to seven-foot noble fir Christmas tree. I always let the girls pick the tree, but I'm in charge of how we decorate it. I only allow white twinkle lights and color-coordinated decorations on the large tree displayed in our family room. I like the tree to match the decor, so the ornaments and ribbons change every few years, depending on how I have the house decorated. Burgundy, gold, pink, purple, turquoise, lime green, and white have all been highlighted throughout the years. Colored lights, ornaments made at school, or any decorations that didn't match the color of the year could be used to decorate Christmas trees each girl had in her room. I know it is wrong and rather shallow of me, but no one ever said I was perfect.

Sadly, my decorating tradition was upturned once Tiara learned to crawl.

The first year Tiara could get herself close enough to the tree, she thought it would be a great idea to bite the lights! Yes, take a big bite out of a twinkle light. I remember I was cooking dinner in the kitchen when I heard this loud, crunching sound. I looked around the corner and saw Tiara on all fours and a strand of lights in her mouth. I screamed at the top of my lungs, which scared her into releasing the strand from her mouth. I quickly shoved my fingers in her mouth to try to get out any pieces of hard plastic that could have broken off and caused her to choke or cut up her mouth. By some miracle, I got out all the bits, and she didn't get electrocuted.

Now what? Did this mean I had to take off all the lights? I so didn't want to get rid of the lights. Of course, I immediately unplugged them, so the temptation to bite them would dissipate. But I knew in my heart, I had to take them off. I decided to remove only the strands she could reach, so half of our tree had lights, and the other half was dark. The tree looked so tacky, it was painful to look at. The next year, she was walking, and I tried using lights again. Well, the same thing happened except it was a little bit worse. Since she could stand, she grabbed onto a branch with one hand and a strand of lights with the other and started pulling. The tree began to topple onto her, but luckily, I was close enough and was able to catch it before it fell on top of her. So, I took off all the lights and all the decorations on the bottom half of our tree.

By the time we get to Christmas 2006, we still did not have lights on our tree, and we no longer had the tradition of going to pick out a fresh tree. We were forced to use an artificial one.

Remember how I said Tiara was having so many respiratory issues because of her weight gain the year before? Well, when we brought home the Christmas tree the year before, she seemed fine at first, but then we noticed an increase in her respiratory issues. I knew she must be allergic to the tree, so we took it out of the house and placed it on the front lawn so that we could see it from the living room. The tree was precisely in the same spot it had been inside the house; now it was just on the other side of the window, on the lawn. After a few dismal days of staring at the bare tree in the front yard, I went out and bought an artificial tree and decorated it without lights. So this year, the decorating process was pretty simple: Get out the ladder, climb into the attic, pull down the fake tree and all the other decorations, and set up! Yes, I'm the one who climbs into the attic, not Lou. Lou hates the attic, and I hate listening to him complain about how tight the space is, so I do it.

CHAPTER 15

Cruising

We survived the holidays, but despite being so thin and active, I couldn't keep Tiara healthy. She was plagued with respiratory infections so often, I decided to pull her from school in January until the flu season was over. You are probably thinking: Why remove her entirely from school? Just send her on the days she feels well. I couldn't do that because of her one-on-one aide. She was fortunate to have an aide, and if she wasn't going to attend school for the day, her aide needed to be reassigned to another student or classroom that needed the help. Protocol dictated I had to call the school by seven thirty a.m. if she was going to be absent. Often, Tiara wasn't even awake by then, so I had no idea whether she would or would not be attending for the day. I got tired of guessing how she would feel upon waking, and it didn't seem fair to her aide. Also, many of the children in her class chronically showed up with runny noses and sometimes even a fever. Their parents put them on the bus sick, instantly putting Tiara at risk. Last but not least, Tiara hated school, and it just seemed easier to keep her home with me until April. She was thrilled to be staying home with Mommy all day, and even though I didn't get a break, I knew she was being cared for properly.

It was during this time that I started weekly walking dates with friends, since I couldn't get to the gym anymore. My walking friends changed throughout the years, except for my Tuesday morning walks with Rorie, which continue to this day. Tiara especially loved Tuesdays because Rorie was one of her favorite people. Tiara would squeal with delight whenever she saw Rorie's house and start chanting her name.

"Rorie, Rorie, Rorie," she'd say over and over again while pumping her arms up and down.

"Hi, T, how are you today?" Rorie would ask while leaning over to pat Tiara's leg. "I love your fancy shirt; you look so pretty."

Tiara would strike a pose and flash a smile while saying, "TT, pretty."

"Yes, T is the prettiest! Are you ready for our walk?" Rorie would ask.

"Yay, go, go, go," Tiara would declare.

I would put on her headphones, turn on her music and push, while she danced and sang in her wheelchair. Going on long walks in her wheelchair was an activity Tiara and I both enjoyed, so when she didn't attend school, we always walked.

As spring of 2007 arrived, Tabitha was in eighth grade and still playing every sport at Carden Hall. Trinity was in her last year of preschool, Tiara was home with me all day, and Lou was working at least fifty hours a week, so we thought it was the perfect time to get a dog.

Tabitha had been asking/begging for a dog for years. She called a meeting with Lou and me and proceeded to document point by point why she needed a dog.

"I'm going to be one of those weird kids that never have the joy of loving a dog, walking a dog, or sleeping with a dog."

On and on she went until we felt like we would be the worst parents in the world if we didn't get her a dog. We considered all the obstacles. Let's start with the fact that Tiara and I are both allergic to dogs, Trinity was terrified of dogs, and I didn't know how to train a dog because I didn't grow up with one. Lou grew up with a sweet but extremely misbehaved Old English sheepdog, so he wouldn't be much help on the training front, and last but not least, who the heck was going to take care of this dog?

Lou and I started researching hypoallergenic breeds. After lots of research, we realized a standard poodle was our only option. At that time, there weren't a bunch of poodle mixes, like there are today. I wanted a small dog, but Lou said a little dog wouldn't be safe around Tiara. She might fall on the dog and kill it. As for Trinity being terrified of dogs, we decided it would be good for her to learn not to be afraid. Lou started looking at standard poodle breeders, and I read books about the care and training of poodles. Tabitha and Lou decided they wanted an apricot standard and found a breeder in Las Vegas. Lou called up the breeder and asked her if she had a dog that would be safe around a special-needs child. He gave lots of background on Tiara, described our family dynamics, and funny enough, she had one apricot standard available, whom she thought would be an excellent fit for our family. She had kept Bailey from the last litter to try to sell him to someone who wanted a show dog, but no one had come along. He was handsome, smart, six months old, and house-trained. He sounded perfect for us, but how could we meet him, when he was in Vegas?

After talking with Lou for twenty minutes, the breeder said, "I'm leaving for a show in Los Angeles tomorrow. If you want to meet me in LA tomorrow, I'll sell him to you."

My eyes widened as I overheard their conversation and realized we were going to do this. I was terrified, but I knew Tabitha needed a dog. Lou arranged the pickup details, and the next night he and Tabitha drove to Los Angeles to pick up Bailey. It was love at first sight for Tabitha as she cuddled in the back seat with him all the way home.

She kept telling Lou: "Dad, he is so beautiful! I love him so much; I can't believe it!"

When they arrived home, they let Bailey out of the car, and he bolted inside. He started running in the same circular path that Tiara always ran. Family room—kitchen—dining room—living room, all while circling the two-sided fireplace.

Now what? That's right; he must need to go pee. I took him out to the front lawn and told him, "Go pee."

He went pee. Wow, maybe he needs to go poop too? I had no idea how often he needed to be let out. Let's say, after I obsessively kept taking him out to pee every hour, I realized that dogs don't need to pee that often. He was so smart that he would stand next to the door and wait to be let out when he needed to relieve himself.

Our family of five was now a family of six, with the most beautiful show dog you have ever seen. Best of all, Tiara just pretended he didn't exist, and Trinity got over her fear within a few weeks. Bailey immediately became a beloved family member, but I wasn't prepared for his need to follow me everywhere. If I was doing laundry, he walked behind me to the garage and waited while I loaded the machine. He sat in the kitchen as I prepared the meals, and found a way to follow me everywhere I went and stay out of Tiara's path, all at the same time. He hated it when I left the house and usually tried to run out into the car so that I would take him with me. That was his only downside. Aside from his constant love and need to follow me everywhere, he was perfect. Oh wait, I forgot his love of chewing up all of my and Tabitha's underwear. Okay, aside from that bad behavior and the need to walk him three miles a day, he was perfect.

Soon after Bailey joined the family, we had a trip planned for my parents' forty-fifth wedding anniversary. My parents wanted the entire family to take a cruise to Alaska to celebrate. They were paying for the whole trip; we just needed to show up, which wasn't an easy task for Sarah or me. My kids were fourteen, eight, and five, but Sarah's kids were only five, three, and nine months. Both of our husbands were in the car business and rarely had time off work. So, the scheduling was a bit stressful, but we figured out a way to make it happen. Because we all knew taking Tiara was going to be extremely difficult and possibly a nightmare, my parents agreed to pay for Grandma Cindy to come with us because she was so helpful with Tiara.

I knew we had to make this trip for my parents, but Lou and I were scared. There were so many things that could go wrong, and we never took Tiara anywhere unless there was a hospital nearby. I consulted Tiara's team of doctors and Holland America cruise line to confirm that a qualified doctor would be on board the entire time. They also assured me that if there was an emergency, Tiara could be helicoptered to the closest hospital. Despite these assurances, I was still afraid of being trapped on a ship in the middle of the ocean with my medically fragile child. Well, let's say that a few things did go wrong but not in the way I expected.

The first part of the trip was a success. The six of us took a flight to Seattle, and Tiara managed not to throw up on the plane—success number one. We stayed in a large, beautiful suite with high ceilings and dramatic decor the first night in Seattle. We spent the entire night doing dance and plank competitions. We ordered food in, not wanting to take a chance of anything going wrong at a restaurant. The next morning, we woke up, packed up our stuff, and were driven on a large bus with the rest of our family, who had arrived on a different flight, to the ship.

Unfortunately, during the night, I noticed Tiara sounded congested, and I was already planning on taking her to the ship doctor once we got on board. I had to get her on antibiotics before she developed pneumonia. We brought Tiara's wheelchair, and she was getting pushed along through the check-in process, as her cousins and sisters entertained her with their silliness. She was having a great time until we hit the gangplank, and it was time to board the ship. She looked at the large ship, saw the expansive body of water, and immediately put her hands over her eyes and started shaking her head from side to side while saying, "No, no, no!"

We hadn't expected this. As Lou propelled her wheelchair forward, I tried explaining what we were doing and reassuring her she would be okay. She was having none of it. With her hands still tightly covering her eyes, she put her head in her lap and refused to look or talk to anyone. She was talking more at this point in her life, so it was obvious she did not want to board the ship because she was afraid. We were shown to our beautiful cabin with a balcony. Grandma Cindy, Tabitha, and Trinity were staying in the cabin to the left of us, and my sister's family was staying in a suite to our right. All of our balconies connected for afternoon wine hour. My parents were on another floor, far away from us, in a larger, more luxurious room.

Once we got settled, I immediately wheeled Tiara to the doctor's office. I met with the doctor, provided him with a letter from Tiara's neurologist explaining her condition and medications, and then asked him for a Z-pack for her congested chest. He readily complied, and off we went back to our room. On the way back to the room, I accidentally took a different elevator. This elevator had a glass-paneled wall that looked straight out to the vast ocean. Once Tiara saw it, she started yelling and hid her head in her lap again. After day one, we realized Tiara's fear of the ocean wasn't going away.

She refused to leave the room except to eat meals. After several days, we tried getting off the ship to explore a town, but she was so stressed out, I had to take her back to the boat. She just kept her head in her lap and refused to look at anyone or anything. So basically, Lou, Grandma Cindy, and I took turns sitting in our room watching *Hannah Montana* with Tiara every day. The good news is that everybody else in our family was having a blast until Tabitha came down with strep throat the day before she was scheduled to go on a super-fun excursion with her dad. I took her to see the doctor, and he gave her a prescription for Augmentin. Poor Tabitha didn't leave her bed for two days, until her fever broke, and the antibiotics kicked in.

As the trip progressed, Tiara was eating less and less, and getting her to the restaurants for meals was getting exhausting. We were all wearing those seasickness bracelets, and the water was calm, but I could tell she wasn't feeling well, and was worried she had seasickness but couldn't tell me. Trinity, on the other hand, was having the time of her life. Miss Independent went to the kid's camp for hours each day and was up for any activity anyone offered.

And now it's time to share the horror that occurred the second-to-last night of our vacation. Our family, except my parents, all had dinner together in the main dining room at six o'clock. My parents didn't eat with us most nights because they enjoyed eating much later than us. On this particular evening, my dad, Lou, and Ray had made plans to meet at the casino after the rest of us had gone to bed. After dinner, we returned to our rooms, but we weren't all ready for the night to end. My sister and I had some wine on the balcony while Tiara watched *Hannah Montana* and the other kids played. Once my sister decided it was time to put her little ones to bed, I went inside our room with Tiara and got ready for bed. Tabitha wanted to stay up late and play poker, so Lou, Tabitha, and Ray decided to play cards in Grandma Cindy's room until it was time to meet my dad at the casino. At about ten forty-five, Lou staggered to our room via the connecting balconies, after he had consumed a fair amount of chardonnay, to get changed for the casino. I was dead asleep in the bed by myself.

He looked at the bed and yelled, "Tiffani, where is Tiara?"

I woke with a start and looked over at her side of the bed. I looked back at Lou.

"She's with you, right?"

"No, she's not with me, she fell asleep with you."

That's when I really woke up and realized she did fall asleep with me, and now she was gone! My barely verbal child, dressed in pajamas and a diaper and who had refused to leave our room, was now walking around the ship alone. I started screaming for her and threw open the door to our room. I hysterically called her name while running up and down the hallway, while Lou got the rest of the family to start searching. Grandma Cindy called the front desk, Lou and Ray took off searching in different directions, and I raced to the elevator after I couldn't find her in the hallway. I thought she might get on the main elevator because the walls were mirrored, and she loved to look at her reflection. As I waited frantically for the elevator to arrive, the doors opened, and there was Tiara, holding hands with an older couple. She ran to me, and I picked her up, sobbing hysterically. We will never know exactly where she went or for how long she was gone, but apparently, this couple got on the elevator in the lobby, and there she was by herself, looking in the elevator mirrors.

By the grace of God, their room was on our floor, and they had recognized her as a part of our group. They were planning to knock on doors until they found us. We were also told that someone had spotted her in the lobby and another person had seen her knocking on room doors.

We figured that she had woken up after ten o'clock and decided to knock on the front door to our cabin. Knocking on doors is one of her favorite activities. She knocks, and then one of us says: "Who's there?" and she says, "TT." She can repeat this knocking game for a solid thirty minutes. Well, the cabin doors are super heavy and insulated. They lock upon closing, and it is nearly impossible to hear someone knocking from the exterior of the door. We had learned this our first day on the ship, which is why we used the balcony doors to communicate with one another. She must have gone out the front door and assumed I was going to answer when she knocked. When I didn't answer, she must have started knocking on other doors. She probably got bored when no one answered and decided to look at herself in the elevator mirrors.

After the trauma of the event wore off, all Lou could say was: "I'm so glad it was with you and not me. If I lost her on my watch, you would have killed me."

He was right. After that event, we kept a chair propped against the front door and piled things on top of it, a booby trap of sorts. We figured if she tried to get through a pile of clothes, then move the chair, we would hear her before she could leave the room.

By this point, Lou and I were desperate to get off the ship and go home. We were so tired of watching the same episodes of *Hannah Montana* over and over again and were now paranoid she would somehow escape. Besides, I could tell she wasn't feeling well. On the last morning of our stay, before the ship docked, she refused to leave the room to eat breakfast. Lou went down to the buffet and brought back some food, but she wouldn't eat. I needed to give her all her medications, which consisted of three different anti-epileptics, the antibiotic, a probiotic, and her allergy pill. I had taken away any medicines that were not necessary, but she still had to get down ten pills with a little bit of pudding. She fought me, but not taking them wasn't an option. She had to get on a plane, and I didn't want her having a status seizure during the flight, so I found a way to get them down.

We packed up our stuff, disembarked the ship, and were on our way to the airport in a shuttle when I smelled an unpleasant but familiar odor. Diarrhea in her diaper. Not uncommon, because she was on antibiotics, and she always got the runs during a course of antibiotics, despite giving her a probiotic. But when she had diarrhea, it usually leaked out the sides of her diaper. Now, what was I going to do? Of course, I had packed an extra pair of clothes and diapers, but I wasn't sure what I was dealing with until we got off the shuttle. As we exited the shuttle, I could see that her pants were wet with diarrhea around the outline of her diaper. This was going to be a disaster. We had to check in our luggage and go through security, so I had to get her cleaned up before we got in the security line. Grandma Cindy came with me to the bathroom, and we were able to get her cleaned up, but I had to change her clothes. Now I was out of extra clothes, and we still needed to go through security, wait for the flight to be called, board the plane, and endure the two-hour-and-fifteen-minute flight home from Seattle to Orange County. I said a prayer that she would make it, but I wasn't feeling hopeful.

We made it through security and found a spot to sit in the extremely crowded airport, when another poop blowout occurred. I looked at Lou in a state of panic and ordered him to go to the gift shop and try to find some clothes to buy for Tiara. Anything. I could see that the diarrhea had once again leaked through and was on the airport chair. OMG, what was I going to do? Sorry, but I had to leave the chair dirty because I was going to run out of baby wipes at this point. I quickly ushered her to the bathroom and started another cleanup, but I didn't have a clean pair of pants to put on her. In addition to the clothing issue, Tiara was not happy. Her butt was getting raw and rashy from all the poop, and she pulled at my hair as I cleaned her up. I tried my best to remain calm and not break down in a fit of sobs. Lou finally found a small pair of men's elastic-waist shorts, and my mom brought them to me in the bathroom. A little sigh of relief released from my beyond-stressed body.

As we exited the bathroom, we heard an announcement that our flight had been moved to another gate. Great, now we had to pack up all our crap and move gates. At least we didn't have to see who was going to sit in the dirty chair. I'm still so sorry about having her soil the chair. As we moved to the next gate, I noticed that Tiara was looking pale. Once we found a new spot to accommodate all thirteen of us at the new gate, Tiara started screaming at the top of her lungs. Then I saw her chest begin to heave. I grabbed a large Ziploc bag from my carry-on and shoved it in front of her face, just before she started puking. She continued to cry in blood-curdling wails between each heave and vomit.

I don't think there was anyone in the entire airport that wasn't looking at us by this point. My mom and Grandma Cindy were racing around looking for more Ziplocs, paper towels, and replacement clothes while all the other children in our group pretended not to be completely horrified. My dad and Ray tried taking the other kids for a walk while Lou helped me with Tiara, but just then, they announced our flight was boarding. I was desperate to get home, but terrified of being trapped on a plane for two hours. Instead of pre-boarding with her, Lou and I decided to wait until the end to board with her. She continued to vomit, and each time she threw up, she screamed as if in pain. When we finally had to get in line to board the plane, every passenger was looking at us as if saying, "Are you freaking kidding me? No way that kid is getting on our flight!"

"Sorry, people, but she is." I hardly remember the flight home. I do know that she vomited several more times, but luckily, we had plenty of bags to catch the puke, and I remember that she eventually fell asleep for a bit. Somehow, we made it to Orange County and safely to our home.

Unfortunately, the bodily fluids excreting from both ends of her body didn't stop that day. She continued to vomit and have diarrhea for days. It got to the point that I needed to take her to the emergency room because I knew she was dehydrated. We visited the ER twice in the following week and she finally stopped vomiting. I think the cruise was so traumatizing because of her fear of the water, that her body just freaked out and couldn't deal with the stress. It took Tiara weeks to recover from that vacation.

CHAPTER 16

Surviving August

Just before our memorable cruise to Alaska, Tabitha graduated eighth grade. Yes, she did win the best overall female athlete award and was preparing to try out for the Newport Harbor High School (NHHS) volleyball team. Trinity finished preschool and was starting Carden Hall in the fall. She was so thrilled to be following in her big sister's footsteps that she often wore old Carden Hall uniforms to preschool. Tiara, on the other hand, was not excited to return to school, but I was ready for a break. August was always the most excruciating month of the year. If you have a special-needs child, you know this well enough, but for those of you who don't, let me explain. Once school ended in June, Tiara and the other students in her special day class attended summer school. The summer school started the week after the regular year ended and concluded at the end of July. The summer school day was short, from nine a.m. until one p.m., but it allowed the kids to stick with a routine. Once August arrived, it was blazing hot outside and there was no routine or any designated daily activity. Trinity wanted to go to the park, go the beach, go swimming, have friends over, or plan amusement park adventures.

Loving Tiara

Well, Tiara could go to the park, as long as it wasn't too hot, but beach days without Lou were a little dicey for me to handle on my own. Since Tiara wasn't a fan of the ocean, we couldn't sit too close to the water or she would freak out, and I couldn't keep an eye on Trinity in the water if we didn't sit close to the shore. Playdates were awkward unless Trinity went to a friend's house, because at our home, Tiara would follow the girls around, which upset Trinity and often scared the other child. We couldn't go swimming at the pool because Tiara would aspirate the water and end up with pneumonia, so it felt like we were in prison during August. Every August, Lou and I would feel like we may not survive the month. When he came home from work, I was ready to leave and have him watch the kids so I could get some errands done. He would be exhausted and didn't want me to go.

Whenever I felt like I couldn't endure another minute of my life, I would imagine the following: *Living in a dilapidated house in the ghetto, with peeling paint, bars on the windows, and dirt instead of grass in the yard. In my vision, it was always a hundred degrees, the house didn't have air-conditioning, the floors were plywood, the single couch was dirty, the kitchen table and chairs were green plastic, meant for the outdoors, and I didn't have anything I needed for Tiara. No music, no toys, no healthy food, just a life of misery.* This vision, which I sometimes needed to conjure several times a day, reminded me: it could always be worse, Tiffani. Be grateful for what you do have.

We, somehow, survived another August, and it was time for school to start.

Tabitha made the freshman volleyball team, even though she was convinced she wouldn't. After a week of playing on the freshman team, the junior varsity coach asked her to move up to JV. Wow, I was so excited for her, but she didn't feel the same. Let me give you a little background so you can understand. During this time, the girls NHHS varsity volleyball team was ranked as one of the top in the nation. Players like Misty May-Treanor and April Ross had attended and played for her coach, Dan Glenn. It was serious business, and the competition was extremely stiff. Tabitha hadn't ever played club volleyball before, so she was a newbie when she tried out for the team. She honestly thought she might not make the team, as lots of girls got cut. Once she made it, she was in a constant state of stress, worrying she wasn't going to do well enough. So, when the JV coach saw her natural athletic ability and wanted to move her up, I instantly got carried away and had visions of her getting scholarships to play in college. Tabitha didn't have the same idea.

"Mom, I'm not doing it! I will not move up to JV!"

"What? You have to. She offered you the spot. You can't say no," I protested.

"Yes, I can, and I will. All my friends are on the freshman team, and I want to stay with them. I'll be too stressed on the JV team, Mom."

Lou and I were super disappointed, but it was her decision, not ours. So, she stayed on the freshman team and had a great season. I loved watching her play, and luckily, we had a reasonably reliable caretaker at the time who watched Tiara during the games. Trinity always came to the games with me, because she loved cheering on Tabitha. Unlike Tabitha, Trinity wasn't a super-competitive athletic sort of child. She was playing her second season of AYSO soccer and refused to touch the ball. If the ball came near her, Trinity ran the other way. Lou practiced with her in the backyard, but it didn't help; she continued running away from the ball. It drove Lou so crazy that before one game, he told Trinity: "If you kick the ball, I'll buy you an ice cream after the game."

Bribery at its finest, and it worked. Trinity ran after the ball and made contact. Bribery went against our parenting rules, but I didn't blame him. We never believed in bribing our kids to get good grades, to finish a task, or for any reason at all, except for Tiara, of course. We always had to bribe her, but that didn't count; she lived by her own set of rules. We never had to bribe Tabitha for anything, but we soon learned Trinity responded well to bribes. No one ever said we were perfect parents. We were trying to survive and did the best job we could.

Tiara was attending school more than not attending, when she suddenly developed a new type of seizure. One morning while sleeping in her twin bed for once, she suddenly rolled off the bed and smacked her face on the floor. It happened so suddenly, it seemed weird, and I didn't realize it was a seizure; I just thought she fell. When I picked her up, I saw that she had broken off part of her front tooth. Both of her front teeth were extremely long, like cute walrus teeth. Now, she only had one long tooth. This was when Lou and I decided to get rid of the bed frames, in case she fell again. So tacky, but we knew it was safer for her. While napping on our bed the next day, the same thing happened, but this time, I realized it was a drop seizure, not just a fall. During this fall, she chipped her other front tooth, despite the bed being closer to the ground. At least her front teeth were matching, but now I had to worry about more drop seizures.

What if she had been standing up and just fell to the ground? She could break a bone or worse. Most children with drop seizures wear helmets to protect their faces and heads from serious injury. There was no way Tiara would wear a helmet. After realizing she had two drop seizures in two days, I called her neurologist. Her doctor added another medication to her regimen and increased one of her current medications that had room for increases. Since there was a max dose for each drug based on Tiara's weight and she usually was on the maximum dose of all her medications, we were lucky she had some room for an increase. She was now on four anti-seizure drugs.

As I expected, her doctor recommended I have Tiara wear a helmet. Tiara hated to have anything on her head except fun holiday headbands or one of Tabitha's fancy hats. If, by some miracle, I found a way to keep a helmet on her all day, which seemed impossible, she would overheat because she doesn't sweat. In my mind, forcing her to wear a helmet wasn't an option. It was a quality-of-life issue for me. I couldn't torture her by forcing her to wear a helmet, to keep her safe. If she was going to fall and hit her head and suffer a concussion or worse, so be it. I thought she would rather endure an injury than wear a helmet every day. So, I had to get a waiver signed by her physician so that she could attend school without a helmet. Another tough decision, which wasn't popular, but I believed it was in her best interest. Luckily, the new medication we added along with the increases in the other one helped minimize the drop seizures to only a few per month. People in the general population are probably horrified at imagining their child having a few drop seizures a month, but in the world of intractable epilepsy, we were grateful for so few. Of course, she still had daily complex partial seizures and absence seizures, but they didn't pose any real danger to her life.

As 2007 continued, something exciting was about to happen. Grandma Cindy was moving to Southern California. I had been asking her to move here for years, but she wasn't quite ready until this year. Lou's parents had gotten divorced when he was nineteen, but the divorce wasn't final for many years. Usually, she would visit us once a month, but the visits were a little tricky. She often arrived late Thursday night and left Sunday night. She was amazing with all the girls and wanted to help and be involved in everything they were doing, but Tiara wasn't always on board. Tiara was used to me doing everything, so by the time she warmed up to Grandma Cindy, the visit was over. I just knew that if she lived closer, she would be a massive help to me and would get to spend more time with the girls. Finally, she moved to Newport, and it was terrific, just as I had hoped. She rented a condo around the corner from us and during the weekends, spent lots of time with us. Weekends were always the hardest time for me because Lou was working, so, there was no designated plan. Trinity and Grandma started a Friday-night tradition. Grandma would come over after work, and they would go out to dinner and then have a sleepover at Grandma's. Tiara would get to see Grandma for a little bit before they left and then had me to herself for the rest of the night. Trinity would get one-on-one attention from another loving adult, and I got a bit of a break.

Of course, Tabitha was still around with her friends, but they were teenagers and relatively self-sufficient, as long as I had a refrigerator filled with food. Grandma moving here was also a massive godsend because now that Tabitha was playing club volleyball, she had long weekend tournaments, and Grandma Cindy always offered to watch both Trinity and Tiara so that I could attend. I somehow managed to never miss a game.

Loving Tiara

On Sundays, Trinity, Tabitha, Mom, and I attended Mass at ten a.m. while Dad watched Tiara. My dad is an atheist and would much rather babysit Tiara than attend church. He drove Tiara around, stopping for french fries and diet coke at McDonald's, or she napped on his couch while he read. After church, our entire family, including Sarah and her kids, met for lunch at Fashion Island. We usually couldn't find a restaurant that appealed to everyone, so we often ended up in Atrium Court, a fancy food court, where everyone picked food from different restaurants. But we always made sure Tiara got her food first, otherwise she had a tantrum. Tiara could use a fork and a spoon, but she piled so much food on the utensil, it wouldn't fit in her mouth. She ended up with food all over her face, hands, and the floor, unless I fed her. I didn't feed her because I wanted her to learn, but my parents were so embarrassed by the huge mess she created, one of them would wait to eat their lunch and spoon-feed her small bites. She ate fast, which often resulted in her choking. I don't remember how many times I have performed the Heimlich maneuver on Tiara, but it was at least once a year. Later during a hospital stay, the doctors were shocked to learn how often I performed the Heimlich and told me it wasn't normal. They said we needed to look further into her swallowing issues. Great, another study and another problem.

After lunch, Tiara always needed a nap, so we would usually leave before everyone else. Tabitha and Trinity would stay behind with the rest of the family to shop and walk around the mall. It gave the girls more time to be with family, without worrying about Tiara's needs and tantrums. Often, Tiara would jump out of her wheelchair and run off through the mall. Once we caught her, she would drop to the ground and lie in the middle of the walkway and refuse to get up. It could take several minutes to convince her to get up and return to her chair. It was rare for Tiara not to have a tantrum, run away, or lash out at Tabitha or me during an excursion.

As you can see, she was rather embarrassing for the other children, so they were usually happy when she wanted to go home for a nap. My nephews thought she was funny, since she was always burping and farting in public without any awareness that it was inappropriate, but the girls, not so much. There were also the few times I thought I could handle bringing Bailey, Tiara, Trinity, and Tabitha without Lou. I'll admit that was a stupid move on my part. There was one episode in which my mom was watching Tiara in her wheelchair and holding Bailey's leash, while I poked into a home store. Tiara decided to get up unexpectedly and took off running. My arthritic mom couldn't handle holding the leash of our sixty-five-pound dog while running after Tiara, so she had to make a snap decision. Tiara or the dog? Of course she chose Tiara, and luckily, I saw the event unfold through the store window and came running out to help. That was the last time we included Bailey on our Sunday mall excursion.

CHAPTER 17

Trying Again

During this phase of Tiara's life, her behaviors escalated so much that I reached out for help. Her Regional Center caseworker, Torrey, had been with us since the beginning and was an incredible support to our family. After having our yearly meeting in October 2007, she suggested we try behavior intervention again. We had tried behavior intervention a few years prior, but it wasn't helpful because the therapist quit on us after a few weeks. Tiara was too challenging, and the therapist said she couldn't help us. Now that Tiara was getting violent during transitions, and while driving, I had to try again. The situation was getting out of control. Her behavior had been out of control for a long time, but I dreaded working with a behaviorist unless I was guaranteed it was going to help.

Once the behaviorist referral was approved, we set up a two-hour appointment at the house when Tiara was at school. Mike then came for another home visit with Tiara present, and he observed her during school. Based on his reporting, he recommended fifty hours of in-home parent consultation over six months. The Regional Center approved his recommendation, and then I got to figure out where I had an extra fifty hours to spend with this guy.

Okay, I admit I'm rude, but if you have never worked with a behaviorist, don't judge. Let me try to describe how it works. During our first meeting after the authorization, he and I spent two hours trying to identify all of Tiara's behaviors, but we ran out of time. The only reason I'm able to recall any of this is because I still have the report. Step one: I needed to identify the first behavior we were going to deal with—falling to the floor. Step two: we came up with an operational definition for this behavior. He determined the description to be "dropping her body to the floor." Step three: we labeled the course of the behavior.

"The act usually begins with Tiara sitting on the floor in a public community location, such as a grocery store, store in the mall, or on a basketball court. Tiara will be verbally prompted to get up; however, she will often remain on the floor. She will sometimes then lie down on the ground. This behavior usually leads to physical aggression as her parent attempts to pick her up off of the ground or elopement."

Now that we had the behavior identified, defined, and laid out, it was time for me to start recording data. Yay me. So, in addition to dealing with these behaviors, I now had to take notes on them. I needed to determine the antecedents to each behavior, which meant exactly what Tiara was doing before she dropped to the floor. Was she tired or hungry, were we getting in or out of the car, was she frustrated? You get the point. Then I got to write down exactly what I did once the behavior occurred and how I resolved it.

I reported fourteen episodes of dropping to the floor in thirteen days. I also reported twenty-two cases of physical aggression, seven inappropriate car behaviors, and three incidences of elopement during a five-day reporting period. I collected data for two weeks until Mike and I met again to review what I reported. Based on the data, he explained why Tiara was engaging in certain behaviors, and we decided first to tackle dropping to the floor, since it led to other inappropriate acts. Mike suggested using a daily visual schedule for Tiara, the PECS system I mentioned earlier in the book. I so hate this system, but once again, I agreed to give it a try.

Instead of downloading the usual stick-figure images from the Internet, Mike thought it would be more useful to use actual pictures. He suggested I take photographs of our family, the places we visit, and the activities we participated in, so they would be more recognizable to Tiara. It was a fabulous idea, but how the heck was I supposed to have time to do all this? Of course I did it, just like I'm supposed to. I still struggled with my perfectionism issues, if you haven't figured that out by now.

His next suggestion was to use start directives instead of stop directives, such as "Nice hands, Tiara," instead of "Stop hitting, Tiara." He presented Lou and me with a list of sixteen suggestions for helping Tiara with her behaviors. Some of which were impossible, such as "teaching her self-help skills to make her more independent."

We had been working on her self-help skills her entire life. At nine years old, she still wore a diaper, couldn't dress herself, and required hand-over-hand assistance to wash her hands, to name a few. Perhaps I sound rude, but the whole process was so frustrating. I tried to keep a good attitude and follow the program, just in case there was some chance it might help, even if only a little bit.

Mike identified getting in and out of the car repeatedly as a big trigger for Tiara. I picked her up from school at one thirty p.m., and then we came home for a while. We had to get back into the car at two fifty p.m. to pick up Trinity from school and again at five p.m. to pick up Tabitha from volleyball. Of course, I knew Tiara didn't enjoy picking up her sisters at different times in the afternoon, but how could I avoid picking up my other kids? Could I carpool? More kids in the car, longer commute times, and less attention on Tiara equals disaster.

Mike and I continued working together for several months, when he became almost as frustrated as I. We would spend two hours picking apart a behavior and then come up with solutions as to how I could help change the behavior. I clearly remember when we both acknowledged Tiara was way too smart for both of us and would always find a way to win. We decided to address the issue of her not wanting to get into the bathtub. We spent another two-hour session talking about how to get Tiara into the tub each night without a full smackdown wrestling match. He gave me strategies to use, leading up to the bath, during bath time, and when finishing her bath. It sometimes took an hour of coaxing to get her into the tub. Whoever happened to be home at the time took a shot at trying to convince her how amazing it would be if she got into the bathtub.

Nevertheless, she usually went into strike mode and refused to move. Once we eventually found a way to get her in, she was fine, but she fought us all the way. Mike gave me a plan to implement for the next two weeks, and I was supposed to take notes on how everything worked until we met again. It was like Tiara was a secret spy and heard our entire conversation and knew how to beat us at this "game."

On the first night that I was supposed to implement the plan, Tiara decided to walk into the bathroom, take off her clothes, and get into the bathtub without me even asking. Are you freaking kidding me? It's like she read my mind and decided, "Watch this, Mom: I'm going to mess with your stupid behavior plan!" But of course, she couldn't be completely compliant, not Tiara. While bathing her, I gushed her with positive reinforcements for getting in the tub by herself. Guess what. She refused to get out of the bath. I drained the water, sang the clean-up song, and tried to coax her out, but no, she wouldn't budge.

Unfortunately, all the tools Michael gave me had nothing to do with getting her out of the bath, only getting her in. That was my final straw! When he came back a few weeks later to review, I told him what had happened, and he just shook his head in disbelief. We both decided there wasn't much more he could offer us since Tiara kept switching behaviors on us, and all the tools I learned had been a waste of time. I was grateful to be done with yet another behavioral intervention program. At least I could now tell her pediatrician, neurologist, and psychiatrist that I had once again tried working with a behaviorist, but it wasn't successful. Now they would stop recommending behavior intervention as a solution to my problems, at least for a little while.

Tabitha (14), Tiara (9) and Trinity (5)

Original image by Mara Blom Schantz

www.artisticimpressionsbymara.com

CHAPTER 18

Schooling

Trinity started junior primary, the fancy term they use for kindergarten at Carden Hall, and Tabitha was a sophomore at Newport Harbor High School, my alma mater. I forgot to mention why Lou and I send our girls to private schools, even though we both grew up attending public schools. Here is why: When I was in third grade at Newport Heights Elementary, Proposition 13 passed. Yes, I know it is bizarre I remember that, but it had a significant impact on me. Leading up to the proposition passing, all the teachers were very concerned with the schools losing money. At that time, we had music, art, PE, swimming lessons in fourth grade, a fifth-grade trip to Knott's Berry Farm, and a sixth-grade trip to Disneyland.

Because we lived so close to the beach, the public schools held a week of swimming at the high school to make sure all the children were water safe. Because I was a good swimmer, this was my chance to shine. I often got picked almost last in dodgeball, soccer, and flag football during PE each day. If I had allowed myself to run and sweat, I would have realized I had natural athletic ability, but because I was afraid to look ugly, I never tried too hard. After Prop 13 passed, the swimming program, along with other school resources, were cut. I was disappointed, and I hate feeling disappointed. As an adult, I've realized that jealousy and disappointment are two emotions my soul can't tolerate.

It's weird, but even as a child, I could feel a shift in the atmosphere of the school. The teachers didn't feel secure in their jobs, as they had before, and they worried about supplies for the classroom. I could feel the stress coming off the teachers, and I didn't like it.

Before high school, I didn't know what the difference between public and private schools was, but once at Newport Harbor, I learned quickly. I took honors English my freshman year and happened to be in the same class as a few students who had attended Carden Hall, kindergarten through eighth grade. I was blown away by their knowledge of grammar and how easy school was for them. Every essay I wrote came back with an F in grammar and usually a B/B- for content, and I had worked hard on these essays. The Carden kids always received better grades than mine. I then saw these Carden kids playing sports, winning elections for student council, and rising to the top of the class in everything. They knew how to study, write fantastic essays, do the math, and give public speeches without appearing stressed. I was especially envious of their confidence. I wanted to be a song leader, which required performing a solo dance in the theatre while students watched, but I couldn't do that. I couldn't risk making a mistake during the tryouts, or worse, not make the team.

Because I wanted my future children to be like the Carden kids, I told myself that if I ever had kids and lived in the area, I would send them to Carden Hall. Hence the reason Tabitha and Trinity went to Carden Hall, even though our budget didn't allow for such expensive schooling. As for public vs. private high school, I let Tabitha chose. She went to orientation night at Mater Dei, the local private Catholic high school, and hated it with a passion and declared she would never go to the "fake, ra-ra school!" Okay, then, Newport Harbor it was.

Unfortunately for Tiara, there weren't any private school options. I tried finding a private school that would fit her needs, but none existed at the time, and I suspect that if I found one, it would have been out of our budget. So, I'm grateful I wasn't forced to make that decision. So, TT was stuck with the public school system, which I detested. But I tried to focus on the positives and found a way to make it work for us all.

Tiara was supposed to be in fifth grade at this point in her schooling and was still in Bob's special day class for students in third through sixth grade. Bob loved to get the kids out of the classroom and into the community, as teaching them life skills was his main objective. Bob took the class on weekly walking trips to Target and took out the school van at least once a month to different places in the county. They were teaching the children how to function in the community. Tiara still had multiple daily seizures, and it was stressful taking her off campus for the staff and myself. If the van trips were too far from school, I would often keep her home from school that day. On the days they took walking trips, I made sure to be close to where they were walking in case an emergency arose.

In addition to the seizures, I worried about her getting overheated, picking up a new virus, or fleeing from the group. The odds of her running off and getting lost were pretty low, since she had a one-on-one aide, but the chances of her putting her hands on lots of dirty public items and then putting them in her mouth was almost a guarantee. I always carried hand sanitizer in my purse, and every time we got into the car, I sanitized both of our hands immediately. This obsessive hand washing wasn't going to happen at school or on a field trip, no matter how much I requested it happen. There is only so much you can expect from the aides and teachers. I'm not criticizing them by any means, because it's a very tough job working in a special-needs classroom, where all the kids are functioning at different levels, and germs get continuously spread.

Soon after Tiara turned ten in October, there was a massive shift in her medical condition. Our stubborn, bossy, noncompliant child, who was also loving and sweet at times, turned into an actual terror overnight. She went from having two to three daily seizures to ten or more each day, accompanied by violent mood swings. She was known for having bouts of violence and bad behaviors, but this was an entirely new beast. I couldn't figure out if the increase in seizures was causing the change in behaviors or if it was something else. She had seen Dr. E at CHOC, but once this change occurred, I knew I had to get her back to UCLA neurology right away. Of course, it takes months to get an appointment, but luckily, one of the neurologists on her former team had recently opened a TSC clinic at UCLA. Dr. Wu was a neurologist and an epileptologist, meaning she specializes in seizures. She was the best of the best, and many of my friends' children were her patients. Because the TSC clinic had openings once a month, we were able to get Tiara in quicker than usual. After meeting with Dr. Wu, we learned that puberty was the reason for this sudden change in her medical condition. Adolescence can be horrible in typical healthy children, but experience it with a special-needs child, and you can't quite imagine. It sucks. The changes in hormones cause an increase in seizures and aggression. She was relatively young to be in puberty, likely a side effect from Depakote, but there wasn't anything I could do about that. It was happening whether we liked it or not.

Just when I thought our life couldn't get more complicated, I received a progress report from Trinity's first-grade teacher. She said that Trinity was having trouble with her penmanship and suggested I get her a tutor. Really? A freaking tutor to teach my left-handed child how to write correctly, when I was already paying $800 a month in tuition? Yeah, I don't think so! As a lefty, I knew Trinity was having a difficult time in school because Carden Hall was obsessive about perfect penmanship. Trinity worked so hard to get her letters correct, that she couldn't finish her work on time. She was falling behind in her work and feeling bad about herself as a result. She even got sent to the booth (an old phone booth in the front office) one day to finish an assignment, which devastated her. Getting sent to the booth was a punishment, and neither of us felt it was fair to punish her for being slow. I asked to have a conference with her teacher and the director for her grade. Before the meeting, I asked Trinity how she felt about Carden Hall. She said: "I hate it, Mom! I don't want to go there anymore."

I had no idea she hated it. I knew she was frustrated, but this was news to me. I took a few deep breaths and said, "Well, it is the middle of the school year, we can't just pull you halfway through the year. Let me talk to your teacher, and then we will come up with a plan."

I could feel in my gut a new school was on the horizon, and I wasn't excited about the change. Once I met with Carden Hall, I realized how dire the situation had become. My sweet, kind Trinity was falling behind the other kids in the class and losing her self-esteem in the process. Carden Hall said she could transfer during the Christmas break if I found another school for her to attend. A few days later, we walked around the vacant public-school campus and peeked through the windows of all the classrooms.

I said: "If you leave Carden Hall, this is where you will have to go. Are you good with this?"

"Yes, I want to go here," she replied.

I was hoping she would say it looked horrible and way too big, but in truth, it was a charming school. Now I needed to change her school, on top of everything else. If Lou and I had learned anything in raising our girls to this point, it was that we wanted them to feel good about themselves and be happy. I couldn't allow Carden Hall and its teaching methods to destroy my child's spirit. I loved Carden Hall for Tabitha, but it wasn't a fit for every child.

The week before Christmas break, I started the process of enrolling Trinity at Woodland Elementary. The next day, I went to Woodland to find out what I needed to do so that Trinity could become a student. I explained to the front office secretary that I needed to enroll my daughter so that she could start school after winter recess. She was pleasant enough until she asked me: "Did you just move to the area?"

"No, we live down the street. Trinity is transferring from Carden Hall."

Her pleasant demeanor was instantly gone, and she became judgmental and outright rude.

"I see," she said with pursed lips and a scowl. It was as if she suddenly hated me because Trinity was a student at Carden Hall. You either love Carden Hall, or you hate it. There aren't many people who land in the middle of the pack. It is extremely conservative, very traditional, and over-the-top strict. Children with behavior problems aren't tolerated and will be asked to leave if the issues can't be resolved quickly. Carden Hall is like the devil to those who love California public schools.

As a result, this lady was negatively judging me, and I could see she wasn't going to make this process easy for me. After seeing her immediate negativity towards me, I mentioned that Tiara attended Killybrooke and Tabitha went to Newport Harbor. She sighed a slight breath of acceptance at hearing my other two children attended public school, but I still had to do a lot to win her over. I knew from experience you always wanted to get along with the ladies in the front office. Whether it's the front office of a physician, a therapist, or a school, you need them on your side.

Woodland Elementary was for kindergarten through second grade, and each grade had five or six classes. I spoke to a few friends who had children in the school, and they told me which teachers to request and who was known to be the meanest/worst first-grade teacher. Once I went to the district and completed the address-verification portion, I had to pick up her vaccination records and fill out twenty pages of repetitive paperwork until she was officially enrolled. Now that she was officially a student, it was time for her class assignment. I walked into the front office and cheerfully greeted "the lady" as I handed her the completed paperwork.

She reviewed everything and said: "Let's see. Where do we have room for her?" She picked up a roster of first-grade classrooms and looked at the number of students in each class.

As she scanned the list, I sweetly asked: "Do you have any space in Mrs. Earl's classroom?"

"No, it's all full," she quickly said without any hesitation. Mrs. Earl was supposed to be fabulous, and I was hoping Trinity could be in her class.

"We only have space in Ms. Clay's classroom."

Really? You only have space in the worst teacher's classroom, I thought to myself. I forced a fake smile and thanked her, pretending not to know that no one liked Ms. Clay. I knew she was lying, but I wasn't going to challenge her when she already wasn't a fan of mine.

Several months later I met a new family who just moved to the school and guess what. There was space for their child in Mrs. Earl's classroom. Oh well, what could I do? Trinity ended up loving Ms. Clay, so it didn't matter in the end.

I was nervous for Trinity to start school after Christmas, but she was thrilled. She was no longer required to wear a uniform and could bring a backpack to school, which wasn't allowed in first grade at Carden. On the first day, we walked onto campus and saw hundreds of children running all over the playground. They were playing handball and tetherball, jumping rope, swinging on the swings, and running around the jungle gym. I had the biggest pit in my stomach and wasn't sure how Trinity was going to assimilate, even though she didn't seem nervous. She had already met her teacher and knew where her classroom was, and now she wanted to play before class started. She looked around the playground and spotted a girl she knew.

"Hey, Mom, I think that's Paige from church. I'm going over to say hi."

I was a bit stunned because I didn't recognize Paige, but Trinity seemed to know her. She dropped her backpack at my feet and took off running. I watched her walk up to Paige and have a short conversation. She then looked over at me and waved goodbye. What? Does she want me to leave her here? I waved her over to me. She came running.

"Trin, do you want me to leave? Don't you want me to walk you to class when the bell rings?"

"No, Mom, go. I'm fine. Paige said I could play with her and her friends."

"Okay then, love you, babe!" Off I walked to my car with tears in my eyes. I saw lots of other mothers sitting in groups, watching their children play, but I was sent away. That kid always surprised me. She was so independent, and I loved it, even though it meant I wasn't able to stay and watch her play. She was her own unique person and somewhat fearless. Despite being assigned to the alleged worst teacher, Trinity loved everything about her new school. I, not so much, but I learned to adapt. I volunteered in the classroom each week and joined the PTA. We weren't allowed to volunteer in the classrooms at Carden Hall, and they didn't allow fundraising, so it was very different for me as a parent. Trinity was invited to join a Brownie troop and continued to make friends quickly.

CHAPTER 19

Cutting Everything

As you can see, there were no breaks in our life to enjoy the holidays or each other. If it wasn't Tiara and her medical issues, it was Trinity's issues with school or Tabitha's chronic strep throat and anxiety. I sometimes wondered why God didn't give me at least one easy child. I never questioned why Tiara was born with tuberous sclerosis, but I did question why all three girls struggled with different issues. I know the saying "God only gives you what you can handle," but sometimes I questioned how strong he thought I was. When Tabitha turned sixteen in January and passed her driving test on the first try, my life got easier. My parents gave her their extra car, a white 1994 Chevy pickup truck, and she now drove herself to school and volleyball practice.

During this time in Tiara's life, she developed a new obsession with cutting. Tiara loved to look at books, pictures in magazines, and especially, photo albums. One day I found her sitting in front of her bookcase with pages torn from her books, scattered all over the floor. This wasn't wholly unusual because she had ripped up books in the past, but this time she was cutting the pages with a pair of children's safety scissors. At first, I was furious because she had destroyed more of her books, but then I was rather impressed with her fine motor skills. She really struggled with these skills, and she was cutting well, so I was excited. This new hobby of hers soon took over our lives. If I didn't give her a magazine to cut, she would take any book, photo album, homework, or bill within her reach and start cutting. After she cut up my favorite design book, along with some library books, I moved every book into the garage. The main problem was how to obtain enough magazines to keep her happy. She would go through three to eight magazines each day. I started begging everyone I knew for their old magazines. I thought my problem was solved when one of Tabitha's friends brought over bags of old *Country Living* magazines that his mom collected. She didn't want them anymore, and when she heard about Tiara's new hobby, she gave them all to us. Well, Tiara decided she didn't like looking at pictures of country decor and refused to cut them. So typical of Tiara. As the months went by and we were getting more and more desperate, my aunt and uncle started going from store to store picking up the free magazines left in the racks outside the stores. This was great, but the newsprint many of them were printed on wore off onto Tiara's hands and got all over the house. We finally hit the real jackpot during a visit to her new dentist, Dr. Mathias, who we started seeing right after the disastrous root canal. We were in the waiting room, and I was trying to stop Tiara from tearing up every single magazine in the room when they called us back for her appointment. We couldn't get her to sit in the chair and hold still, which was normal, but then I suggested we give her a magazine to tear.

Dr. Mathias agreed to try it, and Tiara became so preoccupied, she was able to clean Tiara's teeth and complete the exam. It was her best visit ever. When I told Dr. Mathias, I was struggling to find enough magazines for Tiara to cut each day, she offered us her leftover magazines from the waiting room! From then on, her office saved the magazines for me each month, and I would drive the twenty minutes to her office and pick up the huge inventory. Of course, by this time, I had acquired other magazine resources, but the dentist's office had Tiara's favorite kinds of magazines: *People, Us, Vogue,* anything with beautiful people on every page.

As you can probably imagine, magazine cutting was the messiest of all her hobbies, but it also kept her sitting longer than anything else, so I didn't care about the mess. I swept up piles of magazines at least five times a day, but she wasn't eloping or terrorizing me as much, so I was grateful. Somehow, she made it through the flu season without any hospital admissions, but as we moved into spring, she developed pneumonia, which landed her in CHOC for five days. During this visit, the team performed a CT scan on her lungs, and they discovered what appeared to be a tumor forming in the left lobe of her lungs. I wasn't surprised, even though lung tumors were rare in TSC females under eighteen. In my gut, I had known she would develop tumors in her lungs. I didn't know any other children with lung tumors, but I also didn't know any other TSC child who had suffered from chronic cases of pneumonia like Tiara. She had more medical issues than anyone else in our local TSC community. When they discovered the lung tumor, they also were able to see that the tumors in her kidneys were increasing in size and number. After these discoveries, I decided to transfer her pulmonology and endocrinology care to UCLA so all her physicians could confer through the TSC clinic. UCLA is a teaching hospital, and they have the best doctors, but when she got sick and became a patient at CHOC, it was a problem. Some CHOC physicians resented me taking Tiara to UCLA for her testing and follow-ups because it put them at a disadvantage when treating her. I did what I thought was best for her and believe me, doing everything in Orange County would have been much easier on us both, but I needed her to be with the best doctors in the country, which UCLA provided.

Tabitha was finishing up her sophomore year of high school and playing great volleyball. Her high school volleyball coach required them to do track in the spring, along with club volleyball, so she was super busy and always exhausted. Because she was so strong, she was doing discus and shot put for the track team and hated every minute of it, even though she was great at it. Trinity finished first grade in public school and was looking forward to summer and being on the swim team again. Once school ended for both girls, Tabitha had her final club volleyball tournament in Reno, Nevada. Since Lou had friends in Reno and Tahoe, we decided to drive up, with Trinity and Tiara, as our family vacation. Tabitha would travel and stay with her team, I would watch all the games, and Lou would hang out with the little girls with his friends. Supporting a child who is so involved in a competitive sport is almost a full-time job. Trying to disperse my attention evenly to all three girls was tough, and I know I didn't always do a good job. It's evident Trinity was the child who received the least amount of attention during her childhood, and I acknowledge that fact. I have apologized to her throughout the years, and she understands the reason why, but it still doesn't fix the fact that she didn't receive as much attention as Tabitha and Tiara.

Once we returned from Reno, Tabitha started training for varsity volleyball tryouts, which up until this point in her life, caused her more stress than any other single event in her life. She wasn't a fast runner and needed to be able to run under a seven-minute mile to make varsity. There were no exceptions to this rule. You could be the best volleyball player in the world, and if you couldn't make the timed run, you didn't make the team. She ran and ran and ran every day in between morning and afternoon practice sessions. She made the timed mile, and if you asked her today, she would still tell you it was the most significant accomplishment of her life. Once the season started, there were two games a week and weekend tournaments. Because varsity played five matches instead of three, I had to bribe Trinity with candy and chips from the snack bar so she would agree to tag along. Tabitha's team did so well that they ended up winning CIF, Division I, and went on to win state. It was such a fun four months, except for Tabitha continuing to get chronic strep throat. We finally decided that I needed to take her to a specialist because she could hardly breathe while doing so much exercise and was always getting sick. The surgeon said her tonsils were so big, they were blocking airflow to her lungs. She often used her inhaler ten times during a three-hour volleyball practice, which wasn't safe. She refused to stop running or playing, even if she couldn't breathe, so I was always worried about her.

We had her tonsils removed in December after school was out and before Christmas. The surgery changed her life, because she was finally able to breathe well while exercising, for the first time in years. As she was home recovering from surgery, a big surprise arrived for the girls: a trampoline. I had been begging Lou to let me buy the girls a trampoline for a while because I knew jumping was good for Tiara's brain. I also knew Tabitha and Trinity would love it, and it was something they could all do together. He was so worried it would be too dangerous, but after months of research, I finally found the safest trampoline on the planet, and he agreed. Of course, it was the most expensive, but worth every dollar. Just another purchase to add to our ever-mounting credit card debt.

The girls were thrilled to have a trampoline, and no one ever got hurt because it had such a safe design. As we approached another Christmas, it became clear that Trinity was struggling in school again. While volunteering in her classroom, I noticed her repeatedly staring off into space, doing nothing. I also saw that she was struggling to read, but when she left Carden Hall a year earlier, she was a good reader. I asked her teacher what she thought about Trinity's inattention.

She said, "Trinity does stare off into space, and sometimes doesn't finish her assignments, but she is such a sweet girl and doesn't cause any problems."

Oh good, she isn't learning anything, but she is quiet and friendly, so we will ignore the issue, I thought to myself. While working in her class, I was horrified to see how a handful of misbehaved children disrupted the entire classroom. It was so chaotic, I wasn't sure how anyone could concentrate. After the Christmas break, I decided it was time to explore other options for Trinity, because I refused to let her fall through the cracks.

Tiara focused on her cutting

CHAPTER 20

Breaking Bones

Tiara was consumed with a frantic energy I had never seen before. I didn't know if the increased energy was a side effect from a medication or her new normal. I loved that she was moving and running, which was keeping her thin and in shape, but like all things with Tiara, it was excessive. She would run and run around the basketball hoop and shoot over and over again until she was completely overheated. Once I was able to drag her away from the basketball hoop, I cooled her down with cold rags and ice water. There was no happy medium with Tiara; it was from one extreme to the next. Despite being thin and full of energy, she still suffered from chronic sinus infections, bronchitis, and breathing issues related to her asthma. She managed to make it through the first part of the year without getting pneumonia, an incredible miracle, as I was bogged down with trying to take care of her sisters.

It became glaringly apparent that I needed to find a new school for Trinity. She wasn't falling behind, but she wasn't learning anything either. Her reading scores were the same as they had been the year before, and she was struggling in math. None of her teachers mentioned learning disabilities at this point, so I didn't consider having her assessed. I did start searching for other local private schools that might be a better fit than Carden Hall. Since cost was an issue, my choices were between three schools. Two were Catholic, and one was seriously Christian. So Christian that you needed to declare "Jesus Christ is your Savior" or they wouldn't allow your child to attend. I believed that Jesus was my Savior, but I felt uncomfortable with the whole concept of having to declare my personal beliefs for my child to attend a school, so I crossed that one off my list. We are Catholic, and I love being Catholic, so we had two options left. Both schools had a good reputation, but one was only a mile from our house, and her best friend from preschool was a student there, so I chose that one. I loved the principal the moment I met her. She was kind, compassionate, smart, and a go-getter. It felt like the perfect fit.

You may be wondering if Trinity wanted to change schools again. Actually, she did. She was starting to have issues with her new friend group and was nervous about moving to Kaiser the next year, which was the public school for third through sixth grades. Even if I didn't move her to private school, she would still be changing schools, so she decided she would instead go to Catholic school with her best friend. She was thrilled to be reunited with her best friend and could hardly wait for the next school year to commence.

As we moved into spring, Tiara was still obsessively playing basketball for hours each day. One Sunday afternoon, Grandma Cindy offered to watch Tiara so Trinity and I could spend some time alone.

We left the house at about two p.m. and received a frantic call from Grandma Cindy within an hour.

"You need to come home. TT's hurt; I think she broke her arm. I'm so sorry. Hurry," she begged into the phone.

Trinity and I rushed home to find Tiara holding her right shoulder with her left hand, while Grandma Cindy held ice to the area.

Tiara kept saying: "Owww, TT sad, TT cry, TT sad." Tiara usually referred to herself in the third person. I looked at her upper arm, just below her shoulder, and I could tell her arm was broken.

"What happened?" I asked.

Grandma Cindy then explained: "Tiara and I were playing basketball. She went to go pick up the ball and then climbed up into the planter where the tree is."

This was typical behavior and nothing unexpected. She did this every day. She liked getting as close as possible to the metal hoop so she could stare at it from different directions.

"All of a sudden, she started trying to walk along the ledge on the fence, towards the basketball hoop. I tried convincing her to stop and go back to the planter, but she wouldn't listen to me. I would have tried pulling her down, but I knew she would fall if I tried. I kept begging her to turn around and all of the sudden she lost her balance and fell off the ledge onto her arm."

The ledge was only about six inches wide, and she had never tried doing this before. Grandma Cindy was shorter than Tiara at this point, and the ledge was at least two and a half feet off the ground, so there was no way Grandma Cindy could have safely gotten Tiara off the ledge. My mother-in-law was the best babysitter in the world. She never left Tiara unattended, so I knew this was a total accident, but it still sucked. I wasn't sure what to do. Should I bring her to the emergency room on Sunday afternoon or wait to bring her to an orthopedic doctor in the morning? I called Rorie's husband, Matt, who was an ER physician, and asked his advice. Like he often did when I called, he told me to come over to the house, and he would look at it.

Tiara wasn't crying but was in obvious pain. I drove the five minutes to their home, and when he looked at her arm, he said: "I'm pretty sure it's broken, but I'm not sure if they can cast it since the break is so close to her shoulder."

"Would it affect her recovery if I wait to bring her to the doctors until the morning?"

"It should be fine to wait, as long as she can tolerate the pain."

Thank you, Lord! Neither Tiara nor I wanted to sit in the emergency room, where she would be picking up germs that would inevitably lead to another hospital admission. I brought her home and tried having her sit on the couch to relax. That was a joke. She kept trying to go outside and play basketball with the arm that wasn't broken.

The next morning, I called her pediatrician, told him what had happened, and asked for an immediate referral to an orthopedic doctor. His nurse called around until she found an office that would take us right away. We drove to Orange, and luckily, this orthopedic group had an X-ray machine in their offices, so we didn't have to make an additional stop. As predicted, her upper right arm was broken right below her shoulder. It was a clean break, and the doctor was in complete shock Tiara wasn't sobbing and in horrible pain. He was baffled by her high pain tolerance. In addition to seeing her broken arm on the X-ray, the doctor also saw that her bones did not look as they should for a child who was only eleven years old.

He said: "I'm surprised this is Tiara's first broken bone. Her bones are more translucent than they should be for her age."

He pointed to the X-ray up on the wall: "Do you see how you can almost see through her bones?"

I shook my head and said, "Yes."

He went on the explain, "They aren't supposed to be translucent like this. I don't see this that often, or normally this severe, but I do see bones that look like hers in children who have intractable epilepsy and take numerous anti-epileptics. I'm sorry to tell you this, but this won't be her last broken bone. She will continue to break bones because of how brittle they have become from the medications."

My heart just sank, and I held back tears. I teared up as I was writing this because I remembered standing next to her while she sat on the patient table. I was worried she would try to jump off suddenly, so I had my body positioned in front of her, with my right hand on her leg. I wondered how much more we could endure. Daily seizures; horrible behaviors; the tumors in her lungs and kidneys were multiplying and would soon cause problems that needed to be addressed with either medication or surgery; puberty; and now the potential for numerous broken bones. It was too much.

The doctor suggested I start giving her high doses of calcium because she didn't drink milk. Hmmm, I'm sure she would love enduring high doses of crushed calcium. Oh, but you probably think I could have just given her those Yummi gummy calcium bears. Well, I was under strict instructions not to give her any gummy candy because it was so hard to brush her teeth, and the sugar from those types of candy could lead to another cavity, which would have to be filled under anesthesia. So, do I give her calcium and try to reverse the bone density loss and risk more cavities and root canals or do I forgo the calcium and hope she doesn't break any more bones?

I was always trying to figure out what was the best option for Tiara. I tried calcium tablets rather than gummies for a while, but her mouth broke out in canker sores. After the cankers sores appeared, I gave up trying to get calcium into her system and figured I would deal with the next broken bone when it happened.

After discussing the bone-density issue, we moved on to her broken arm. "So, do you have to put a cast on her arm?" I asked.

"Her break is too high up and close to her shoulder, so we won't be able to cast it. I'll put her in a sling, which she will need to wear twenty-four hours a day for the next few weeks, except when bathing."

I shook my head in dismay. How the hell was I going to keep her in a sling twenty-four hours a day?

"I'm not sure how I can keep her arm in the sling," I said.

"We have a sling that is like a sock and is very difficult to remove. I think it should work for her. I'll go get it, and we'll see how she does."

He left the room and returned with the sock sling. The minute he started putting it on her arm, she started fighting him. I helped him by holding her other hand down, and he was able to get it on her. The second he finished putting it on and stood back to look at her, she started pulling and tugging at it with a vengeance. It took her thirty seconds to take it off and throw it across the room with her left hand.

She was proud of herself for getting it off so quickly. She had a big smile and kept saying: "I did it, I did it!"

I looked at the doctor and said: "Now what?"

"Well, if she doesn't keep it in the correct position, it won't heal properly."

I pretty much knew that, but I needed some help on how to keep her arm in the correct position.

"What about if we put her in a long-sleeve T-shirt and then we safety pin the sleeve to the front of her shirt?" He demonstrated his idea by showing me on his button-down since Tiara was wearing a short-sleeve shirt. She hardly ever wore long-sleeve shirts, but it seemed like a reasonable approach.

"Okay, I'll try that when we get home," I said.

"Also, make sure she keeps her arm as still as possible," he added.

I then asked: "She keeps trying to play basketball with her left arm. Is that okay?"

"I would suggest she refrain from any physical activity for the next few weeks until her arm sets properly."

I nodded in agreement but knew his suggestion was going to be impossible to follow. We left his office and drove straight to the T-shirt store. I needed to buy a bunch of long-sleeve cotton shirts that would be thick enough to hold the safety pins in place without them tearing through the fabric when she tried to move her arm. I also needed to cut off the other arm because I knew she would get too hot in long sleeves every day. We picked out a bunch of bright-colored, inexpensive long-sleeve T-shirts and went home to start our T-shirt–sling project. The long-sleeve T-shirt idea worked reasonably well, but I could not stop her from playing basketball. Inside the house, she kept running from door to door, trying to get to her basketball hoop in the backyard. I finally gave up when she started pounding on the glass of the back door in the kitchen. She had broken the glass on the front door panes as a young child while trying to get outside, and I knew she wouldn't stop pounding until she got what she wanted. I let her out to play and watched her like a hawk. I also retrieved the ball each time she shot a basket so she wouldn't try using her right arm to pick up the ball. We had lots of basketballs, but she was shooting one after another, so I had to move quickly to retrieve them.

Because she refused to comply with the doctor's orders not to engage in physical activity, her school refused to let her attend while healing from her broken arm. It was too much liability for them, so once again she was home with me all day until her caretaker arrived in the afternoon. I had finally started using the services provided by the Regional Center to get her a caretaker in the afternoons, so I could pick up Trinity from school without incident and take her to softball practices without Tiara trying to jump out of the car or hurt one of us. Because Tiara was so violent, the Regional Center agreed to provide a caretaker to protect me for twenty-five hours a week. This wasn't respite care, because I didn't have to find the caretaker myself. These caretakers were trained in dealing with extremely aggressive behaviors and came in the afternoons when Tiara was most difficult. We went through several caretakers until we found TL, who was a perfect fit for Tiara and our family. It was tough having a person who was not family in our house every afternoon while we were trying to help with homework, make dinner, and do laundry. Trinity and I decided to stay away from the house in the afternoon as much as possible because when I was home, Tiara would follow me around, and TL would have to follow Tiara. If I was home, Tiara wanted to be with me, so she would grab onto my leg or arm and not let go. Then TL would try to release Tiara from me, and Tiara would hold on tighter and swat TL away from us. I would try removing myself from the situation, but it was practically impossible. I would walk away with Tiara hanging on my leg and dragging next to me, while TL was holding onto Tiara. So, it was just easier for Trinity and me to stay away as much as possible. But at some point, she needed to do her homework, and I needed to prepare dinner. TL left at six or six thirty each night, so she would sit with us at dinner and help Tiara get her food into her mouth instead of all over the floor. She then bathed Tiara after dinner, which was a massive help with our night routine. Once she left, all I had to do was give Tiara her breathing treatments and medications before bed. Easy-peasy. If only that were true.

When TL first started working with Tiara, she was so strict that she and Tiara were constantly battling on everything. Within two weeks, Tiara had TL eating out of her hands and, yes, TL was still strict, but not like when she first arrived. Tiara won over everyone with her charm and beautiful smiles. She might hit and kick you, but the next minute she would give you the best hug you ever received while she told you, "Sorry, sorry, love you, love you." It was almost impossible to stay mad at Tiara. She wouldn't allow anyone to ignore or be mad at her. If she felt as if you were angry with her, she would taunt you with big smiles, sideways flirty glances, dance moves, hugs, kisses, or repeated words of love until she felt like you weren't mad at her anymore. She could understand everything we said, and even though she didn't have a large vocabulary, we all understood what she was trying to say or convey 98 percent of the time.

Once Tiara was cleared to go back to school, she was not excited to return. Each day was a struggle getting her into class, but luckily, she only had one month left of school. I'll never forget her graduation from sixth grade. Lou, Tabitha, Trinity, TL, and my parents arrived early to get seats, but Tiara refused even to sit down. She ran and ran and ran around the school playground in her new purple-and-black tank dress, while TL chased her. It was mid-June and about seventy-eight degrees, so she heated up quickly. Her teacher, Bob, tried to get her to sit with her class and wait for the graduation to start, but she refused. She ran until the commencement started and then sat with us. Bob told us to walk her up to the stage when it was time for her class to graduate. Luckily, the school had Tiara's class walk across the stage early in the program, so we didn't keep her in her chair too long. Once her class filed onto the stage, Lou tried to walk her up to the stage to stand with her class. She refused to let go of him, and each time he tried to release his hands from hers, she would grab onto him. He finally gave up and walked through the sixth-grade graduation while holding hands with her. We thought we were done, but Bob whispered into Lou's ear not to leave yet. Now what? After the rest of the sixth graders walked across the stage, each teacher handed out awards to students in their classes for various things. Bob gave Tiara an award for being most athletic, and when he called her name, we all looked from one to another. Tiara had resumed running from basketball hoop to basketball hoop while was TL trailing behind her.

We knew there was no way we would get her attention away from playing basketball to walk back onto the stage to accept an award. If we tried, she would most likely drop to the ground in protest, and then we would put on a show for the entire school. So instead of drawing even more attention to our group, Tabitha decided to walk up and accept Tiara's award on her behalf when she realized neither Lou nor I were getting out of our seats. Just like a famous movie star that is too busy to accept their award at an award show, Tiara was too busy playing basketball to receive hers. As soon as Tabitha collected Tiara's honor, we told TL to take Tiara home and cool her down. We had already doused her with water numerous times, but I could tell she was on the brink of severe overheating. The rest of us stayed for the remainder of the graduation while Tiara got into TL's air-conditioned car and sang along to her favorite music all the way home.

Tabitha finished her junior year, and I was getting panicky about the college situation. Tabitha refused to discuss college, so I took matters into my own hands. I figured she could get into college with the help of her volleyball skills. I knew she wouldn't get a scholarship because I saw firsthand the level of expertise the girls needed to receive scholarships. Several of the girls from her team the year before received full-ride scholarships to schools like USC, UCSB, and UCLA, but these girls were close to six feet tall and practically lived on the court. They were incredible athletes. Tabitha was a great player, but she wasn't in their caliber, which was fine. There is a spot for everyone, or so I've been told. I hired a company to put together a recruiting video of Tabitha playing volleyball that I could send to potential schools. I started researching Division II volleyball schools in California, which I thought she might like. Yes, I was being overbearing and doing the work she should have been doing, but she refused to talk about college at all, so I wasn't sure what else to do.

Trinity finished second grade in public school and spent the summer hanging out with Tiara and me. I enrolled Trinity in a few different day camps from nine a.m. to noon for several weeks so she wouldn't be stuck at home with TT and me all day, but as August approached, all the camps were over. One August morning, I took the girls to the park before it got too hot. During our typical park visits, Trinity would play on the jungle gym and practice going across the monkey bars, while Tiara would run from basketball hoop to basketball hoop. The jungle gym and the basketball courts were a bit of a distance from each other, so I was always running from one area to the next.

Trinity would yell at me: "Mom, come watch me go across the bars."

I would run over to watch her while keeping an eye on Tiara at the same time, but Tiara usually took that opportunity to try to run off. The school I took them to was enclosed with a gate, but that didn't mean Tiara wouldn't attempt to scale the gate, where she might fall and break another bone. During this particular visit, all three of us started out playing basketball. Within ten minutes of arriving, Tiara wanted to go home, which was unusual. I usually had to beg her to leave, so I was surprised she didn't want to stay. I convinced her to stay a little longer because Trinity hadn't even practiced her monkey bars yet. Her goal was to get across all the bars by the end of the summer.

Something about Tiara wasn't right, and she already looked overheated, so I decided we needed to leave. Upon arriving home, Tiara immediately flung open the car door and walked quickly toward the front door. As I rushed to unlock the front door, Tiara started vomiting everywhere. She was walking and throwing up at the same time. I was shocked. For some reason, I didn't feel like she had stomach flu. She was projectile vomiting, and it seemed different than how she normally vomited. I had a funny feeling about it. I quickly got her to the couch, while Trinity fetched the "throw-up bowl." I was holding the bowl up to her mouth to try to catch the vomit, but she kept trying to lie back on the couch. Every time she stopped throwing up, her eyes would roll back into her head, and it seemed like she was passing out. It scared the crap out of me.

I took her temperature, and the thermometer read ninety-six degrees. That was weird. She kept dozing off and then would suddenly wake up a few minutes later, start throwing up in the bowl, and then immediately fling her chest back down onto the couch. Her eyes continued to roll back into her head.

I called the pediatrician's office and told the front office receptionist what was happening and said I was bringing Tiara right in to see Dr. Michelis.

The receptionist said, "I'm sorry, but Dr. Michelis doesn't have any openings today. Let me connect you to the nurse."

Before she could transfer me, I said, "I know you are new and don't know me or my daughter Tiara, but I promise, if you ask Dr. Michelis, he will tell you to have me come right in."

She refused to accept my explanation and tried to transfer me to the nurse again.

I then said, "Okay, I'm not wasting my time talking to the nurse because she will tell me to bring Tiara right in, so I'm leaving my house right now and coming there. I'll be there in five minutes, so you might want to tell Dr. Michelis we are on our way."

I hung up the phone and got Tiara and her throw-up bowl into the car while Trinity followed behind carrying my purse and a few rags for cleanup. Tiara was so weak from the constant vomiting, I had to wheel her into the office in her wheelchair. Our favorite receptionist checked us in, but they didn't show us to a room right away. Tiara started vomiting in the overcrowded sick side, and parents began fleeing to the parking lot with their children. They were exiting the room so fast, it was as if the building was on fire. I didn't blame them and would have done the same thing in their position. The new receptionist kept glaring at me through the window from behind her desk. Finally, a nurse came to get us and showed us to a room. As we were going to the room, our favorite receptionist apologized and explained that the rude new girl was trying to make us wait. Like I couldn't figure that out?

As soon as we were in a room, Dr. Michelis came in right away. He was always so attentive to Tiara and took great care of her. I explained my concern about her low temperature and weird vomiting.

He took her temperature himself: ninety-five degrees. He was shocked and couldn't figure out what was going on with her. We thought maybe she had eaten something poisonous in the garden when I wasn't looking or had some weird infection that could lower her body temperature. Either way, he decided it was an emergency and called 911 for an ambulance. This wasn't the first time he had called 911 from his office for Tiara. I called my mom and asked her to come pick up Trinity because I didn't want her coming in the ambulance with us to CHOC. Once the medics arrived, they loaded her onto the gurney and took her out to the ambulance. I followed the stretcher, and as I passed by the rude receptionist, who had a look of horror on her face, I smiled and said: "I told you it was an emergency!" Sorry, but I couldn't help myself.

Once we got to the hospital, Tiara stopped throwing up, and her temperature was returning to normal. They did a bunch of blood tests, which all came back normal. After three hours of resting in the emergency department, she was suddenly sitting up and moving around and wanted to go home. The doctor said he couldn't find anything wrong with her, and she was getting so anxious to leave, she kept trying to get off the bed and run down the hall. Because I couldn't get anyone to discharge us or help me control her, we finally just walked out without permission. Since we arrived in the ambulance, we had no car, and Tiara was barefoot because I had rushed her to the pediatrician's office without putting on her shoes. I suspect we looked like a mother/daughter duo who had just broken out of the hospital without permission, which we kind of were. We sat waiting on the curb outside the hospital, with Tiara's chest still covered in stickies from the EKG leads, and several Band-Aids on both arms from the numerous failed attempts to get her blood. Luckily, Lou worked close to the hospital and came right over to pick us up and take us home.

A few days later, the vomiting thing happened again. Back to Dr. Michelis's office we went, but he couldn't find anything wrong with her and suggested we meet with a gastroenterologist. You might be wondering what happened when I saw the rude receptionist during this visit. Well, she had received a stern reprimand for the way she had treated me on the phone, and she apologized to me. I felt a bit sorry for her during her apology, but she needed to learn when a real emergency was happening and when a parent was just overly dramatic. I think she learned her lesson, but I can't be sure because she didn't last very long at that job. She was gone within a few months.

Once we got home, I called the gastroenterologist's office right away and sweetly begged the doctor's secretary to squeeze us in as soon as possible. As I have mentioned several times, a new patient appointment with a subspecialist is usually scheduled six weeks to three months from the date you call. The doctor received a message from me and a personal phone call from Dr. Michelis, so she found a way to see Tiara within ten days. It was so kind of her, and I truly appreciated her making time for us because Tiara continued to vomit every other day.

Each time she vomited, her temperature would drop anywhere from ninety-seven to ninety-four degrees, and it was terrifying. I was living in a state of constant panic, trying to figure out what was wrong with her. Ten days later, while waiting to see the gastroenterologist, Tiara started throwing up in the waiting room. I hadn't brought her vomit bowl with us, so I grabbed a trash can when I saw her chest starting to lurch. She threw up twice while waiting to see the doctor. The doctor went through every possible diagnosis, based on Tiara's records, and said she couldn't explain why she was vomiting so often. She felt as if something else was going on that wasn't related to a GI issue, possibly a neurology issue. Despite her belief that it wasn't a GI issue, she offered to run more blood tests and schedule some scoping procedures if I wanted to proceed with this route. She also gave us the option of starting some new stomach meds. I agreed to try the stomach meds, and if they helped at all, then I would have Tiara move forward with more testing. Just like we both thought, the stomach meds did nothing to help with the vomiting. I knew in my heart it wasn't her stomach. We didn't proceed with any further GI testing or appointments.

CHAPTER 21

Vomiting Mystery

It was now September, and school had started for all the girls. Tabitha was a senior and co-captain of the volleyball team; Trinity was a third grader at St. Joachim; and Tiara was now a seventh grader at TeWinkle Middle School. Tiara hated seventh grade with a passion. She was the only girl in the class, and the boys were all in puberty and super rowdy. I walked her into class the first day and was pretty horrified myself. During the first week of school, I repeatedly got hit by a male student while waiting with Tiara for her aide to show up. I pulled Tiara from the class and requested a meeting with the principal and teacher. Here we go again. No school for Tiara until this classroom is safe for her to attend. After meeting with the principal and teacher, it was determined that the class did not have adequate help to control all the hormonal special-needs boys. I agreed that Tiara would return to school once another permanent aide was hired for the classroom. Within a week, the issue was resolved, and Tiara returned, but only for a short while.

Most days, the school nurse would call me between eleven thirty a.m. and one p.m. to ask me to come pick up Tiara because she had thrown up at school. I knew she wasn't contagious, even though I had no idea what was wrong with her, but I picked her up anyway. I finally stopped bringing her to school and asked to have her transferred to home-health schooling, for medical reasons. Tiara didn't want to be there, and it wasn't like she was missing anything. She wasn't feeling well, so why not let her relax at home with her Mommy and do her favorite stuff? The district approved the transfer to home health. A teacher was supposed to come to our house for an hour each day and teach Tiara, but I never asked for a teacher, and no one followed up. I could have cared less about Tiara learning her colors, which she had been working on since she was three.

I needed to put my resources into figuring out what was wrong with her. She was losing weight and getting weaker every day. I would take her to the pediatrician's office three times a week, even though he believed it was related to a neurology issue and told me there was nothing he could do. Tiara would cry to see the doctor, so I brought her to see Dr. Michelis all the time to appease her and myself. Whenever Tiara felt sick, she would immediately start asking: "Doctor, doctor, call, call." If I didn't bring her to see a doctor, she would obsessively ask until I couldn't handle it anymore. It broke my heart to hear her beg to see a doctor, and I didn't have a doctor that could help her.

At this point, I believed it was a neurology issue, but I didn't know how to prove it. I finally got Tiara into to see Dr. Wu at UCLA, but she did not think it was a neurology issue. She claimed it was a gastroenterology issue, even though the gastroenterologist said it wasn't. No one wanted to claim it as their problem. I was continually researching, documenting, and trying to figure out what could be wrong with her. I finally got Dr. Wu to agree to an inpatient EEG since Tiara hadn't had one in years, but that didn't happen right away. They were always booked, and I begged to get her in ASAP. I knew in my heart it was a neurology issue, but no one believed me, except Dr. Michelis, and he couldn't do anything to help, except call UCLA and encourage them to find an appointment for Tiara. While waiting for an EEG opening, I kept hounding Dr. Wu to come up with a plan for Tiara. I couldn't just sit around and wait.

She told me to take Tiara to the lab and get blood work as soon as she started throwing up. I know, crazy or what? But I did it, because I had no choice. I brought her to the lab during a vomiting attack and had them take her blood. She had also told me to take her temperature rectally during an attack, because no one believed ninety-five degrees was an accurate reading. So, every time Tiara had a vomiting attack, I took her temperature rectally numerous times, and kept records. Guess what. Her temperature would drop from ninety-eight to ninety-five within minutes and stay at ninety-five for hours. The blood taken during the vomiting session came back normal, so her neurologist gave me another job. Once Tiara started vomiting again, I was instructed to rush her to the emergency room so they could take an X-ray of her abdomen during the attack. Another crazy idea, but I did it. I think her neurologist thought I would never follow through with her suggestions, which would keep me off her back until an appointment was available.

It was during this last ER visit that the brilliant doctor she had seen before looked at me and said, "This is a seizure."

"What do you mean?" I asked.

"Kids with tuberous sclerosis can have seizures that present weird. I have never seen a vomiting seizure before, but I know they exist, and I am sure this is what is going on. There is no other explanation," he declared.

I asked him to call UCLA and relay this information to her neurologist. He called UCLA and told the on-call neurologist his theory and told them he was once again releasing Tiara from the hospital. The moment he declared it as a rare seizure, I knew he was right! A flood of relief spread through my body. I now knew what was wrong with my baby. I just had to prove it and fix it.

The next day I called Dr. Wu to discuss what the ER doctor had told me. She still wasn't convinced it was a seizure and said the only way to confirm his theory was with overnight EEG monitoring. I had waited over a month for an opening, and now there was a cancellation for the day after Thanksgiving, which was only a week away. Not ideal, but I could care less about Thanksgiving. I needed Tiara to have an EEG right away. Thanksgiving night, I packed up our things, which was a lot of stuff, as I was expecting to stay for at least a couple of days. Every inpatient EEG visit in the past had lasted from three to seven days. I was praying it would only be three days, but I packed enough for a week, including bags of magazines. Now that she was too weak for basketball, she was back to cutting with a vengeance.

We arrived at UCLA at six a.m., as instructed, but weren't given a room until two p.m., because of some emergency. Unfortunately, this wasn't surprising because the system was overwhelmed with patients. I always expected a long wait for anything we did at UCLA. In the past, I typically went to these appointments by myself because Lou would be working or with the other girls and I felt guilty having him take off from work or having us both be with Tiara. But because Tiara was so weak, continually vomiting, and I had bags of stuff to carry, I asked Lou to come with me and help. For the first time, I didn't think I could handle it on my own. He is the sweetest man and had offered to come in the past, but I always told him it wasn't necessary. Tiara didn't get hooked up to the EEG recording until five o'clock that night. It felt like a whole day of recording had been lost, and I was frustrated. I told myself to stay positive and focus on the fact that she was finally getting the testing she needed.

Once Lou left, to go home and take care of the other girls, Tiara and I got in her bed with a huge stack of magazines. I put on her favorite music, and she just cut away. I sat next to her, making sure she was always in the view of the camera. I was supposed to click a button each time I saw a seizure. After I clicked a button, I then recorded on a piece of paper what I saw, along with what time it started and ended. Since she was having so many seizures during this time of her life, this job kept me pretty busy. She didn't have a vomiting episode that first day, so I was hoping that the next day she would, because the sooner she vomited on camera, the sooner we would get to go home. Sad, but true.

The next morning, she was as busy as ever. The room looked like a bomb had gone off, with magazines, crayons, markers, and books everywhere. As she got off the bed and was walking to the desk area, she suddenly dropped to the ground in a drop seizure. Just as she started to fall, I tried to jump across the bed to catch her, but I wasn't fast enough. At the same moment she was falling, a nurse was opening the door to our room, but she wasn't able to catch her either. Somehow Tiara managed to keep her head up as she fell, and it didn't smack on the ground. Maybe it was my earth-shattering scream that scared her and helped her to keep up her head. Either way, they sent for a doctor right away to check her out, but she seemed okay.

I was shaking, especially since I hadn't seen her have a drop seizure in over a month. With drop seizures, there is never a warning or an aura, like with her other seizures. With complex partial seizures, sometimes her facial expression changed, or she tilted her head a certain way, which signaled me a seizure was approaching. I taught her to sit down on the couch if she knew a seizure was coming, and if I wasn't sure whether she was having a seizure or not, I would ask her: "Tiara are you having a seizure right now?"

"Yep, seizure, seizure, seizure."

She got good at identifying her seizures and moving to a safe location. Shortly after the traumatic drop seizure, Lou showed up to spend the day with us. The doctors came by for rounds, and luckily enough, Dr. Shields, from the vigabatrin study, was doing rounds that day. He told me they had seen the drop seizure on the EEG film, along with lots of other seizures. He started to explain all the seizures they had captured in twelve hours of filming and then said we were free to go home.

"What? Why are we going home? We just got here, and you haven't seen the vomiting seizure yet."

He explained that he didn't need to see the vomiting seizure; he had seen enough. I was so confused. I then started talking to the whole team, which consisted of at least five people.

"We can't go home yet. You haven't seen enough."

Dr. Shields then said, "We captured lots of seizures, and we have seen enough."

I was so confused, and kept asking them all: "What is the next step? Now that you have seen all the seizures, what are we going to do?"

No one answered me. They just looked at me with pity in their eyes. I was desperate for them to help her, and they were telling me to go home. Why weren't they telling me what to do? I needed a game plan for Tiara; she was wasting away.

I asked about the vomiting seizure. None of the doctors were convinced the vomiting was a seizure because they had never seen a vomiting seizure. Finally, after begging for some guidance, Dr. Shields told me how to prove the vomiting was a seizure.

He said: "The next time she starts vomiting, give her Diastat. If she stops vomiting, it is a seizure; if she doesn't, it's not!"

"Okay, I can do that, but what is the plan aside from that? What about all these other seizures and the fact she can't go to school and is losing weight every day? What are you going to do?"

None of them had anything to offer. When they left the room, I started to cry in frustration, looked at Lou, and said, "Why won't they help? Why aren't they coming up with a plan?"

I will never forget his response. "Tiffani, they don't know how to help her."

He explained how he felt watching me talk to them.

"You can't see it, Tiffani, but I could see it in their eyes. They were just letting you talk because they don't know what else to do. That is why they are sending her home. They can't make a plan because there is no plan to make; they have nothing left to offer her."

"That can't be true! They have to find a way to help her," I cried. I was mad, angry, hurt, frustrated, and devastated. How could they not have a plan? I knew she had tried every seizure medication that existed, in every different combination, but there had to be something else.

We packed up and went home. A few days later, Tiara had the vomiting seizure, I gave her the Diastat as instructed, and the vomiting stopped instantly. I now had proof that it was a seizure. Thank you, Lord! I emailed Dr. Wu and told her the news. I was expecting a big plan or revelation after she received my email, but that didn't happen. She acknowledged my email and said the team would meet at the end of December to discuss Tiara's results, and hopefully, come up with a plan of action. I still wasn't feeling she believed it was a seizure, and even if she did, what could she do about it? Tiara's medications were all at maximum levels, and there were none left to try. Despite all these obstacles, there had to be something they could do to help Tiara. I refused to give up hope!

A few days after getting home from UCLA, Tiara started vomiting like crazy, and when I gave her the Diastat, it didn't work. I took her temperature, and this time, it wasn't low, but high. She must have picked up the stomach flu when she was in the hospital for testing, but I wasn't convinced. Was this a regular flu or a crazy seizure? I couldn't get her to keep down her seizure meds, so I called Dr. Wu, and she said we needed to drive straight to UCLA. If Tiara missed a dose of her seizure medications, she most likely would go into a status seizure, and they wanted that to happen at UCLA, rather than another hospital or at home. I had been up all night and was beyond exhausted, but I called Grandma Cindy and asked if she could drive up with me. I got a stack of towels, clothes, and a bowl, and we drove to UCLA with Tiara vomiting the whole way. Of course, the ER was overflowing with people, so she waited for hours, and she continued vomiting in a bowl until they found her an extra gurney in the ER hallway. I kept telling everyone about the vomiting seizure, and they took her in for a CT scan to rule out hydrocephalus or any other emergency neurology issue. After about five hours, they moved her into a room in the ER and hooked her up to an EEG. She started having prolonged seizures lasting twenty minutes because of the missed medicine. After they admitted her to the hospital, she was agitated, so she kept pulling my hair and hitting me.

One of the nurses was so rude about Tiara hitting me that she kept threatening to restrain Tiara if she didn't stop. Of course, I didn't like getting hurt, but Tiara was sick with the flu and suffering through prolonged status seizures; she needed a way to vent her frustration, which was why she hit me. She was so sick that all the monitors kept alarming. She kept having seizures, and yet she still had enough strength to try to beat me up. The nurses decided Tiara was too sick to stay on the general floor and needed to be moved to the ICU, where she could have her own nurse. The charge nurse called neurology and asked to have her moved to the ICU. They said no, they didn't want her moved to the ICU, and she could stay on the floor. It was weird because the nurses kept calling the doctors in charge, asking to move Tiara to the ICU. The first doctor said, "Yes, move her to the ICU," and the second said, "No, we can wait it out."

I'm sure it had something to do with money or lack of space, but the charge nurse seemed terrified something terrible was going to happen to Tiara while on her floor. She finally took matters into her own hands and reassigned the nurses for the entire wing, so Tiara had her own nurse to sit with us and monitor her vitals and EEG throughout the night. Tiara continued to throw up all night and experience status seizures. They gave her some of her anti-epileptic medications through her IV, so the seizures were lasting closer to ten minutes instead of twenty minutes. The next morning, Dr. Wu came by to discuss last week's hospital stay. I was so excited to discuss the results because we hadn't had a chance to talk since Tiara had come down with the flu. I was waiting for her to give me this big game plan after reviewing the EEG recordings, and yet she wasn't saying much. Once again, I was perplexed. I finally just asked her straight out: "Why doesn't anyone have a plan for Tiara? What is our next step? I feel like you aren't telling me something."

She looked at me and said, "We have no medical options left. I have done everything I can for Tiara, and there is nothing medically left for me to do. I'm sorry."

Wow, and that was it? There was nothing left. This is what Lou had been telling me, and I had been refusing to believe him until Dr. Wu actually looked me in the eyes and told me the truth. I don't remember what I said to Dr. Wu, because I was in a state of shock. Tiara was violent, having ten or more seizures a day, vomiting daily, losing weight, and couldn't go to school, and the doctors had nothing left to offer her. After breaking this news to me, Dr. Wu suggested we start Tiara on Keppra again. We had used it in the past, and it caused Tiara's behaviors to be even worse, but Keppra was available in IV form, and the doctor felt as if we needed to try it again. I was nervous about trying it again, but as she told me, we were out of options, so I consented. She also said she would talk to Dr. Mathern, the neurosurgeon who had performed brain surgery on many of the other TSC children. She would ask him to consider Tiara for brain surgery even though she hadn't been a candidate in the past.

Lou had come back to the hospital to sit with us, and I took a break and went downstairs to get some food. I wasn't feeling that well but figured I was just hungry, exhausted, and heartbroken. Well, I was wrong. Within minutes of finishing my meal, I started feeling super nauseous. All of a sudden, I found myself throwing up in Tiara's hospital bathroom. Apparently, that flu was extremely contagious. I laid a sheet on the bathroom floor and alternated sticking opposite ends of my body over the toilet. Lou called his mom and asked her to come pick me up and drive me home. I refused to go, so he told the nurse I had the stomach flu and asked her to kick me out. He knows how stubborn I am, and he couldn't reason with me, so he just went over my head. By the time Grandma Cindy arrived, I had agreed to leave and had been vomiting and having diarrhea for hours. I had no idea how I was going to make it home in the car. The nurse gave me a diaper and a Benadryl, which she said helps stop nausea. They use it on the kids undergoing chemotherapy all the time. I took the pill, put on a Depend's diaper, and started my slow shuffle to the parking garage. Of course, there was LA traffic, but I made it home without throwing up or messing up my diaper. Thank you, God!

By the time I got home, it was already eight o'clock at night. Tabitha was taking care of Trinity, and they both looked horrified when I crawled into the house. I was so weak; I could barely walk. Neither of them wanted the stomach flu, so they stood at a distance from me. Tabitha put me into bed and told me not to get up. In the middle of the night, I crawled to the kitchen for coconut water. I was too weak to walk and must have been spiking a fever, because I was shaking and had the chills. After getting the coconut water, I crawled to the front bathroom and remember sleeping on the cold floor for a few hours. I forced myself to keep drinking the coconut water because it is so hydrating. Years earlier, a man at the health food store told me they used to use coconut water through an IV during the war if they didn't have access to glucose for rehydration. Because of this, I always drank coconut water when I was dehydrated.

I woke up at six and called my mother-in-law. She had promised to drive me back to the hospital in the morning, but when I called her, she told me she had been up all night vomiting. Oh no. How was I going to get back to UCLA? I didn't have a car, and I needed to get back to the hospital to check on Tiara. Of course, she was with Lou, so she was fine, but in my mind, if I wasn't there, she wasn't going to be okay. Plus, Lou needed to get to work. I called my dad and asked him to drive me to UCLA before he left for work. He didn't have court until later that morning, so he was able to do it. I had stopped throwing up, my fever had disappeared, and I was weak, but I was in Super Mommy mode, so I pretended to be just fine. I didn't want Lou sending me home again, so I used my best acting skills to pretend I had miraculously recovered in less than twelve hours.

I noticed Tiara was feeling better, and her seizures were a lot less, but she seemed anxious and moody. She kept crying, and I wondered if the Keppra was causing this or if it was something else. Tiara didn't usually cry unless in extreme pain, and it was rare to see her cry. She was a fighter, not a crier! That day, they released her to go home at five p.m. It was a Friday. Hello, traffic on the 405 Freeway south from Los Angeles to Orange County? You couldn't find worse traffic if you searched the entire state. The horrible traffic at this time of day was a known quantity, but I didn't care. We were both extremely weak and exhausted, and we had to get home. It wasn't like I could take her to a coffee shop and hang out for two hours until the traffic dissolved. Grandma Cindy had offered to get a ride back to UCLA and drive home with us, but I thought that was silly. She had been sick the entire night too, and I could drive my kid back, no problem. Well, if I would have known what was going to happen, I would have accepted her help.

Once we got in the car, Tiara started crying and yelling, and her mood was unpredictable. She didn't seem like herself. It took us at least twenty minutes to get on the freeway, which was not even five miles from the hospital. When I finally managed to maneuver the car across five lanes, into the carpool lane, in hopes it would move faster than three miles an hour, she leaned her body toward me and placed both her hands around my neck, as if to choke me.

I immediately said, "No, no, TT. Hands to yourself, please."

She moved them away from my neck briefly but then moved them back to my neck.

I looked over at her and could see her eyes didn't look right. She looked a bit insane, and I instantly started freaking out to myself. I was seriously fucked! Sorry for the language, but I love to swear, and in this circumstance, I was terrified for my life. I had to formulate a plan quickly. I knew from experience I couldn't show her my fear because that would encourage her behavior. When she wasn't in her right mind, it was like dealing with a wild animal. You had to move very slowly, very cautiously, and figure out what was your safest move.

Should I try to be the alpha and get her to submit, while attempting to navigate stop-and-go traffic, or should I act compliant and try to redirect her attention? I decided to start singing all her favorite songs while she clutched my throat. She immediately started to calm down and removed her hands. Once she removed her hands, I needed to decide whether I was going to try to keep driving or exit the freeway and call for help. If I pulled over to safety and called a family member for assistance, it could take them hours to get to us. That would be hours alone with her in the car, and I knew my safest, yet scariest, option was to keep driving. I sang and sang at the top of my lungs while driving in the stopped traffic. Every time I tried to take a break from singing, her hands would resume their position on my neck. When I was desperate for a break, I would call up either Lou or Grandma Cindy and ask them to sing to Tiara on speaker. They could both hear the panic in my voice and complied without asking any questions. "Silent Night" and "Twinkle, Twinkle, Little Star" were the songs that seemed to calm her the most, so I sang them over and over and over again. It took us three hours to get home and once there, things weren't much better. By the next morning, I was convinced she was going to murder me, and I knew it was the Keppra. I called the on-call neurologist at UCLA, and it happened to be the resident that had treated us the past week. She wasn't my biggest fan, I don't remember why, but I do remember her looking at me like I was crazy. I didn't care what she thought of me. I only cared that she knew Tiara and her huge med list and agreed to switch the Keppra for a similar medicine that had the same properties but was more expensive and sometimes difficult to obtain. Of course, I was supposed to wean her off the Keppra slowly, but forget that, I did it faster than allowed because I feared for my life. If she killed me, we would have more significant problems than a quick titration schedule. Within a week, she was on the new medication, Vimpat, and her mood was returning to her usual mean self, but not psychotic.

CHAPTER 22

Fading Away

Christmas was approaching, and I was starting to feel as if this would be Tiara's last Christmas with us. She continued to vomit daily, was so thin that none of her clothes fit, and was continuously in a drugged state from daily doses of Diastat. She seemed to be fading away before our eyes. Luckily, the team at UCLA agreed to complete the testing for Tiara to have brain surgery, because that was the only medical option left. I was thrilled, though not everyone else in my family felt the same way. They were scared for Tiara to have brain surgery. I felt like it was her only option, so I needed to make it happen. For her to be approved to have brain surgery, she needed a PET scan at UCLA, a MEG scan at UCSF, and then the team of doctors at UCLA would discuss the results and come to an agreement. Then we would meet with the neurosurgeon and see if he'd agree to do the surgery. As I am sure you can imagine, getting everything done seemed as if it was going to take a lifetime, and we didn't have any time to waste.

We got an appointment for the PET scan right after the new year, but I wasn't convinced she was going to live long enough to complete all the tests and have the surgery. I kept begging Dr. Wu to admit Tiara into the hospital so we could get the tests done quicker, but she didn't agree. I had the worst feeling in the pit of my stomach every time I looked at Tiara. For the first time since her birth, I started researching SUDEP, sudden unexpected death in epilepsy. I spent hours a day searching the Internet, trying to find anything that could help her, but found nothing. All I read was confirmation that she could suddenly die of a seizure.

It was Christmas Eve, and Tiara was so excited about the party. She loved parties. Every Christmas Eve we would all go to the four p.m. Children's Mass at our church, which was crammed full of people, and then immediately after it is over, we would go to my parents' house for dinner, and the kids would get to open all their presents from my parents. Since the spoiling had continued through the generations, the grandkids were beyond excited to get to Nana and Grandpa's and open their loot. My parents let them open everything during appetizers, all at once, so then they could play with all their new gifts the whole night. My parents would even move their cars out onto the street and sweep their three-stall garage so the grandkids could ride their new scooters, set up any big items they received, or play ball in the garage.

This year, we decided Tiara wouldn't be able to sit through Mass, and Grandma Cindy offered to babysit and then meet us at my parents' at five o'clock. I was nervous about leaving Tiara but had trained Grandma Cindy how to do the Diastat, so I thought she could handle it. I felt like I needed to go with Trinity and Tabitha to church and try to pretend our lives weren't falling apart and their sister wasn't dying. Lou was working and was scheduled to be home by four o'clock, so I knew he would be there to help if his mom needed it. The moment I sat down in the church pew my phone started vibrating. I picked up the call and walked outside because it was Grandma. "Tiara just threw up!"

"Okay, take her temperature with the ear thermometer."

"It says ninety-six degrees."

"Okay, give her the Diastat, and she should stop throwing up. If she throws up again, call me back."

Once I got back in the pew, all of my family had already figured out what was wrong, and everyone except the little kids were sad and scared. I stared at my phone for the next thirty minutes, but it didn't vibrate. We had arrived forty-five minutes early to get seats in church, and just as Mass was starting, my phone vibrated.

It was Lou. "I just got home from work, and Tiara has thrown up three more times since my mom gave her the first dose of Diastat. What should we do?"

"Crap. Give her another dose but watch her closely and make sure she is still breathing. If you get worried she isn't breathing right, call 911."

"Got it, see you at your parents' after church."

The next hour seemed to go so slow. All I wanted to do was run out of the church and drive home as fast as I could and take care of Tiara. The problem was that I was finally spending some quality time with my other girls, and even though they weren't sick, they still needed me. They needed their mom just as much as Tiara needed me, and I hated always having to choose Tiara. But most of the time, I didn't feel like I had any other choice. Once Mass ended, we raced over to my parents', and I ran into the house looking for Lou, Tiara, and Grandma Cindy, but they weren't there. I frantically called Lou, and he finally picked up.

"Where are you?"

"Tiara is too drugged, and she can't walk. I put on her pajamas, and she is laying on the couch," said Lou.

"What? Lou, she has been waiting for this party all day. She has been talking about it constantly; she has got to come. I will be right there."

I got to our house in five minutes flat, and Tiara was happy to see me, especially when I said, "Let's get on your party dress, we are going to Nana's."

She gave me one of her big smiles, then I dressed her[?] quickly, and Lou carried her to the car. I grabbed her pink vomit bowl, which we took with us everywhere, a handful of towels, and all of her nighttime meds, and off we went. There was no way I was going to let her miss Christmas Eve because, even though I didn't say it out loud, I thought it might be her last one. At the house, all the kids had already started opening their presents because they didn't know if we would make it back. Tiara sat on the stairs with Grandma Cindy and watched everyone. All her cousins have always been so sweet and kind to her. Each time they opened a present, they would bring it over and show her and try to get her attention and see if she liked the gift. They kept trying to include her even though she was too drugged out to get excited.

Once everyone went into the garage to play with all their new toys, she followed them out to play basketball on the mini hoop my parents kept for her in the garage. The problem was that she was too drugged to walk on her own, and she refused to sit down, so I had to hold her up while she tried to play basketball, which was somewhat hazardous for us both. She was an eighty-pound rag doll that refused to give up and wanted to play like her cousins, even though she couldn't hold herself up. Once again, her stubborn personality kept her going. Anyone else would have passed out long ago.

Within the first hour, she started throwing up, even though we had already given her two doses of Valium, which was the most we were allowed to give her within the prescribed time frame. Tabitha grabbed her bowl, and we took turns sitting with her on the garage floor as she threw up off and on for the rest of the night. All the adults were silently crying to themselves and trying to act brave for the younger kids, but they were all thinking the same thing as me: "This is her last Christmas."

Tabitha had taken over my photography duties and would only take pictures of Tiara and me, as I am sure she felt the same as me. We all knew Tiara couldn't live this way for much longer.

Christmas Day wasn't much different, except I was hosting the dinner for twenty-five people and didn't feel like doing anything except sit with Tiara on the couch and try to savor each moment I had with her. Everyone brought lots of food, so I didn't have much to make except desserts, and everyone was helping me. For once, I didn't even care what we ate or what the house looked like. By the time everyone arrived around two o'clock, I had already given her two doses of Diastat, and she was sitting on the couch with her bowl and throwing up off and on. The Diastat wasn't working anymore. My relatives who weren't used to the vomiting and hadn't seen Tiara in a few months were nervous when they saw how she looked. The mood was somber. My Aunt Joan had to excuse herself the moment she saw Tiara, and walked straight outside and started sobbing. She was crying to my mom and then to me.

She kept saying to me, "You have got to do something more, Tiff, look at her!"

"If there were something I could do, I would have already done it. All we can do is wait for her to have the tests and pray they agree to do the surgery and it helps."

I had watched my grandparents die, so I knew what the process looked like. Every time I looked at Tiara, I knew she was on that path, and I couldn't figure out how to get her off.

CHAPTER 23

Waiting for Surgery

Tiara was still alive but wasn't able to do much each day except sleep, listen to music, or masturbate. I feel bad discussing this, because it is so private, but she was doing it so often each day, everyone who entered our house saw it. Since being a toddler, when she had lots of seizures each day, she would masturbate on the edge of the sofa, the edge of the bed, or any surface she could find. Guests didn't usually know what she was doing because she wasn't using her hands, so we just ignored her and pretended it was normal. She would straddle her body on the edge of the sofa and rhythmically move forward and backward until she almost fell asleep. I imagine her brain felt on fire or like a puzzle without all the pieces in their places. I could only guess how horrible she felt, and if the masturbating calmed her, then it was my job to let her do it. It was a bit embarrassing when people would come over and she straddled the couch, but what was I going to do? I couldn't send her to her room unattended. She was suffering, so if rubbing up and down on the couch gave her comfort, then who was I to stop her?

She spent most of her days in the living room, listening to music and coloring on the couch, the walls, and sometimes her paper. We rearranged the living room furniture so both sofas faced one another. Tiara liked to sit on the slip-covered sofa with her CD player, crayons, markers, magazines, and books spread all over. Whoever was watching her sat across from her on the gold couch. She no longer watched television and would only listen to music or have books read to her. She liked to hold the CD player up to her ear while listening to the Dixie Chicks or Sarah McLachlan. I guessed she could feel the vibrations from the music, and it comforted her. She wouldn't wear headphones or listen to any other music choices at this point, so the family was forced to listen to these CDs over and over every day for months. I had two to three CD players of the same model and numerous copies of each CD because they were frequently destroyed. Despite having backups, I often ran into an emergency and had to call Grandma Cindy to go out and buy us another CD player or create another CD on the computer. We were all just waiting for the tests to be completed, scheduled, and reviewed and a decision to be made as to whether she would get the surgery or not. Not having the operation wasn't an option for me.

She completed the PET scan earlier in the month at UCLA, and she now had to get the MEG scan at UCSF. There was a MEG scan at UCSD, but they didn't have an opening, so we needed to get her to UCSF. That was problematic for us since she was a horrible flier because of her motion sickness and irritability, so we realized we would have to drive her up north for the test. We got a date for the test in the first week in March and decided Lou would take the day off and we'd drive straight to San Francisco, spend the night, get up, do the test, and drive straight back home. Funny enough, the three of us had a great time. Tiara was fabulous on the drive there, because she had the attention of both her parents and her music. Our only problem was her urine issue. Around this time, Tiara had suddenly started holding her urine for hours, like any average adult. The problem was a Depend's diaper cannot sufficiently accommodate a considerable rush of urine all at once like a toilet, so it gushed everywhere. So, every few hours we had to stop, change her clothes, wipe her down, and clean up her seat. By the time we pulled into the hotel driveway, our car smelled worse than a litter box.

Lou's best friend, Damon, had arranged for a hotel for us right next to the hospital. It was this cool Japanese hotel that had a traditional Japanese bath, which was a perfect square with stool to sit on. Tiara was terrified of it, but Lou had a blast figuring out how to use it. Lou is obsessed with baths, and we had an ancient, regular-sized tub, which didn't accommodate his large frame, so whenever went to a hotel, he couldn't wait to use the tub.

Tiara loved the hotel, and the next morning we drove straight to UCSF Medical Center. Once we got into the hospital, we met the technician, who was so kind and informative, but she told us Tiara would have to lie still for at least twenty minutes, without moving at all, to complete the test. Every time she moved, the test would start over, and there were three parts. OMG, how were we ever going to do this? She then went on to tell us that if they sedated her, the results wouldn't be as accurate, so they highly recommended we try without sedation. Besides, they hadn't ordered sedation, so if she needed it, the test would need to be rescheduled. Since I wanted the most accurate results possible, and we didn't have time to reschedule, we needed to make it work. Lou and I positioned ourselves on either side of her and started singing every imaginable song and telling her every story we could think of. She did well, but we ended up staying in the tiny room for over an hour, in order to get the whole test done. On the way back to the car, we were feeling so elated. We did it! We survived the drive up and the hotel stay and finished the test; it felt so great. It was as if we had won the Lottery!

Once we got to the car, we realized she was soaking wet with urine again. Oh well, no biggie. Lou held up a beach towel as a little tent so I could change her in the parking garage before we started our seven-hour drive home. When I pulled down her diaper, I realized she had just started her period for the first time. Wow, what great timing. I wiped her up, put on the diaper, and got into the car. I knew her violence had been stemming from hormone changes, and once she started menstruating, the theory was confirmed. Two weeks after the MEG scan was completed, I received an email from Dr. Wu asking if Tiara and I could come to UCLA in two days to discuss the results the Dr. Mathern.

Two days later, we met with Dr. Mathern, and he reviewed all the results with me. He explained that Tiara had tumors on both sides of her brain in many different areas, where the seizures were originating.

"Typically, what happens in a child with tuberous sclerosis is that if you remove an active tumor, one which is causing seizures, a nonactive tumor might then start causing seizures. So just because you remove a problem tumor doesn't mean the seizures will stop, because most likely another tumor will decide to start causing seizures. When tumors on both sides are actively causing seizures, the team has to decide which area is causing the seizures that are most detrimental to the child's development and welfare. In this case, we are hoping to eliminate the vomiting seizure, but unfortunately, there are a couple of potential areas in her brain that could signal a vomiting reflux, and one is on the right side of the brain, and the other is on the left side. Because both sides of the brain have numerous tumors that we could potentially remove, we need to look closer at all the test results," explained Dr. Mathern.

Initially, the team was convinced Dr. Mathern should take out a few of the more active tumors on the right side, but after the MEG scan results came back, they decided the left side would probably benefit Tiara most. Since her most-active tumors on the left were in the frontal lobe area, they felt strongly that removing them could help with her violent behaviors. After explaining the options to me, Dr. Mathern said if we wanted to proceed with the surgery, he would attempt to take out two or three tumors in the left frontal area of her brain. He explained the risks and the reality that the only reason he was offering this surgery to us was that she had no other options. He wasn't convinced it would help but would try. If it didn't work, he would consent to a second surgery to remove the active tumors on the right side of her brain, and if that didn't work either, there was nothing left to do.

He looked at me and said, "Does Tiara have a father?"

"Yes, he is wonderful; he is working." He looked at me with this sideways glance as I then went on to say, "My husband will agree with whatever I decide, and I have already decided we want the surgery. So, what do we do now?"

He seemed perplexed by my attitude and said even though I had already agreed, he needed me to sign some consent forms. He explained we had to wean Tiara off Depakote for two weeks before the surgery. I wasn't scared of her having brain surgery, but I was terrified of her not taking Depakote. Depakote was her most potent and most effective anti-epileptic, and her seizures were out of control. How could she survive without it? He said it wasn't negotiable; she had to be off for two weeks before the surgery because of bleeding issues, or he wouldn't perform the surgery next month. Now I was scared. He didn't have a date for the surgery yet but said it would be at the end of April.

That meant I better get the rest of our life in order before the surgery. Despite being preoccupied with Tiara's seizures for the past few months, I also had to deal with Trinity's school issues. Luckily, she loved St. Joachim and had made lots of friends but was still struggling academically. After speaking with her teacher, I realized it was time to rule out any learning disabilities. During this time, we had Kaiser PPO insurance, which no one understood or had ever heard of. The dealership Lou was working at only offered Kaiser, so we didn't have a choice. Everyone in the family switched to Kaiser doctors but Tiara. Tiara also had CalOptima because of her disabilities, so whatever Kaiser wouldn't pay for, the state would pick up the tab for. Or that is how it was supposed to work. I don't want to talk about it because I could write an entire book about our healthcare system and the horrors of trying to keep a person alive and get them the services, treatments, and the medications they need. Let's just say I hated the insurance companies, but I was at their mercy and couldn't live without them.

Anyways, I took Trinity to Kaiser for an assessment with a pediatrician who specialized in learning disabilities. I filled out a bunch of worksheets before the appointment, similar to ones I had completed for Tiara in the past, and he spent an hour talking to us about the results. Just like that, he confirmed my suspicion: Trinity had attention deficit hyperactivity disorder—ADHD. Awesome.

"Really, Lord, my hands are more than full and you still think I can handle more?"

This doctor didn't recommend medication at the time and gave me some suggestions and resources that could help Trinity. On top of everything else I needed to get done before Tiara had brain surgery, I needed to figure out how to help my youngest child with her ADHD. Oh, and let's not forget, I also had to throw Trinity her birthday party because she would be turning nine on April 5, and Easter was the next weekend. Yay me! We had celebrated Tabitha's eighteenth birthday in January, and she had developed senioritis and was eager to graduate in two months.

I forgot to tell you what happened with the college plans for Tabitha. As you know, I had hired a guy to put together a video of Tabitha playing volleyball so I could get her into some colleges. Well, it turned out, all the schools I contacted were more interested in her athleticism for discus and shot put rather than volleyball. When I mentioned this to Tabitha, she went crazy on me and told me she would never do either of those sports ever again. As it was, the discus coach was mad at her because she refused to do track her senior year. He had big aspirations of her winning CIF and going on to compete in state, but because volleyball was over and she wasn't required to participate in track, she didn't. She hated track, and I felt bad for the coach, but it was her life. Anyways, despite all I had to do, I kept trying to get Tabitha motivated to apply to some colleges that she would most likely be able to get into. She never said she didn't want to go to college, nor did she ever say she did. She took the SAT once and then refused to talk about her future.

When time was running out for finishing college applications, she finally screamed at me one day: "Mom, I am not going to college, and if you don't drop it, I will drop out of high school!"

Well, that shut me up real quick. "Why didn't you just say you didn't want to go?" I asked.

"Because I didn't want to talk about it, and you should have figured it out."

Of course, I should have figured it out, how dumb could I be? Lou didn't graduate from college, and he supported us, and besides, we didn't have any money saved for college, so why argue. Lou and I had a few more discussions with her, but at the end of the day, we supported her decision. Tabitha was a born salesperson like Lou and a hard worker, so we knew she would be fine. The hardest part of her decision was going to be dealing with the closed-minded parents in our community who thought you were a loser if you didn't go to college. These were the same parents whose self-esteem was based on the accolades their children received or which college they attended. I didn't hang out with these types of superficial people, but they were everywhere in our community. It would be hard for Tabitha to avoid them.

Tiara (12) on New Year's Eve,

waiting for surgery.

CHAPTER 24

Hoping to Survive

Surgery was scheduled for April 28, 2011, and I was able to wean her off Depakote and complete all the necessary physicals, just in time. The morning of the surgery, we carried Tiara from her bed to the car, hoping she would continue sleeping on the drive to UCLA. She woke up right away and started saying: "Picture, picture, brain, brain?" For days, I had explained we were going to the doctors for surgery on her brain, to help with her seizures, but she didn't understand. I finally gave up and let her believe she was getting pictures taken of her brain, like usual.

Once we arrived at the vacant hospital, we headed to the check-in office. Tiara started dancing and singing to the music blaring through her headphones from her iPod. She had finally learned to wear headphones and listen to music from a small iPod shuffle we attached to her shirt. It was a lifesaver for everyone. She started singing loudly because the empty hall echoed her voice, and she loved hearing her voice broadcast throughout. She was having a blast. A few other people showed up to check in and weren't thrilled with Tiara's performance, because they were stressed. Every person was either checking in for surgery or was a family member of a surgical patient; you could feel the tension in the room. Lou and I pretended not to notice their irritation, and let Tiara have some fun.

Within a half hour, we went upstairs to the pre-op area. TT was tired from dancing, a perfect time to put on her hospital gown and have her lie on the gurney while they prepared her for surgery. Only one parent was allowed to stay with Tiara before surgery, so Lou kissed us goodbye and went to the lobby to wait for me. I was given a white surgical jumpsuit to put over my clothes, and both of us were given matching surgical caps. TT thought our outfits were funny, so we kept taking selfies and laughing at our pictures. I was trying to make light of the situation despite being nervous about her brain surgery. About two hours later, Tiara was pushed on a gurney through the halls into the surgery room. The anesthesiologist walked us to the room and introduced me to her partner who would be assisting, because the surgery was so long there would be a whole team working on her in case people needed a break. Wow, I hadn't even thought about how the doctors would get nourishment or go to the bathroom. Once I kissed her goodbye, I prayed the surgery would help; even though the doctors said it might not. I was praying for a miracle. They anticipated the operation would last eight hours and told us they would be calling my cell phone with updates.

I found Lou in the cafeteria.

"Where should we wait?" he asked.

"Let's go to the car, get our pillows and snacks, and then we'll find a spot."

"Okay." We walked to the parking garage holding hands while I talked about TT's last moments before they sedated her for surgery.

"You get the pillows, and I'll take the bag of food," I said.

"I don't want to bring our pillows, it's weird. People will wonder why we have pillows with us."

"Like I care what people think? I want to rest on those wooden benches outside the cafeteria, and without a pillow, I won't be comfortable."

"Fine, I'll bring a pillow for you, but I'm not taking one for me," explained Lou.

"Do what you want, but you'll be bummed when you don't have one. Our daughter is having brain surgery, and you're worried about looking funny? Who freaking cares?"

He grabbed both pillows and followed me to the benches. We each took a side, propped our pillows on the armrest, and lay down. I draped my bare feet across his chest, and he rubbed them, as he often did at home. He scrolled through his phone as I attempted to nap.

Dr. Wu found us there, three hours later, and told us the good news.

"You guys look comfortable," she said. We both sat up when we saw her approach.

"We are. I love this spot. But how is Tiara doing?"

"She's doing good. We just finished placing the electrodes directly onto her brain. We do this first to verify the areas Dr. Mathern will be removing. As you know, we were planning to remove three tumors from the left frontal lobe. We identified the tumors, saw seizure activity, and confirmed our original plan. As the technician was about to remove the electrodes from her brain, the screen lit up, indicating a seizure, coming from a different tumor on the left that we hadn't realized was causing problems. We were all surprised and decided to look closer. Because this new tumor was so close to the other ones, the team decided we should take all four."

"That's great news! It seems like the more you remove, the better," I declared, and Lou nodded in agreement. "So now what happens?"

"Dr. Mathern and his team will remove the tumors, and we'll go from there. I'll talk to you later."

"Thanks for the update, Dr. Wu. We'll be in this spot all day if you need us for anything." She smiled in agreement and walked away.

"I'm so excited, Louie, this is great news! I mean, four instead of three, that has to be helpful, right?"

"Hopefully. It seems like good news, but I don't know," he said.

We both called our family with the update and went back to waiting.

All day, I kept praying: "Please, Lord, let her wake up, let her not be violent, and let the throw-up seizure be gone." I didn't dare hope for seizure-free because I knew it was ridiculous to think the seizures would stop completely, but we needed the violence gone.

Once we hit the seven-hour mark and hadn't heard anything more, we started to worry.

"Should we call the operating room and ask for an update?" I asked Lou.

"If you want to."

"I do, I just don't want to bother them while they are working on TT."

"She said we could call, so call if you want," he said.

I decided to call. Everything was fine, but because Dr. Mathern was taking the additional tumor, he expected the surgery to last longer than anticipated, maybe nine hours. And so, we waited. Once the sun started to set, we moved inside to the surgical waiting room. The room emptied as everyone else's surgeries were complete. There were only a few families left waiting when I saw Dr. Mathern walk in. I waved him over, and he smiled.

"Well, she did great! It was longer than we planned, but hopefully, taking out the fourth tumor will be helpful."

"Is she already in recovery?" I asked.

"No. My resident is closing her up, and she should be in recovery within an hour." I must have looked worried because he then added: "This resident closes up my patients all the time, don't worry. She is in good hands."

I sighed a breath of relief. "So, everything went well?"

"Yes, here are the before and after photos of her brain. You can see here the four areas I removed. You can keep these," he said while handing me the two large photos. "They should be calling you back to recovery in about an hour. I'll check on her in the morning. Try and get some rest."

"Thank you so much, Dr. Mathern," I declared while he gave us both a hug before leaving us.

After fourteen hours of surgery, they called me to the recovery room, and Lou went home for the night. I saw my angel asleep with a big, red bandage on her arm. I couldn't believe she picked red instead of purple, her favorite color. She always surprised me. As I approached her bed, I heard the nurse complaining that Tiara seemed too sedated, but she started waking up right then.

I leaned over the rail of the bed and whispered, "Hi, TT, Mommy's here."

Before I could even react, she lifted her arm, swung at my face, and said, "I'm mad at you!"

She loved this phrase, and I heard it several times daily, but I wasn't expecting it at that moment. Every hope I had dared dream for her was gone in an instant. I willed myself not to break down sobbing. I had just been telling the nurse Tiara's medical history and how I prayed she would wake up without the violence. The nurse looked at me with pity in her eyes and said: "She's probably just grumpy from anesthesia."

"Probably, she always wakes up angry."

I pushed aside my devastation because now she was trying to pull off the bandages wrapped around her head. I grabbed her hands and said, "TT, stop. Gentle hands. You can't pull on your bandages, sweetie."

"No, go away! I'm mad at you," she said while trying to release her hands from my grip. She refused to stop fighting me, so the nurse asked the doctor for a sedation order, even though they don't usually do that. They like to see the patient wake up and make sure they are okay before they start sedating them, but in this case, it was necessary. Once the sedation took effect, she stopped fighting and fell asleep. I sat next to her bed and prayed she was going to wake up happier next time.

They moved us from recovery to a room in the ICU for the night. They had just finished remodeling the hospital a few years before, and the ICU was gorgeous. Everything was white, brand new, clean, modern, and state of the art. The rooms were large, with high ceilings and lots of windows. The entrance to each room was double glass sliding doors, so everyone walking by could see in the room. This allowed staff to check on their patients without having to walk into the room. Each room had a nurse station right outside the door with a window, so the nurse could chart and look in on the patient regularly. I loved the setup.

Everything seemed fine during the night, until her face started to swell. When the neurosurgery team stopped by the next morning, they seemed concerned about the swelling but said, "Some patients swell more than others. We will keep a close eye on her."

I learned that the neurosurgery team arrived between six thirty and seven a.m. every day. During hospital stays, I always tried to be awake, with at least a cup of coffee in my system before the first team arrived. Because neurosurgery arrived so early, they were usually my alarm clock. Once I spoke with them, I would rush down to the Starbucks coffee bar, which unfortunately didn't open until seven. Then I was ready for the day. I took my shower, brushed my teeth, washed my face, and put on a clean pair of clothes before bed each night, so I could wake up and be ready for the day. It's a great hospital tip for those who live in hospitals with their children or significant others.

Tiara continued to sleep.

"What time does Tiara normally wake up each morning?" asked the nurse.

"Anywhere between three a.m. and seven a.m.," I said, laughing. "But if she sleeps through the night, by seven thirty, at the latest. "Don't you think she is just tired from all the sedation?" I asked the nurse.

"Could be, but the doctors like to see the surgical patients wake up sooner than this," she said.

"Do you think it's because we had to give her the extra sedation?"

"I'm not sure."

Unlike the nurse, I wasn't excited for Tiara to wake up. She looked so peaceful sleeping, and I was terrified she would repeat last night's behavior and start pulling at her bandages the minute her eyes opened. When she still wasn't awake by eleven o'clock, the ICU team was worried. I had been staring at her monitors all morning, when I noticed her intracranial pressure (ICP) was creeping up. When I asked the nurse about this, she said: "I need to page Dr. Mathern and let him know."

Her response worried me, and when the neurology team showed up a few minutes later, I started peppering them with questions. They all gathered around the monitors and stood staring at Tiara's ICP.

Suddenly her nurse appeared and said: "Dr. Mathern has ordered a CT of her brain, stat. Transport is coming for her right now."

"Is something wrong?" I asked.

She ignored my question and started preparing Tiara for the trip to CT. The energy in the room changed. It went from concern and questioning to an all-out emergency. The neurology team stood silent, watching the monitors until transport arrived and pushed her gurney out of the room. I followed behind the gurney and, looking back at her room, I saw the entire team watching us with a sense of dread. The CT scan was fast, and by the time they wheeled us back to her room, Dr. Mathern was waiting for us

"I just reviewed Tiara's CT, and she has cerebral edema, swelling of the brain. We need to address this immediately. I need your consent to put a drain in Tiara's skull to relieve the pressure. Once you consent, I'll explain everything further, but I need to get started on this now. We will be putting her back on the ventilator for the procedure. Do you consent?"

"Yes, do what you need to," I said.

"Thank you. Let's go in the hallway and talk, while my resident prepares Tiara for the procedure."

Dr. Mathern led Lou and me out into the hallway to explain the following: "What has happened to Tiara is a rare complication, which has only happened to me with one other patient."

"Okay, why is this happening to her?"

"Let me try and explain. Everyone's brain resides in a box, which is basically the skull surrounding the brain. Tiara's box is abnormally small and can't accommodate the swelling, which is a normal part of the healing process after brain surgery. It also appears that Tiara is an excessive sweller, which I couldn't have anticipated before surgery. The rapid swelling caused her sodium level to drop dangerously low, resulting in more swelling and seizures. Seizures bring more blood to the brain, which exacerbates the problems. It is a horrible cycle, which needs to be stopped right away. I plan to place the drain in her skull, and her intracranial pressure should drop. Her ICP is at twenty-five and should be under ten. If her ICP doesn't fall by the morning, the next step will be to place her into a drug-induced coma, to calm the brain even further. If for some reason, step two doesn't work, which I'm confident it will, my last resort is to open her back up. If I have to bring her back to surgery, we will remove the skull, releasing the pressure on the brain. I'm hopeful the drain will resolve the problem, and if it doesn't, I'm confident, step two will work. Do you have any questions?"

"No, I think we understand. Thank you," I said.

"Okay, I need to get in there and help. If you think of any questions, just let me know. I'm sorry this happened," said Dr. Mathern.

Luckily, Lou had returned to the hospital in the morning, so at least we were together when we heard the news. I wasn't surprised by this complication because this was Tiara's norm. She was always the most complicated patient in every situation, but I was hopeful the drain would fix everything. After Lou and I both cried, he started calling our family, and I paced. I wasn't allowed back into her room until the procedure was complete.

Once the drain was in position, her ICP dropped to nine, but unfortunately, didn't remain there. By Saturday morning, her ICP was creeping back up into the teens, and Dr. Mathern declared step one wasn't enough. He needed to place Tiara in a drug-induced coma. Putting her in the coma reduced the pressure temporarily, but it still wasn't enough. It was inconceivable to watch her brain waves show constant seizure activity while she lay utterly motionless. The seizures wouldn't stop, so her ICP couldn't go down.

Dr. Mathern showed up and said: "I can't just allow her ICP to increase; it's too dangerous. I need to draw a line in the sand. If her ICP reaches thirty, I have to take her back into surgery."

"Is having another surgery safe?" I asked.

"There are no guarantees. Tiara is fighting for her life, and I will do everything in my power to help her."

"Okay," I murmured through my tears. For the first time, I asked God, "Why is this happening? Please, help her. I need you to fix this."

I never took my eyes off the ICP monitor. I had watched it every waking moment for the past forty-eight hours. Her first surgery was Thursday, and on Saturday afternoon, I watched as her ICP hit thirty. This was it. She was going to have another brain surgery. I called everyone in my family and told them to rush to the hospital because they were taking Tiara back into surgery, and I didn't know if she would make it. If her brain continued to swell, she would die. While preparing for surgery, her ICP continued to rise and at one point, reached fifty.

Trinity had gone to a birthday party at Color Me Mine because I didn't want her to miss it. When Tiara was in the hospital, I always tried to have Tabitha and Trinity continue their lives as typically as possible. I called Sarah. "Can you please go get Trinity from the party and bring her here? Everyone else is already on the way."

"I'm already driving there now," she said through tears.

"Thank you. Try and act nonchalant, I don't want to scare her."

"I'll try. I have to go. Love you."

"Hurry, but drive safe! Love you."

Sarah calmly made an excuse as to why Trinity needed to leave the two-hour party forty-five minutes early and sped up the 405 Freeway to UCLA. Even on Saturday, there was a significant amount of traffic, and I kept calling them, telling her to hurry. Everyone in the family had said goodbye to Tiara except Trinity and Sarah. I needed them to say goodbye, just in case Tiara didn't make it. My sister and Trinity came running down the hall as transport was wheeling Tiara out of her room. Trinity was so confused and wasn't sure why it was so important to get there to see Tiara before the surgery.

I looked at Trinity and said: "Kiss TT's toe and tell her you love her."

Trinity looked at me like I was crazy and rolled her eyes at me, implying "Whatever, Mom." But she did what I asked and said, "I love you TT" as leaned over to kiss her toe.

They rolled Tiara away for her second brain surgery in two days. This time, I wasn't allowed to go with her. We all stood there, wondering if we would ever see her alive again.

We weren't quite sure what to do with ourselves as we waited. Dr. Mathern said it should only take a couple of hours. We went to the cafeteria and bought snacks for all the kids. After a few minutes of staring at each other blankly, Tabitha asked: "Can I go home? I don't want to sit here and wait for hours."

"That's fine. I'll call you when Tiara comes out of surgery."

Trinity and her cousins then all declared at once: "Can we go home too?"

"Yes, everyone, go home. Lou and I will wait; we'll call you as soon as we know anything." Tabitha, Sarah, and Ray left with the kids, while my parents and Grandma Cindy waited with us. After four hours, we received word from the operating room that Tiara had survived the surgery and would be brought back to her room shortly. She made it, thank you, God!

Everyone left for the night, while I waited for Tiara in her room, not knowing what to expect.

Dr. Mathern appeared and explained what he had done during the surgery. "Once I removed her skull, her ICP immediately dropped. I removed the packing, which usually protects the brain from pushing against the skull during swelling, but her brain box is too small to accommodate anything extra. I discovered a bleed she had developed and took care of it. After several trials, I decided it was safe to keep her skull in place and stitch her back up. The alternative was to leave her skull off and have her return to surgery sometime in the future."

"I'm so glad you were able to put her skull back on. I was terrified you might not be able to do that."

"I'm glad too. I'll see you tomorrow. Hopefully, it will be a quiet night," he said.

"Thank you," I said exhaustedly.

It was ten o'clock by the time Tiara was situated in her room. The plan was to keep her calm so her brain could continue to heal. Any movement could cause a person's ICP to increase, which is why they wanted her to remain as still as possible until she stabilized. She had survived the surgery, but she wasn't out of the woods yet. I finally sat down on my pull-out bed to get some sleep, when I noticed her ICP was increasing again. I hadn't slept in over twenty-four hours.

"Why are the numbers going up again? This isn't supposed to be happening, God," I thought to myself.

Within minutes, the fellow (a doctor above resident but below attending) in charge of Tiara's care came running in.

"We need to hook Tiara back up to EEG. Her ICP is increasing, and we think seizures are the cause."

The EEG team arrived in minutes, and I watched in horror as they removed her head bandages, which had only been placed hours before. With the bandages gone, I saw her fragile skull held together by large staples, which ran the length of her head. It was frightening to look at, and now they were gluing leads directly onto the incisions. The sound of the air gun punctured the quiet, as the toxic-smelling glue made me feel nauseous. The techs were gently moving her head from one side to the other, to place the leads, even though Dr. Mathern said she needed to remain still.

Several nurses and techs scurried around her to change drips, give meds, and adjust the ventilator settings. The EEG was finally set up, and the data was bleak. The seizures were constant.

At two a.m., just when I thought I couldn't take more bad news, the fellow came in and said: "Neurosurgery wants another CT, stat."

"No. It's too much," I declared.

"I know it's hard, Mrs. Goff, but it's in Tiara's best interest."

"Is it? It doesn't feel like it. She just got out of surgery four hours ago, and you want to wheel her down the hall, transport her to the CT scan machine, back to her gurney, and back up to her room, when she is not supposed to move? It seems insane. Can I refuse?"

"Yes, you can refuse, but you will be going against neurosurgery's orders."

I stopped, took a breath, and thought about what I was doing. *What if you don't allow the CT and she needs it? You don't have a choice, Tiffani. You have to let them do another CT*, I reasoned with myself.

"Okay, she can have the CT."

I walked beside Tiara's gurney, back down to the basement for the fourth time in forty-eight hours. I remember grabbing a blanket to put around my shoulders because I was shaking. I didn't know if I was cold or if my body couldn't handle any more stress. Every time she had a CT, I had to wait outside the door, in the basement hallway. This time I was so exhausted, I remember sitting on the disgusting hospital floor and not caring. I sat there crying, waiting for them to bring my baby back out. I tried calling Lou, but my phone didn't have service. I begged God for help.

"Please help me, somebody."

"I need help."

"I can't do this."

"She can't die."

"Please, let her live."

"Give me the strength to help her."

By the time we got back to the room, I wasn't much better, and one of the doctors came and sat with me. We talked for a while, and from that night on, she came to visit me every night before I went to bed.

The CT showed that her brain needed to be calmed even further. She was already sedated, but they needed to shut down her body as much as possible to let her brain heal. She stayed in a deep coma for several days until her ICP stabilized, and then they slowly started backing down on the medication to allow her body to wake up and see what would happen.

Even though Tiara was on super-high levels of numerous anti-epileptic medications, she was having more seizures than could be counted. Days later, they slowly brought her out of the coma and allowed her to wake up. It was my worst nightmare. Each time she opened her eyes, I thought she was going to look at me, but her eyes just darted from side to side. I knew the eye darting was seizures. That night, I sat next to her bed in a state of constant panic as I watched her have continuous seizures.

I asked the nurse, "Can you please page the fellow on duty? Tiara is having so many seizures. This is horrible."

The fellow finally arrived. "You need to put Tiara back in a coma. She is continuously seizing," I told her.

I've been monitoring her EEG, and we know she is having a lot of seizure activity, but we need to let her wake up and see what happens."

"She's not ready. This is a bad idea. I'm her mom, I know her better than anyone else, and you need to trust me. She needs to go back into a coma, right now."

"I'm sorry, Mrs. Goff, but I can't do that. You realize the eye darting isn't seizure activity, don't you?"

"Yes, it is!"

"We don't see it on the EEG," she said.

"Just because it doesn't show up on EEG doesn't mean they aren't seizures!" I said angrily. Again, I was dealing with someone who didn't believe what I knew was a fact.

"I'm sorry you are so frustrated, but we need to wait this out. I'll talk to you again in the morning. Try and get some rest."

Tears of frustration ran down my face. She was dying before my eyes, and no one was stopping it.

By the next morning, everything had gotten worse, just as I knew it would, and the team decided to have Tiara undergo another CT scan. I didn't expect the results from this CT to be any different from the CT twelve hours ago, but I was wrong. As we returned to her room from the basement, I saw Dr. Mathern walking toward me. It seemed odd because the team had already been by, and he usually came by to visit in the late afternoon. He looked devastated.

"I need to talk to you. There is something I need to show you on the computer."

He led me to the nurse's station outside Tiara's room and motioned for me to sit in the chair. My friend Carol had just shown up for a visit, and she paced the hallway as I spoke to him, sensing that something terrible was about to happen.

He pulled up an image of Tiara's brain onto the computer and said something similar to these words: "We have just discovered that Tiara has suffered two severe strokes at the base of her brain, which is the worst place to have a stroke. They most likely happened when her ICP was extremely elevated. The areas of her brain where the strokes occurred are responsible for receiving and relaying information to the body, including breathing, swallowing, hearing, and many other functions. If she ever wakes up, she will most likely be in a wheelchair, with a trach, a G-tube, and will be blind. I'm so sorry; I don't know why this happened," he said with tears in his eyes.

I heard the entire devastating prognosis, but what I listened to the most was "if she wakes up." I was shaking my head side to side, with tears streaming down my face. I then asked the hardest question I have ever asked anyone in my entire life.

"Is she going to die?"

"I don't know," he said, looking completely stricken.

"I have never seen this happen before. I have gone through her surgical chart over and over again. I have met with the anesthesiologist and discussed the case at length with her. I have met with the neurology team several times. None of us can find any mistakes during surgery. I don't know why this happened," said Dr. Mathern.

I believe with all my heart it wasn't his fault and said, "It's not your fault. Now, what happens?"

"We are going to put her back into a coma and give her brain more time to heal, and then we wait and see what happens."

"Okay." I was hysterically sobbing and returned to Tiara's bedside, where Carol embraced me.

After a minute, I pulled away from her and said, "I need to call Lou."

I told him what Dr. Mathern had said. As I was talking to him, he walked out of work and started running to his car so he could drive to UCLA to be with us.

"Lou, please, don't speed. I don't want you to get in an accident," I begged through my tears.

I then found the strength to call everyone in our family and let them know. Tiara might not live. I told Tabitha and Trinity the truth, but Trinity didn't comprehend what I was saying, which was for the best.

I vowed to keep Tiara alive but took back that promise a few weeks later when she seemed to be suffering so much. There were no improvements in her condition for weeks. Every time they tried to wean her out of a coma, the seizures would increase substantially, and so would her ICP. Every few days she'd spike a fever. The nurses would swab every open port on her body as they searched for the source of infection. The doctor would order another antibiotic and continue pumping her full of endless seizure medications. Whether she was in a coma or not, her brain continued to seize.

The only sustenance she received was first through her veins and later through a feeding tube. She was so thin and frail, I feared a bone would break each time they turned her to change her diaper, give her a sponge bath or routine turns to prevent bedsores. I wondered how her emaciated body could find the strength to survive. Looking at her, it seemed almost impossible.

One morning I woke to find her face pinched, like she was in pain. The doctors thought it impossible for her to feel pain while so medicated, but I knew something was wrong. I researched all the medications she was on and brainstormed with her nurse. We figured out that she must be itchy, which is a common side effect of fentanyl. Can you imagine feeling the urge to itch and not being able to scratch, because you are in a sedated coma? Once we gave her a strong antihistamine, her troubled expression disappeared. Seeing her agitated while in a coma felt like a sign.

I no longer prayed to keep her alive. My prayer became, *"Please, God, don't let her suffer. Take her under your wing and do what is best for her."*

I think May 18 was the day I signed the "do not resuscitate" (DNR) orders for Tiara. I kept voicing my concerns to her doctors about her deteriorating condition, and my favorite fellow said, "You may want to sign DNR papers for Tiara. If her heart stops, then she will be allowed to die peacefully. If she doesn't have DNR papers in place, we will be obligated to restart her heart. It can be devastating for a patient in Tiara's condition. Most likely, we would break one or more of her ribs, possibly resulting in a punctured lung. It would be horrible for her. Signing DNR papers gives her a way out. If she were my child, I would do it. It is the most compassionate thing to do under the circumstances."

"That's what I want to do, but I need to talk to my husband first. Can you get me the papers so that I can read them tonight?"

"Yes, I'll bring them to you, and we can talk about it again tomorrow."

"Okay, thank you," I said with tears falling down my face. I sobbed, thinking about all Tiara was enduring. She was on a ventilator, being fed through her veins, had squeezy things on her legs to prevent blood clots, may be blind, could be in a wheelchair on a ventilator for the rest of her life, is on more than eighteen different drugs, is full of infections, and yet her heart is still healthy. If she had had enough, the only way for her to pass peacefully would be for her heart to stop. I had to give her that option.

At the time, I knew it was the right decision, and oddly enough, several nurses thanked me for signing the orders. They said it was heartbreaking to watch, but knowing that she had a way out comforted them. They told me, most parents couldn't bring themselves to sign the papers, and many times regretted it later. Once the orders were signed, I started obsessing on getting a priest to come perform the anointing of the sick for Tiara, but I couldn't bring myself to ask the nurse to call a priest. It was like her whole life was hinging on whether or not I asked a nurse to call for a priest.

Lou agreed we should sign the DNR papers and came to see us the next day.

"Louie, I want a priest to come, but I'm afraid to ask. Will you ask the nurse to call one for me?"

"Of course. When do you want him to come?"

"As soon as possible. I'm afraid she'll die before he gets here."

"I'll go ask the nurse right now. Do you want me to see if he can come today, while I'm here?"

I nodded to say yes while trying to hold in a deep sob.

The priest arrived a few hours later, took one look at Tiara, and broke into tears. He wasn't supposed to be crying; he was there to comfort us. Oh, that's right, he is a human, not a god, and seeing Tiara for the first time was traumatizing to most. He continuously cried while performing the sacrament. Lou and I both cried hysterically through the entire ceremony, but I finally felt safe. The priest explained that since she was a child, she was going straight to Heaven. Now that I knew she was blessed and going straight to Heaven, I wanted to let her know it was okay to leave me. I wasn't sure if she wanted to be alive anymore, and I wasn't sure if it was fair for me to want her to be alive.

After Lou went home and it was only Tiara and me, I grabbed her hand and whispered into her ear, "Tiara, I love you more than anything in this world, but if you don't want to be here anymore, it is okay, you can let go. I will fight for you if you want to stay alive, but if this is too much, God will take care of you. I will find a way to be okay without you; I don't want you to suffer. I love you, sweet girl."

I felt her squeeze my hand, and I saw her eyes flutter. She heard me! *She's going to wake up*, I thought. I watched and waited, but nothing happened.

She didn't wake up, but I knew she had heard me, and that was enough. Now it was between her and God.

At some point during this nightmare, we decided it might be a good idea to put on her headphones and play some music for her. Her iPod was loaded with wild, loud songs from Hannah Montana to John Mellencamp, and Lou and I were scared to play that kind of music for her, but we thought it might help. We were both standing next to her bed as we put the earbuds in her ears. I was watching the monitors to make sure her ICP didn't increase, when all of a sudden, her heart rate increased. I got nervous and pulled out the earbuds. And then she got pissed! Her blood pressure spiked, and she lifted her hand toward me, as if saying "Put them back in my ears, Mom!" At first, I thought her blood pressure was spiking because she didn't like the music, but then we both realized she wanted her music back. Lou quickly put the earbuds back in her ears, and she instantly calmed, and her blood pressure returned to normal. From that point on, we kept an iPod playing in her ears, twenty-four hours a day. Sarah bought her another one and had Tabitha program it, so once one iPod battery died, we would replace it with another fully charged one.

Twenty-five days passed, and the doctors declared that she couldn't just live there in a coma. They had to bring her out of the coma and deal with the consequences. As they slowly brought her out of the coma, she didn't wake up, but her brain started going crazy. She started seizing constantly, and no amount of medication would stop the seizing. They kept adding more and more Ativan, Valium, any drip anti-epileptic they could think of, but nothing worked. The neurology and neurosurgery team were at a loss. Dr. Mathern seemed devastated by Tiara's condition. He visited every day, and even though his part was over, the surgery, he never stopped coming to see her until the day she left the hospital. During one visit, he asked me, "Why do you always smile when I walk in?"

"I don't know. I just do," I said.

"How can you sit there and smile at everyone who walks in the room. Why aren't you mad?"

"I guess because I don't think it's anyone's fault. Plus, it's not going to help me to be angry and miserable, so I smile."

He looked at me thoughtfully. "You are different than other parents."

"I guess."

"I don't think I would smile at anyone, if I were in your position," he proclaimed.

"You don't know that, you might," I said. We then started talking about books or travel, which we did daily.

A few days later, the ICU attending said Tiara needed a trach and a G-tube surgically implanted. Based on her prognosis, they believed she would need a trach for the rest of her life, and she had been using a breathing tube too long already. The trach would help reduce infections, and the G-tube, a permanent feeding tube in her stomach, would allow the tube from her nose to be removed. A G-tube would also enable her to take medications that don't come in IV form. I consented to both, even though I didn't want her to get a trach. I was okay with the G-tube because it is easy to remove, but the trach scared me. Both procedures were performed without incident.

She had been in the ICU for forty days. She hadn't been in a medically induced coma for a week, and she hadn't woken up. The doctors weren't sure why, and neither was I. They kept saying she needed more time to wake up, but she was still having tons of seizures on the EEG, so I could tell they weren't convinced she would ever wake up.

I knew she would never wake up if we couldn't stop the seizures. I racked my brain to try to think of anything that could help her. The team decided to start her on a soy-based ketogenic diet, which would be given through her G-tube. On almost the same day they started the ketogenic diet, I was talking to my favorite neurology nurse practitioner, Sue, who visited us every day. She was always helping me brainstorm things that might help Tiara. While talking to Sue, it suddenly dawned on me, "What about Depakote?"

Depakote was Tiara's base seizure medication for years, and she had to be weaned off it for the surgery because of bleeding issues. She looked at me with wide eyes and said, "Oh, the team may still be downstairs; I am going to go ask them right now." She presented the idea to the team.

Dr. Mathern spoke up first, "It's fine with me. I think it's a great idea."

All the neurologists agreed. Within days of starting the ketogenic diet and Depakote, Tiara opened her eyes and smiled. I knew it was the Depakote, but the nutritionist and doctors tended to believe it was the diet. It didn't matter why, just that she woke up. I knew the minute I saw her smile, she was going to make it.

The nurse ran in and said, "Can she see?"

From the glass doors, I took one of the big pictures that Sarah had blown up of all the family members, and brought it over to her bed.

"TT, can you point to Daddy?" She slowly moved her finger over to Lou's image. I then asked about her sisters, and she got them right too! She could see! It was beyond a miracle. The news spread fast, and before I knew it, Dr. Mathern came bolting into the room. Tiara had been dozing and suddenly woke up and smiled right at him.

"Can she really see?" he asked.

"Yes! She pointed to her dad and sisters."

"Hallelujah!" he shouted while throwing his arms up in the air.

He gave me a big hug. Tiara became somewhat famous in the hospital, as her recovery was thought to be a real miracle. A head nurse who had worked at the hospital for fifteen years said to me one night: "I can always tell when a child will walk out or be wheeled out [to the morgue]. I've only been wrong twice. Now it's three times. I never thought she'd make it. Tiara's recovery is a true miracle."

Soon after we realized Tiara was going to survive, it was time to focus our attention on Tabitha's graduation from high school. Tabitha had stopped coming to visit Tiara and me after she said her last goodbye to Tiara. When it became clear Tiara would survive, Tabitha didn't believe it. I spoke to her on the phone daily, but she didn't want to talk about Tiara's condition.

"Tab, why don't you come see us this weekend?"

"I don't want to come there, Mom."

"But I miss you. I want to see you. TT would be so happy to see you."

"I'll see you when you come home for graduation," she said.

"Tiara's doing better. You should see how great she looks," I said.

"I'll see her when she comes home from the hospital if she ever really does."

"I promise you, she'll come home."

"Well, you said the brain surgery would be fine, and it wasn't. I don't want to go there, and I don't want to talk about it anymore. I love you. I gotta go," Tabitha said and hung up the phone.

I let it go and tried to be excited for her graduation. As her friends planned elaborate parties, vacations, and college move-in dates, she only had plans to continue working for Sarah in her store. She didn't want to leave home to travel or go to college. I surprised Tabitha by coming home for prom pictures and stayed the night so I could pick her up from the after-party.

For Tabitha's graduation, April and Lee Ann, my TSC friends, agreed to each take a shift and watch Tiara in the hospital so everyone in our family could attend. I went home for twenty-four hours and pretended to be upbeat and excited during the ceremony and party afterward, at Sarah's house. It was only my second night home since Tiara had been admitted, and it seemed like Tabitha wasn't coping well. That night, Ray told me he had paid one of Tabitha's friends to complete her economics project because she had refused to do it herself.

He admitted to completing a few of her assignments so that she would pass her classes. Her teachers knew about Tiara and were very lenient on Tabitha, but she still needed to complete a minimum of work to graduate. Now I understood why he had been such an asshole to me the month before, when he showed up at the hospital unexpectedly one night.

I was watching the *American Idol* finale when I saw Ray walking through the glass doors.

"Hi. What are you doing here? It's late," I questioned him.

"I came to visit you and Tiara," Ray said while handing me a plastic bag.

"Thanks, what's in here?"

"Water, a Synergy, and pretzels," he said.

"Thanks. Sit, I'm watching the *American Idol* finale."

He sat down and started watching with me. I wasn't sure why he had come. We started talking about Tiara's condition, and then he said, "I know Tiara needs you, but Tabitha and Trinity need you too."

"I know, but I need to be here with Tiara."

"Tabitha isn't doing well and needs you home. Tiara might not make it, but Tabitha and Trinity are still alive and are suffering without you," Ray said with tears in his eyes.

I looked at him, and replied angrily, "What are you saying? That I should leave Tiara here to die alone, so I can go home and take care of Tabitha and Trinity?"

"Well, yes. They need you, and you aren't doing anything for Tiara by just sitting with her. Sarah and I are trying to help Tabitha, but she's not doing good."

"Well, I can't come home and take care of her. Tiara will die without me. Lou is home; you guys are all there. You all need to figure it out," I said.

"Lou is a mess without you; he is barely making it himself," he said.

"I can't believe you are saying this to me. I can't deal with this."

"You need to hear it, Tiffani. Your other girls are suffering without you, and Tiara probably isn't going to live, but they are," said Ray.

I stood up and said, "You need to leave right now. I'm going to forgive you for what you just said, but I can't talk to you anymore."

He got up from his chair and tried to hug me goodbye. "I'm sorry you're mad, but you needed to know."

"Just go, and don't ever talk to me about this again." As soon as he walked out of the door, I called Sarah.

"Did you know Ray was just here?"

"No! Why was he there?" I told her what had transpired, and she was livid with him. She hung up with me so she could call and yell at him. I forgave him, but I never forgot.

Now that we knew Tiara was going to survive, we had to switch from survival mode to getting better mode. She was still having seizures and wasn't awake much each day, but she tried to start talking. But she couldn't talk because of the trach, which meant there was a hole in her throat, and the vibrations are lost unless you cap the hole.

As soon as she appeared to be waking up more each day, they started weaning her off the ventilator. It was a scary process because she would often get mucus plugs from the new trach. The plugs prevented oxygen from getting into her airway, so they had to be removed quickly. I watched the respiratory therapist remove them on several different occasions and each time, I was stressed.

The team started her on physical, occupational, and speech therapy because she had to relearn everything. Like a baby, she wasn't strong enough to hold her head up. She had lost over thirty pounds and was so weak, she couldn't sit up without support. Nevertheless, I could tell she would someday walk, talk, and be her sassy self again.

Now that Tiara's condition had stabilized and she was attempting to relearn all the skills she once knew, the doctors started discussing moving her to a rehabilitation facility. I was hesitant to consider such a move, even though they told me it was bound to happen whether I liked it or not. Ugh! Everything was starting to change, and I wasn't ready.

I felt safe in the ICU and didn't want to leave, so I panicked when they told me it was time to move out of the ICU and onto the general floor. I loved all the nurses and doctors in the ICU. I knew about their families, their boyfriends, the weddings they had recently attended, where they were going to school at night. I had developed a whole life with the doctors and nurses in the ICU. They put Tiara on the waiting list but said it would probably take a week. I prayed it would take two weeks.

Two days later, her nurse said, "They found a bed for her on the floor. I'm sorry, but we need to move her right away because another kid is coming into the ICU and needs her bed."

I started to cry. I kept thinking, *I know she is getting better, but really, the floor?* I wasn't ready for the floor, and I doubted the nursing staff there could care for Tiara properly. It is my belief, there should be a middle level, where the nurses are trained to the same level as ICU nurses, but maybe they have three patients. On the floor, the nurses don't have the same level of training, and they have more patients than they can handle.

Before I could gather my wits, they started bringing carts to our room to help me move all the junk we had accumulated. Our nurse was leaving for her dinner break, so they sent up this transition person to help. We didn't even have a chance to say goodbye to everyone. The minute we walked into the new room, I thought for sure I would start screaming and have a tantrum like a two-year-old. The room was dark and dingy, and the entry door had only a small window into the hallway, instead of glass, like in the ICU. How were they going to see us in an emergency? Also, it was dirty! No glass, no natural light, no access to help immediately. Tiara and I had been transported from a beautiful, safe space to what felt like a filthy cell.

A nurse greeted us briefly and said she would return to get all the necessary information from me after taking care of another patient. She was very busy with this other patient and didn't have time to do the intake right away. *Are you fucking kidding me*, I thought. *Tiara has been hanging onto her life with a thread for the past seven weeks, and you are too busy to take care of her?* While waiting for the nurse to return, I started cleaning like a maniac. The last thing I needed was for her to pick up another infection, so I got to work with the bleach wipes.

When the nurse eventually returned, she brought the new doctor with her so they could both complete the intake on Tiara. It was as if she had just been admitted for something random, and I had to give them a history. *Didn't someone read her chart before they transported her to this floor? Does anyone here know anything about her?* I kept trying to remain calm, but by the time they both left, I knew they thought I was insane, but I didn't care. It was getting late, and we had been in the new room for several hours, and no one had done anything for Tiara. *Hello people, she needs her trach suctioned, her G-tube cleaned, her anti-nausea medication, her breathing treatment, and you need to start crushing and dissolving all ten of her meds that are due in an hour,* I thought to myself. I kept calling the nurse, but no one showed up. I'd been learning how to do all these tasks while in the ICU, so I just started doing them on my own. The nurse finally showed up with the anti-nausea medication, an hour after it was due. And said she had called respiratory to come for the breathing treatment, but they did all the ICU kids first, so Tiara probably wouldn't get her treatment until nine o'clock, even though it was supposed to be at seven p.m. The final straw was when the nurse brought in all the meds and left them with me.

"Am I supposed to put them in the G-tube, myself?"

She looked at me and said, "Oh, do you want me to give them to her?"

"Well, I have watched the other nurses do it, but I've never done it myself," I said.

She then said, "Okay, I'll do them." She started to push the meds too fast.

"Can you please push them slow? Tiara will throw up if you give them too fast," I said.

"Sure," she said, but completely ignored my request and continued to push them faster than Tiara could tolerate. As expected, Tiara threw up that night; I was so pissed.

I knew from that moment on, I couldn't trust the nurses on that floor. I would have to do everything myself. This thought was validated the next day when Tiara's oxygen level started to drop, which meant she needed her trach suctioned immediately. I rang for the nurse because the person watching the monitors hadn't noticed her levels drop, and no one was showing up, even though the alarm was going off and it was an emergency. While waiting for the nurse to arrive, I knew I didn't have a choice but to suction her myself. I had watched them in the ICU and told myself, "You can do this, Tiffani."

I got out the tubing and sterile gloves and turned on the suction machine. It was important for the process to be sterile. I put on the gloves, carefully removed the tubing from the open package, and attached it to the suction machine with my one gloved hand. I gathered up the tubing in my right hand, which hadn't touched anything else, and fed the tube down Tiara's trach. Once you get down far enough, you release your finger from the hole you are covering on the tubing, which allows the suction to start. I was suctioning, but her oxygen wasn't going up. *She must have a mucous plug stuck*, I thought to myself. I was beginning to panic when the nurse finally rushed into the room. I sighed a breath of relief. I had just stopped suctioning and was giving her blow-by oxygen before starting the next session of suctioning.

The nurse looked at what I was doing and said, "We need respiratory right away. I don't know how to suction a trach!"

She ran out of the room to get help and left me with Tiara to administer oxygen and try to get out the mucus plug myself. Fortunately, I was able to suction out the plug after my second attempt, and by the time she returned with respiratory, Tiara's oxygen had returned to a safe level. Yes, I reported her incompetence to the head nurse.

It was at this point my sweet, understanding disposition shifted to *Everyone here is incompetent, and watch out, I am taking names!* Within a few days of moving Tiara to the floor, she developed stomach pains and started throwing up. She wasn't having regular bowel movements because the soy ketogenic diet caused severe constipation, but no one could agree on what was wrong. One doctor told me the X-ray showed Tiara's bowels were impacted, and another doctor said it was gas. No one could explain her stomach pains or vomiting except to say they thought she had horrible reflux from all the medication. I thought she was constipated but didn't believe the reflux theory, and I thought the vomiting episodes were seizures, but of course they didn't agree with me. Either way, everyone decided she needed her system cleaned out, so they put her on buckets of laxatives for twenty-four hours. It lasted for days. Poop after poop, followed by never-ending diarrhea, and a raw, red bottom. It was so much work for me because I now had to change her diapers, do the meds, and do the G-tube and trach care. I even started changing her bed. The bed changing was hard because she still couldn't sit or move, and she was very fragile. I got good at the nursing thing but was getting worn down. When she was in the ICU, I felt safe leaving her for five minutes without someone else by her side. Now I couldn't leave her for a minute unless a family member or friend was sitting with her.

The doctors decided she needed a Nissen fundoplication surgery to help with the reflux and stop the vomiting. The operation would prevent her from being able to vomit, thereby helping her gain weight and keep her seizure meds down. Another surgery. It seemed like we were never going to get home. The night before surgery, she kept vomiting repeatedly, and her vitals were all over the place. Her temperature dropped, and I knew it was a seizure. The vomiting seizures were back. I paged neurology, and they rushed down to see her, and for the first time in history, they witnessed her vomiting and declared I was right—it was a seizure. She was having surgery in the morning for reflux, which she didn't have. Now what? The neurologists discussed it and thought she should go through with the surgery because it would help by physically preventing her from vomiting up her seizure meds. I agreed to let her go forward with an operation she didn't need.

A few days after surgery, we were transported to a rehabilitation home in Orange County, only twenty minutes from home, and I was thrilled to be leaving UCLA. The rehab home was so different, and once again, I had trouble with the transition. It was much more casual; they administered the medication differently; it had carpet, which freaked me out; but it was like a home. By the morning, Tiara had started to cheer up, so I was feeling happier myself, plus I realized right away I was going to be able to manipulate these people better.

I immediately set five goals for Tiara, which I wrote on the whiteboard next to her bed.

1) Get her trach removed.

2) Get her on solid food.

3) Get her to sit up on her own.

4) Get out the PICC line in her arm.

5) Get her to stand, with help.

Her team agreed that Tiara could go home, once she could sit on her own and stand with help. They expected this would take six weeks.

Before we left UCLA, I had repeatedly begged them to remove her trach. I knew she didn't need it to breathe, but they refused. They kept telling me, "Kids like Tiara relapse; it isn't safe." At the rehab home, I asked if we could cap her trach on day two. They said if she kept it capped for seventy-two hours without a problem, they would consider taking it out. The same day, a speech therapist assessed Tiara and said she had a swallowing issue, but if I watched her closely, they would allow her to eat solid food. Because of this swallowing issue, UCLA had forbidden me to feed her, and she was sinking into a depression.

As Tiara tried her first bite of food in eleven weeks, her face radiated joy. Food was her medicine. As soon as she started eating, everything got better. She sat up on her own, started talking, and was making progress by leaps and strides. The staff and doctors were shocked. One doctor told me he had never seen anything like it. Again, she was deemed a miracle girl. She accomplished all her goals within two weeks and was then cleared to go home. That drive down the 55 Freeway in our car was exhilarating. She hadn't been in a car or seen her house in three months. The whole way home, she kept saying, "Home, home, I did it, I did it!" Yes, you did, TT.

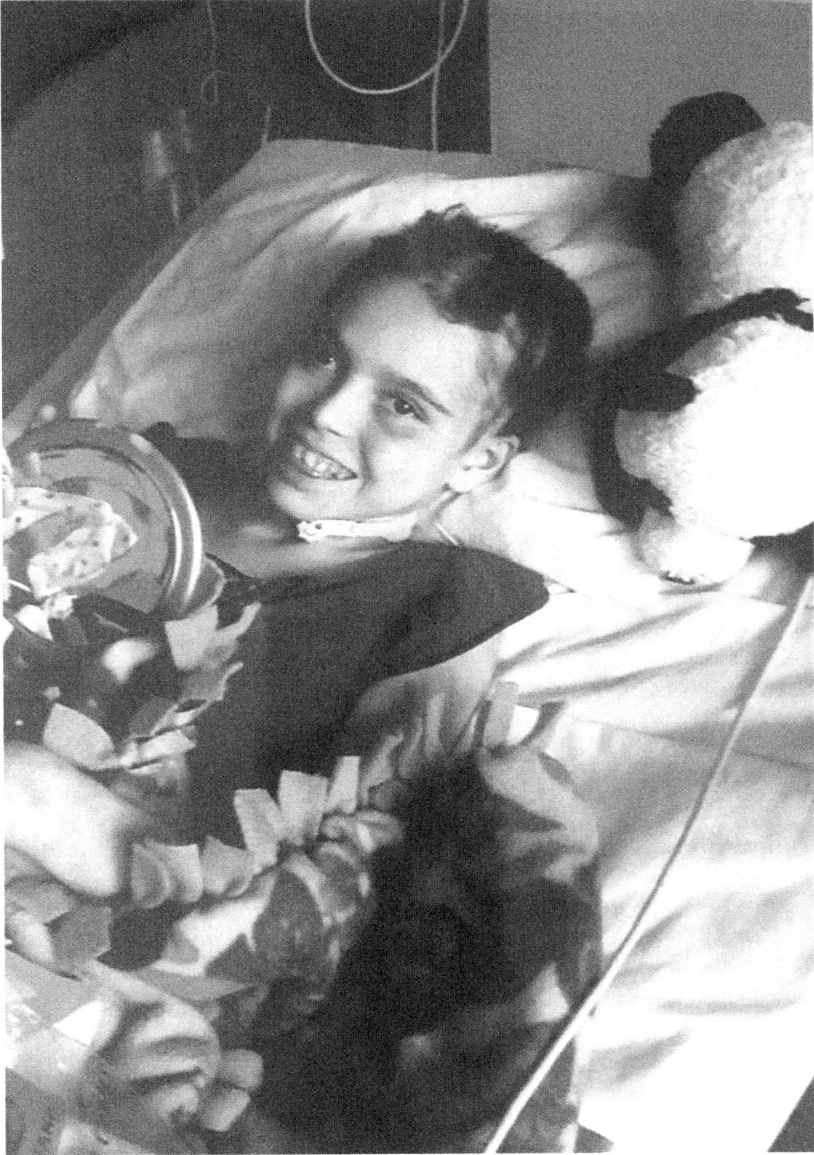

Tiara at the rehabilitation home.

CHAPTER 25

Learning to Live

Every day, for months, after getting home from the hospital and the rehabilitation home, Tiara would look at me, grab my neck in a tight hug, and say, "We did it, we did it, home, home!"

She was so happy to be home with her family, sleeping in her bed, watching her own TV, and wearing her regular clothes. Her bad behaviors appeared to be gone, and although she was still having seizures, she was stable. She was in physical therapy, and it only took her a few weeks until she was able to walk on her own again. She was skin and bones but gaining weight steadily, now that she was able to eat food. The G-tube helped administer her medications, so I kept it in, until one morning it fell out of her stomach and onto the floor. I was shocked, and I screamed bloody murder, and Tiara started hysterically laughing. I didn't realize there was a balloon inside the wall of her stomach that needed to be inflated periodically, to keep it in place. After consulting with her doctor, I decided to let the hole close up and heal. I drove her to the rehab home twice a week for physical and occupational therapy for several months and agreed to have a teacher/speech therapist come to the house one hour a day for her schooling. Other than that, it was just Tiara and me at home, enjoying our life again.

The first time we returned to UCLA neurology for a checkup, every doctor came out of their exam rooms to see her. She was famous. They couldn't believe she had survived and wanted to see her in the flesh. We had arrived a bit early, and I helped her walk, with the aid of a gait belt, to the cafeteria for a snack. At a nearby table, I spotted one of her neurosurgery residents. I tapped him on the shoulder, and he looked at me with shock and confusion.

"Do you remember us?" I asked. "You were on Tiara's rotation after her brain surgery."

He nodded and said, "Of course! I just didn't know—I was shocked to see you both here."

Understanding his reaction, I smiled and said, "You aren't the only one surprised. As far as I know, she shocked the entire UCLA Mattel Children's ICU department and is deemed a miracle girl!"

Our miracle girl celebrated her thirteenth birthday in October, with a dance party at our house. Tiara never returned to school and was enjoying working with her teacher, Miss Beth, at home each day. For the first time in a long time, she was able to focus. Tiara could sit at the table and work for up to twenty minutes at a time. Tiara was learning the names and sounds of animals, new knowledge for her, and was working on her shapes and colors, and attempting to write her name. She was enjoying learning and proud of her progress. She often called me during her lessons: "Mom, mom, look, look!"

"I see TT. What great work. I'm so proud of you."

With a huge smile, she'd pull me for a hug, squeezing until I thought she was going to choke me.

"Okay, TT, that's enough." I'd say while untangling myself from her embrace.

"Sit, Mom, sit," she'd say while patting the seat next to her.

"Not right now. Miss Beth will only be here for a few more minutes, and then we can sit together."

If we were lucky, she would return to her work, but more often than not, she got up from the table and ran off. Some days we could coax her back to the table, other days, we just gave up. She had a smooth transition back to our home life, but mine wasn't as seamless. It took me a while to adjust to the slower life of living back at home. I had spent the past three months talking to neurosurgeons, neurologists, ICU physicians, and nurses all day, every day. My days were spent researching, brainstorming, or going from one medical test to another. I lived in a state of adrenaline and anxiety. At home, there were no stimulating conversations or life-saving procedures to discuss. My days were spent driving to and from school, cooking meals, cleaning diapers, doing laundry, cleaning the house, and doing errands. It was depressing; even though I should have been ecstatic Tiara had survived, but I wasn't thrilled to be back living the same life. I needed more mental stimulation and wasn't sure how to get it. I was bored.

At the beginning of 2012, I came across an article about mommy bloggers. I had never read a blog before, but apparently, companies were paying mommy bloggers to advertise on their websites. Many of these bloggers were making lots of money, more than they would make with a regular job outside the house. I was intrigued. I started researching how to become a blogger and decided I could do it. All you needed was a website, something to write about, and a smartphone. Lou had just bought us a brand-new Mac desktop for Christmas, and I had an iPhone. Money was a constant worry for us, and because I was never able to work outside the home, this was an opportunity for me to make some money. I didn't have the money to hire a website designer, but that wasn't going to stop me. Despite knowing nothing about website design, I figured it out. I spent every free moment at the computer, building my website. I stopped cleaning the house, left all the clean laundry unfolded on the couch, and hardly took care of anyone until my website was up and running. Of course, I took care of Tiara, but she enjoyed having more freedom from my watchful eyes. She would help herself to extra snacks, create huge messes without me yelling, and do whatever she wanted, while I sat glued to my desk.

I finally had my website close to the way I wanted it to look, when disaster struck. Late one night, I was at the computer, when the server shut down. Everything on the screen just disappeared. No matter what I did, I couldn't find my blog. It was lost somewhere in the Internet universe. I put my head down on my desk and started sobbing. Lou heard me and came out of the family room.

"Honey, what's wrong?"

"Everything is gone! Everything I've been working on just disappeared! I can't find it."

He then said sympathetically, "I'm sure you'll find it. Just go to bed, you're exhausted. You can find it in the morning."

"No, I can't, I'll never find it! You don't understand!"

"You're just exhausted. I know you'll figure out how to fix it tomorrow. Let me help you to bed."

"I'm not going to bed; just leave me alone," I said while sobbing with my head on my desk.

It was after eleven o'clock when I started drifting off to sleep and went to bed. I fell asleep but was startled awake at three a.m. I looked over at Tiara—still sleeping. I quietly went out to my desk in the living room, turned on the computer, and waited for it to boot up. I logged onto my website—and everything was there! I'm not sure what happened, but everything was where it was supposed to be. I turned off the computer and went back to bed.

It was official—my website was up and running, and I was ready to start blogging.

My first post was about Trinity at junior lifeguard tryouts and how several adults had cut in line. The line wrapped around the building, and everyone had to wait at least an hour before being allowed to try out. This man and his two kids pretended to stop and talk to the people in front of us and then just stayed there. Anyway, I wrote about this, and I received several comments right away. It was instant gratification, and I loved it. Was I obsessed? Yes! I had found an outlet for my never-ending thoughts, and people wanted to read what I wrote—it was amazing.

Lou often said: "Wow, I'm so glad I bought the family a new computer. If I'd known it would encourage you to become a blogger and spend every waking moment writing about our lives on the Internet, I would have saved the money."

"Don't be mean, Louie," I'd say.

"You know I'm just kidding. If the blog makes you happy, it makes me happy, too."

"Thanks, babe, I love you. Now go away, I need to finish this post."

"Of course, you do. What time are we eating?" he asked.

"I'm almost done, and then I'll start dinner, I promise."

"Okay, if you say so."

Every day centered on writing the blog. I wasn't making much money, but I was making enough to pay my monthly website fees and have a bit left over. More importantly, I found an expanded support system, which I never had before. People from all over the world were reading my posts and reaching out to me. Parents whose children had been diagnosed with TSC said they found my blog and felt more hopeful about the future after reading it. One woman wrote: "I didn't think I could do it. I couldn't take care of my baby with TSC, I was too scared, and then I found your blog. You inspired me and gave me hope. If you could do, I could do it!" Blogging about my life helped different people in different ways. Most of my posts were about Tiara, and everyone in the community was shocked to learn how difficult our lives were. Even my closest friends never knew how hard taking care of Tiara was—I didn't have time to talk on the phone all day, explaining the hell I was enduring. I was no longer alone on this journey. Readers sent me gifts, wrote me notes, and prayed for us. It was like having this amazing extended family at my fingertips. The blog was my lifeline to the outside world and kept me sane at a time when I thought I couldn't make it through another day.

CHAPTER 26

Struggling to Breathe

Miraculously, Tiara made it through 2012 without a trip to the hospital, until the last day of the year. She was struggling to breathe, and I rushed her to CHOC. Just like in the past, once the intake nurse saw her struggling for air and looked up her name on the computer, she was rushed to the back and immediately greeted by a doctor. Her oxygen levels were dropping quickly, while several nurses struggled to get an IV in her, and the X-ray technician took pictures of her lungs. After several failed attempts, the doctor took matters into his own hands and inserted the IV into the side of her neck. I was shocked, as I had never seen this before, but it worked. They put her on BiPAP right away and transferred her to the ICU. Once there, the charge nurse came in with an ultrasound machine to look at her veins. They planned on keeping the IV in her neck for blood draws, because it pulled back, but they couldn't use it to give medications. They needed to find another spot on her body for an additional IV. As the nurse was looking at the ultrasound screen and repeatedly looking and looking for a decent vein, she said, "I wasn't expecting this."

"Expecting what?" I asked.

"Come here, and I'll show you."

I looked at the ultrasound screen. Tiara's veins looked like a bunch of broken paths, thin and ragged.

"Her veins look weird. Are they supposed to look like that?" I asked.

The nurse looked me in the eyes and said, "I have never seen anything like this; I'm surprised."

I suddenly felt the weight of all Tiara had endured through every hospital admission over the years. I held back my tears and asked the question I already knew the answer to.

"Why are her veins like this?"

The nurse responded, "These are the veins of a chronic patient."

She never was able to find a viable vein in either arm but eventually found one in her foot that was stable enough to administer medications and fluids through. Tiara had pneumonia and remained in the hospital for ten days.

Two months later, she came down with a respiratory infection, and her pediatrician gave her a Z-pack because she was no longer able to take Augmentin. They had discovered during her last hospital admission that she had developed an allergy to Augmentin, from overuse. After a few days on the Z-pack, she couldn't stop itching. Her doctor realized she was also allergic to this antibiotic as well. At fourteen years old, Tiara was allergic to three antibiotics, from overuse.

In March, we endured a sleep study at CHOC and discovered her oxygen dropped dangerously low during sleep. The doctor running the study told us that she must sleep with oxygen for the rest of her life. After learning she failed the sleep study, her pulmonologist ordered an X-ray of her lungs while "she is healthy." I took her the next day and received a call from him that evening.

"I just finished reading Tiara's X-rays, and the bases of both her lungs are collapsed. This explains why her oxygen drops so low during sleep," he said.

"Why are her lungs like this?" I asked

"Her lungs are still sick and haven't recovered from the last pneumonia. We need to try to help get them back open. The best thing for her is exercise. She needs to get jumping, running, swimming, anything that will cause exertion and get the lungs pumping."

"Well, I'll try my best, but you know Tiara can't swim, she is unsteady on her feet, and constantly overheats, so this is a big order," I said.

"Well, do your best. Call my office on Monday and schedule a follow-up appointment for a few weeks."

I hung up my cell phone and looked over at Lou. We were eating dinner at the Yard House with Tiara and Trinity like we did most Friday nights. It was Tiara's favorite place for Caesar salad and chicken fingers, and Trinity agreed to go there with us because it was so loud no one would notice if Tiara screamed, burped, or acted horribly. I agreed to eat there as long as we arrived in time to get the happy-hour discount.

"Bad news?" Lou asked.

"You won't believe what her doctor just said." I relayed our conversation to him.

I could never get Tiara to exercise enough to open up her lungs, and it scared me. What an idiot, what was he thinking, giving me that advice? He wasn't looking at her whole person, just the organ he was worried about. I hadn't been impressed with his bedside manner and now was convinced that dealing with him was a waste of our time.

A few days later, Tiara came down with another virus. She must have picked it up while getting the X-ray. CHOC admitted her right away, but this time she didn't receive the same care as the visit before. The ER doctor in January had been very aggressive right from the beginning, and I believed he saved her from going onto a ventilator. This ER physician was the opposite and did not put her on BiPAP or admit her to the ICU right away. He put her on regular oxygen and sent her to the floor. I was not happy with him. She made it through the night without her oxygen dropping too low, but around five a.m., she started desatting into the low eighties, and no one came to help us. I looked out into the hallway, saw a resident, and called to her:

"Excuse me, my daughter's oxygen is at eighty-two, I need some help in here."

The resident came into Tiara's room, stood at the end of her bed, and stared at the monitor. She then walked over to Tiara's side and started moving around the pulse oximeter on her index finger.

"I'm sure it's not an accurate number; she probably just needs a new probe," the resident said.

"It is a real number. She has been asleep and hasn't touched the probe. I watched her numbers drop from ninety to eighty-two. We need to get her up to the ICU, now!" I demanded.

After a solid three to five minutes of her doing nothing and me badgering her to do something, I was done with her and took matters into my own hands.

"I want you to call a code," I said.

I had learned years before that if you ever felt like your child's life was in jeopardy, and she wasn't receiving proper medical care, you could "call a code." Once a code was called, an ICU physician and nurse, along with a respiratory therapist, were required to show up in the room within a minute or two and assess the patient's medical state.

"Let's wait; we don't need to call it yet. Her oxygen could increase," she stammered.

"I'm not waiting anymore. If you don't call it right now, I'll call it myself."

When she didn't start reaching for her hospital phone, I walked over to the room phone on the side table, picked up the receiver, and dialed the emergency number. The light outside her room immediately started flashing, and within seconds a team of people appeared. I explained to them what was happening with her oxygen. The ICU doctor started listening to her breathing, and the ICU nurse, who knew Tiara well, spoke up right away:

"Tiara has a history of chronic pneumonia and respiratory distress. She needs to be brought up to the ICU right now."

She looked at the ICU doctor for confirmation, and he said: "Let's move her, now!"

Once in the ICU, her lungs were immediately X-rayed, and the doctor confirmed that her left lung was completely "whited out," meaning it was full of infection, and air couldn't move through it. She went on BiPAP right away, and they started running more tests. She tested positive for influenza, as did I. For the next few days, we were both plagued with fevers, chills, and body aches, but while I recovered, Tiara's condition only worsened. On Easter Sunday, three days after arriving at the hospital, she was intubated and put on a ventilator, for the sixth time in her life. Two days passed, and she showed no improvement. I could see the worry on the doctors' faces as they repeatedly checked her throughout each day, which wasn't usual. X-rays of her lungs were taken every twelve hours. Soon I learned why she wasn't showing signs of improvement.

Dr. Cherin, who knew Tiara and me well, walked in and said he needed to speak with me.

"I just looked at Tiara's most recent X-ray, and it appears she has acute respiratory distress syndrome, ARDS, in addition to both lungs being whited out."

"What does that mean?"

"Her lungs are getting worse, and she is going to be here for a long time. I'm sorry." He turned and started to walk out of the room, then looked back at me and said, "We will do everything in our power to get her better, I promise."

I could feel Dr. Cherin's worry. Once again, Tiara was fighting for her life. I pulled out Tiara's iPad and started researching ARDS. It appeared that only 40 percent of patients with ARDS survive. I called Lou.

A few days later, as I was sitting next to her bed and staring into space, Tiara suddenly kicked me. Stunned, I looked over at her and saw her grabbing for the breathing tube in her mouth. I lunged over the side of the bed and pulled her hands away from the tube. She started fighting me, just as a respiratory therapist entered the room.

"Hold her hands," I yelled at the stunned RT.

As she grabbed Tiara's wrists, I climbed on top of Tiara's bed and straddled her, so I could put all my weight into holding down her hands.

"Call for a nurse and have her bring in some sedation. Hurry," I ordered the RT.

The RT frantically hit the call button, then resumed helping me hold Tiara's hands because I was starting to lose the battle. We struggled with Tiara for at least fifteen minutes because the nurse had to get an order for the sedation, since there wasn't one in the chart. Up until this point, Tiara was so sick she hadn't been moving, so there had been no reason to sedate her. The nurse finally ran in with the drugs, and as she pushed the sedation through the IV, Tiara finally gave up fighting us. Thank you, God! After I recovered from the trauma of holding her down for so long, I felt hopeful. My feisty girl was back, which meant she must be getting better.

The next morning during rounds, I expected her doctors to say she was improving; instead, they said she was getting sicker. How was that possible? *They must be wrong*, I reasoned. Dr. Cherin said her kidneys were no longer working sufficiently to remove all the fluids that had accumulated in her lungs and the rest of her body. She was now in renal failure. After much discussion, they decided she would need dialysis within the next twenty-four hours if her kidneys didn't improve significantly. Also, they decided to put her in a medically induced coma to calm her brain from prolonged continuous seizures. The mood was somber the next day as she underwent her first round of dialysis. All of this because she got the flu. And yet, if I was honest with myself, it wasn't that surprising. During flu season, the news is always reporting about the elderly and the medically compromised dying from the flu. "Get your flu shot," the reporters warn.

I forced everyone in our family to get a flu shot to protect Tiara, but she wasn't able to get one herself, because of her medical status. Now she might die from the fricking flu. It was more than I could bear, but once again, by the grace of God and his miracles, Tiara recovered. After two weeks, we were able to bring her home. Tiara was so weak, she couldn't walk, and spent the next twenty days recovering in bed.

And then she started vomiting. Her pediatrician told me to take her back to CHOC, even though I knew it was the vomiting seizures. I was scared, so I listened to him. They didn't understand why she was vomiting, but since she was in the hospital, they took the opportunity to administer a swallow test. She failed. The technician and I watched on the screen, as the barium she was drinking flowed straight into her lungs. After they thickened the barium and tested her again, she was able to swallow the fluid without it going into her lungs. And now, we had another reason for her chronic respiratory issues, and I had a new job: making sure everything that entered her mouth was thickened to nectar consistency. Awesome. It wasn't as horrible as I had imagined because I could order cases of SimplyThick in packets, to carry in my purse and car, and large pump containers to leave on the kitchen counter. It is a gel substance that doesn't taste like anything, and it didn't seem to bother Tiara, except when she was screaming at me for her Diet Coke in the McDonald's drive-through and before letting her drink it, I had to mix in the SimplyThick. Like with everything, our family adapted quickly, and soon we couldn't remember a time when we didn't need to thicken water before giving her a sip.

A few months later, after Tiara was walking on her own again, we decided to put our house up for sale. We didn't want to sell, but at this point, we didn't have a choice. We had refinanced it numerous times before the recession, to pay for our living expenses, so we had a huge mortgage that we couldn't afford. We had applied for several loan modifications during the recession and were always denied. We had also pulled out all our retirement money to save the house. I got the house ready, and it went into escrow in the first week, only to fall out of escrow. We were unable to find another buyer and finally took it off the market after three torturous months. We also decided to stop making the house payment but pay all our other bills. We felt like losers, not paying our mortgage, but I couldn't work, and Lou already worked at least sixty hours a week, so we didn't have a choice.

As fall arrived, I sank into a depression because Tiara's aggression and violent behaviors had returned. As she started gaining weight after brain surgery, she started menstruating again. Once her period returned, so did her behaviors. It was devastating. She started hurting me even worse than before the brain surgery, and no one knew how to help. We tried putting her on birth control pills to deal with the hormone shifts, but that didn't work. She also started having more seizures, which also contributed to her worsening behaviors. For the first time in her life, I documented how much she hurt me in the blog.

I posted pictures of my scratched and bloodied arms, neck, chest, and legs. I described how Tiara attacked me, and I would scream for Trinity to lock herself in her room and call 911 on her landline. I wrote about her holding my head down on the cement as she pulled at my hair and dug her fingernails into my skin. I wrote about her jumping out of the car while I was driving, because she saw a basketball hoop she wanted to visit. I wrote about having to pull my car over to the side of the road because she had grabbed my hair and was holding my head in her lap. I wrote about her pooping in her diaper, and when I tried to change it and clean her up, she smeared poop on me.

I often prayed a bus or semitruck would crash into Tiara and me and kill us instantly during one of our daily drives around town. We drove around for hours because she always demanded: "Drive, drive, drive!"

If I denied her a drive, she tended to grow violent, so I usually agreed. Driving calmed her until, without warning, she would suddenly demand, "Go home!" And if I wasn't able to get her home quickly enough, the violence began. It was hopeless.

I told Tabitha about my wish to die. She looked at me and said, "Oh, Mom, you would never get that lucky."

"Probably not, but one can always hope."

Everyone knew I was suffering, but neither Lou nor my children knew how to help. It was an impossible situation.

During my yearly psychic visit at the Orange County Fair, the psychic told me, "You are a wounded bird lying on the ground. Your wings are broken, you can't fly, and ants are crawling all over you, but you are still breathing. You need to take care of yourself before it is too late."

I started crying. I was that bird. I was dying inside but had no way of fixing myself. To fix me, I had to stop being Tiara's caretaker—and that wouldn't fix my pain, only make it worse. I could never let someone else care for her. It would break her heart, and she had endured enough in this lifetime. She didn't deserve me giving up. The only thing that could fix me was for Tiara's violent behaviors and seizures to disappear. I had to keep taking care of Tiara, Tabitha, Trinity, and Lou, and yet, I wasn't going to last much longer.

During this time in our lives, it wasn't uncommon for me to announce to Lou or yell in the kitchen to myself, "I hate my life!"

Lou would look at me, hug me, and say, "I love you, and I love our life."

He would then try to make me laugh, by saying something like, "I bet if there were a *Guinness Book of World Records* for cleaning up the most human poop, you would win. You are a professional poop cleaner, love, and no one can do it as well as you."

I would slightly laugh, punch him in the arm, and think, *Yep, that's me. Tiffani with the law degree is a professional poop cleaner.*

He would kiss me, tell me he loved me, and leave for work. And then I'd start my daily prayer/mantra that I repeated in my head constantly, all day, every day: "Please give me the strength."

Tiara became like a wild animal, and we were all terrified. My parents wanted me to put her in a home, but I refused. It got so bad at one point, that I considered it. I asked her caseworker what my options were if I couldn't take care of her anymore. She researched the local group homes and discovered that, because Tiara had so many medical issues, in addition to horrible behaviors, no home would accept her. I honestly did not have any options.

I continued to share all of the horrors of our lives on the blog, which helped keep me sane, but there was a huge downside. You must be wondering, what could be the downside? My mom and sister hated the blog with a passion. They hated that everyone knew Tiara was abusing me.

Mom got so furious she issued me an ultimatum: "If you don't stop writing the blog, I won't speak to you anymore. It's too hurtful for your father and me to have everyone know your business."

It was her or the blog.

My sister owned a retail store at the time, and my mom worked there once a week. Every day someone would come in and ask about me being abused by Tiara or other topics I wrote about in the blog.

This drove them both crazy. It was a store meant to sell beautiful things, not talk about my horrible life. My original nuclear family was very private, and they liked everyone to believe we all lived this perfect life. A life where everyone was beautiful, everyone dressed wonderfully, we always had our hair and makeup fixed, we had gorgeous homes, all our children were brilliant and beautiful, we only drove black, newer-model vehicles, and we all got along with each other, all the time—the perfect family.

Well, that wasn't my reality, but it was the truth my mom and sister wanted to portray to everyone else. When Mom gave me the ultimatum, I was devastated. The blog was my saving grace, the reason I was able to survive my life. I told her how much the blog helped me and begged her to let me keep it.

"No," she said. "It's me or the blog. You choose, Tiffani!"

I talked to Lou about it, and he said: "Keep writing the blog but just leave out all the bad stuff Tiara is doing."

"I can't do that!" I exclaimed. "The whole point of the blog is to tell the truth and show our reality. Why bother sugarcoating our life? Then my blog will be like everyone else who pretends they have this wonderful life, but it's all a charade. I need to tell the truth, or I can't write."

Lou responded, "Well, I guess either you lose your family, or you give up writing. I can't make that decision for you, Tiffani. You know I love you, and I will support whatever you decide."

I let myself cry.

For my entire life, I had been doing exactly what my mom wanted, as did everybody else in our family. I learned how to be her definition of *perfect* at a young age, in hopes of always keeping her happy. When Mom was unhappy with someone or something, she was scary, so I learned how to keep her anger at bay as much as possible. As a married adult, I mostly made my own decisions, but she still had a significant amount of control over me until Tiara was born. Tiara messed up our whole fake reality of being perfect—and it was a relief to me, but not to Mom. For the first time in my life, I didn't have the time or resources to appease her wishes, and she did not like it.

By now, I had already drifted far from being the perfect daughter in Mom's eyes. I never dressed up anymore; I always wore my hair in a ponytail and only bothered to apply mascara and lipstick. I didn't carry a designer purse unless she bought me one as a present. I traded in my

Mercedes for a Honda to save money, we never traveled, and Tiara walked around with permanent stains on her shirts. I was short-tempered and didn't have time to listen to her daily stories about the plumber who showed up late and dragged mud across her floor, or how Mirna cleaned her wood floors with a new product which almost caused her to slip, or what gourmet meal she prepared the night before. I used to talk to her on the phone every day for an hour about inconsequential things, but now I didn't have time. And my worst sin of all: telling the truth to the point of being rude. It wasn't uncommon to hear her say: "Well, you know how Tiffani is. She is the rudest person I know."

I knew I was becoming a failure in her eyes and couldn't take the pressure of losing her. If I lost her, I would also lose Dad, and I needed my sweet dad. Everyone loved him because he was so intelligent, yet always humble and kind.

I made my decision. I would no longer write the blog. My readers were devastated, as was I. I cried for two days straight. My readers begged me to reconsider. After three days I was so depressed, I couldn't take it. I started writing my blog in email form, to subscribers only. I took Mom off the email list and tried to write it secretly. After a few weeks, she found out what I was doing. I gave up trying to pretend I wasn't blogging and went back to it full-time. I told her I wouldn't write anything embarrassing, and for a while, I kept my promise.

Celebrating Tiara's 13th birthday

Tabitha (18), Tiara (13), Trinity (9), and Lou

CHAPTER 27

Driving to Safety

Things weren't getting better with Tiara, and one day while driving around together, I thought, *Maybe I should consider another brain surgery.* Dr. Mathern had told me he would perform another surgery on her if I got desperate. He was confident he could avoid what happened last time because now he knew how much her brain would swell, and he would do a much less aggressive surgery. I had told him, "No way, I'm not having Tiara go through another surgery." Was I changing my mind? Could I possibly put her through another surgery? I wasn't sure. Suddenly Tiara looked over at me and said, "Ouch. No, hurt, no hurt. Hold my hand, hold my hand."

She had just read my mind! It surprised me for a moment, but then, not really. I had never been more connected to any other human in my entire life. I was always trying to read her mind. Was she in pain, did she have a headache, was she about to have a seizure, was she going to throw up, was she intentionally hurting me, or was it beyond her control? I observed her facial expressions, her breathing patterns, her gait, her moods, and her skin color—anything about her that would give me insight into how she felt or if she was going to strike—and now she was reading me.

I looked over at her and said: "Okay, TT. No hurt. You don't have to have another surgery, and I'll always hold your hand."

"Love you, Mom, Mom. No hurt?"

"No hurt, babe, I promise," I said, knowing another surgery wasn't an option after all.

I needed to find another way.

Tiara's favorite expression had become: "I hate your face!" At first, we all found it funny because we had never heard anyone say that before, and it's the kind of thing you want to say to someone when you are pissed off but don't have the nerve to say it. Tiara had no problem saying it to all of us all day, every day. She was angry; she was frustrated; she was, once again, obese and only seemed to find comfort in food. Watching her eat was like watching an alcoholic drink. It pained me. I tried to control everything that went into her mouth, but she was ferocious. If I refused her food, she would scratch me until she drew blood or pull my hair until I was in tears. For my safety, I always gave in. She ate so fast, she often choked, and I had to perform the Heimlich maneuver on her all the time.

At the end of January, she woke up one night and was panting for air. I now owned a pulse oximeter so I could check her oxygen level without going to the doctor's office. Her oxygen was in the low eighties. I wasn't sure whether I should drive her to the hospital or call 911. Lou told me to call 911. They arrived quickly, and I recognized several of the firemen. They knew us and immediately put her on extra oxygen and loaded her onto the gurney. Upon arriving at CHOC, the ER physician admitted her straight into the ICU, where we stayed for two weeks. Again, she had severe pneumonia. Both her lungs were whited out, she ended up on a ventilator, and her kidneys failed, requiring dialysis, once again. When she was well enough to leave the ICU, they allowed me to take her home instead of making us stay on the floor. I could care for her better at home, and they knew it.

Once Tiara gained the strength to walk on her own again, Lou and I decided to try selling our house one more time. We hadn't made a house payment in almost a year, and the real estate market had improved. The bank was threatening to foreclose, and I couldn't handle the stress of the constant calls and letters. I realized that if we were going to get our house sold, I needed to make it boring so everyone would love it. Our house had lime-green-and-white-striped walls in the family room, tons of art everywhere, and lots of pizazz. Buyers wanted a more neutral palette, so I painted the walls either gray or white. I removed tons of art and decluttered every space to make our house look like a model home. Doing all this while watching Tiara almost killed me, but she had a caretaker in the afternoon, and Grandma Cindy came over every day to help watch her, so I was able to get it all done. Our real estate agent loved the changes. He had new pictures taken, and we put it back on the market. It sold in the first two weeks, and this time it didn't fall out of escrow. The offer we accepted was enough money to pay off our delinquent mortgage, allow us to pay off some debt, and rent a home, with some money left over for our savings. It was a miracle, and we were both thrilled.

But now we had to find a place to live. The house would have to be one story, with no steps or carpet, and on a quiet street (so if Tiara eloped from the house, she wouldn't get hit by a car); it would have to have three bedrooms, two baths, and a yard for the trampoline; it had to cost under $3,000 a month; and the owners must be willing to accept our credit score, which had declined since failing to pay our mortgage. I spent every waking minute looking for houses online, and the inventory was very low. We couldn't find anything in our neighborhood, so I expanded my search to new neighborhoods that I would never have considered in the past. Mom was so angry with me for selling our house in Newport, she was barely speaking to me again. She wanted to lend us several hundred thousand dollars to save the house, but I refused the offer. The house was falling apart, and we couldn't afford the upkeep or the payments. It was time to downsize and live within our means. We were excited to have the financial burden lifted off our backs and just wanted to start over.

Lou and I were terrified of moving Tiara, which is why we had stayed so long in the first place. Now she was going to have to adapt to a new home. If I wasn't packing our lives into boxes or searching the Internet for homes, I was driving every neighborhood within a fifteen-mile radius of our current home. Tabitha and Trinity were starting to panic because I couldn't find us a house. Lou was working all the time, and it was my job to find the house. A week and a half before we were supposed to be out of our house, Trinity asked me: "Mom, where are we going to live?"

"I don't know, babe, but I promise you, I will find us a place," I said.

Tabitha hated the unknown and decided she wasn't going to move with us and would live on her own. She was twenty-one years old, worked a full-time job, and made enough money to pay rent on a studio apartment. It was time, and we were happy for her.

I finally found the perfect house in Westside Costa Mesa. It had carpet in the family room and bedrooms but hardwood or tile in the kitchen, dining room, hallways, and bathrooms. The landlord lived in Colorado and was a little worried about our credit history. After talking for a while, I realized we had gone to high school together, even though he was a few years ahead of me. I knew his stepsisters, and one of them was a big fan of my blog. She commented on my blog often, and I told him to ask her to vouch for me. After speaking to her, he agreed to rent us his home. Thank you, God, because we needed to move out in five days! After we signed the lease and gave him the deposit, I did another walk-through of the house. The carpet was super dirty, and I freaked out. Remember, Tiara can't have carpet because of her respiratory issues. I took pictures of it and sent them to him. He was planning on getting it cleaned, but I made him an offer: "Would you be willing to let me tear out the carpet and replace it with vinyl flooring that looks like the existing wood floors? We had it in my other house, and everyone thought it was real hardwood. We will pay for everything ourselves, and I promise it will look great."

I quietly prayed he would agree, and then he said, "Sure if you want to pay for it!"

"Yes. Thank you, thank you," I said.

I spent the next few days, with Trinity's help, pulling up the old carpet and putting down vinyl flooring. Lou worked and watched Tiara when he was home, and I replaced the flooring in the family room, master bedroom, and Trinity's room before we moved in. Tiara slept in our room, so I finished her room and the sunroom after we moved in.

We moved into our new home on July 3 with help from Grandma Cindy, Bob (her new boyfriend), and paid movers. No one in my family helped me pack a box, move a box, or lift a finger to help us. Was Mom really that shallow and cruel? I guess so. Dad came over by himself after we moved in and brought us a bottle of wine.

When I spoke to my mom and asked her when she was going to stop by and see our new house, she said: "You live so far away now, I'm not sure when I can come visit."

We lived five miles from our old house. She was still upset with me for moving out of Newport Beach; she said it was a poor reflection upon her and my father. Because of the blog, everyone knew we had almost lost our house, which was embarrassing for her. After several weeks she finally came around and "forgave me" for moving out of Newport.

I'm sure you are wondering how Tiara was coping with the change. Well, not so great. The move caused her anxiety to rise significantly, and her only outlet was obsessively eating or beating me up. She was more violent than ever, and Lou was afraid to leave me and go to work each day. Neither of us had found any other options than doing what we had been doing. I talked to her neuropsychiatrist, Dr. Jeste, on the phone almost every day. She was continually trying to find ways to help keep me safe. She suggested I start giving Tiara Ativan when her behaviors escalated. It did help to calm her—when the pill made it into her mouth and not spit back onto my face. By the end of the month, Dr. Jeste urged me to admit Tiara to the psychiatric ward at UCLA. She was afraid for my life. She told me they would help get Tiara stabilized, and then I could bring her back home. She made it sound like it could possibly work, so I agreed.

Dr. Jeste explained that Tiara would need to be admitted to the psych ward via the emergency room. I couldn't drive her to UCLA by myself, so we waited until Lou's next day off work. I was wracked with guilt every time I thought about leaving her at UCLA, and I wasn't sure I could do it. Two days later, we arrived at the UCLA ER, where we met with the on-call psychiatrist. He observed my injuries, observed Tiara's behaviors, and agreed we needed to admit her, but there wasn't a bed available. He said we could stay in the ER and wait for a bed or go home and they would call us when one became available. I opted for the latter, so we gathered all our stuff and drove the hour back home. Two days later, we got a call from the hospital. Lou came home from work to, once again, drive with us. I wanted to back out, but Lou wouldn't let me. As we waited in an ER room, I kept accidentally smashing my fingers into everything. I was so nervous and terrified, three of my knuckles were bleeding from scraping them on the paper towel rack while rushing to get towels to clean up Tiara. By the time they wheeled Tiara up to the psych ward, she had already fallen asleep for the night. The intake process took a few hours, and my hands were shaking so much, I had a hard time completing the paperwork. I had brought a typed med list, a list of her behaviors, and a bio of her history for the nurses and doctors. I described Tiara to the intake nurse, and she seemed a bit overwhelmed with her respiratory issues and extensive medication list. I was sobbing as we prepared to leave and asked the nurse:

"Can I come visit her tomorrow? She is going to be so scared when she wakes up in this place, and I'm not here," I said.

I looked at Lou. "I can't do it. I can't leave her here."

"You have to, Tiffani. This is going to help her. We don't have a choice," he said.

The nurse looked at my tear-streaked face and said, "They normally don't allow the parents to visit for at least several days, but call in the morning and ask to speak with the nurse on duty. She will ask the doctor if it is okay for you to come for a short visit. He may allow you. Just call in the morning."

"Okay," I said through strangled sobs.

Lou ushered me out of the room after we kissed her goodbye one last time. I barely slept, even though we hadn't arrived home until one a.m. When I got out of bed the next morning, it was weird not to have been awakened by the smell of urine from Tiara's diaper. I didn't have to get her medications ready, change her diaper, prepare her breakfast, or set up her breathing treatment. I just had to get Trinity ready for school and make my coffee. After driving Trinity to school, I called the psych ward.

"How is Tiara?" I asked the nurse on duty.

"She's fine. She is missing you and keeps asking for you."

"Can you ask the doctor if I can come see her today?" I asked.

"I already called him. He said it is fine."

I was surprised, since the nurse last night had told me it was rare for them to grant parents visitation right away.

"I can come?" I asked, surprised.

"Yes, you can come. Are you going to come right now?" she asked.

"Of course. I just need to take a shower, get ready, and drive there."

"Wonderful," she declared." What time do you think you will be here? She is quite a bit of work, and we could use your help."

I sighed. Tiara had only been there for seven hours, and they were already overwhelmed.

"I'll hurry!" I was eager to get to her but also disappointed. Did they expect me to drive there every day to help until she fell asleep at night?

When I walked into her room, she was sitting up in bed and wearing three different shirts, two of which were on backwards, and yelling at a nurse's aide who was trying to complete her breathing treatment; Tiara had thrown off her mask and was refusing to put it on. Her face was smeared with food from breakfast no one had bothered to wipe off, and she was pushing the nurse away with her hands.

When she saw me, her eyes lit up, and she started chanting and pumping her fists, "Mom, Mom, Mom! Love you, Mom, love you."

I went over to the bed, and she grabbed me into a huge embrace. The nurse gratefully backed away, and I took over. I cleaned her face, changed her soaking-wet diaper, put on appropriate clothes, got her to finish the breathing treatment, put on her music, and joined her on the bed. The charge nurse came in to speak with us.

"We've had a tough time with her."

"I imagine you have—what is the plan for today?"

"The doctors should come by around one o'clock, and then they will make a care plan. Can you stay with her for the rest of the day?"

"Yes, I can stay, but I can't believe she hasn't seen the doctor yet. I assumed he would come in first thing this morning."

"The team will be here soon," she said.

I kept Tiara busy while we waited. Once they showed up, I spoke with her doctor extensively, and he suggested increasing her Risperdal by a half dose. I was stunned.

"I'm a little confused. I was told you were going to do some psychiatric testing to help figure out how to reduce her violence."

"Well, after reading her chart and the notes from the nurses overseeing her today, I'm not sure that will help anything. She has a very complex history, so let's start with the med increase and see how she does," he said.

"I could have increased her medication at home. Why is she here, if you don't have any special testing or some other way to help her?" I asked.

"Dr. Jeste was very worried about your safety, and the process takes time. We will increase her medication, observe how she does, and then go from there."

"Who will be doing the observing?"

"The nurses will come in every few hours, observe her behaviors, and I will review their notes each morning, before seeing her during rounds," he explained.

"So, she is going to sit in this bed all day and be watched by a nurse's aide who has no idea how to take care of her? Then the nurse will come in every few hours and take some notes?"

"Yes. It's not ideal, but like I said, she is a complicated case."

I stopped and thought about what he was saying and spoke again.

"I'm not sure this is the right place for her. I don't feel comfortable having her stay in this room all day."

"The aides can walk Tiara up and down the hallway, and we have a playroom down the hall, she is welcome to visit," he said.

"This doesn't feel right. I don't feel comfortable leaving her here with just an aide who hasn't been trained in caring for her, and I can't drive up here every day. I might as well take her home. It doesn't feel like this ward is designed to accommodate children like Tiara."

"Unfortunately, it's not. We don't have the necessary resources for children like Tiara, but we were trying to make it work because Dr. Jeste was very concerned about your safety."

"Well, I guess I would like her discharged, then. Thank you."

"If you would like her to remain, we will do our best to give her all the care she needs, but if you want her discharged, I understand your reasoning. I only wish I had something to offer you both," he said.

Tiara was so grateful to be leaving that she had good behavior all the way home. As frustrating as the process was, neither Lou nor I felt like it had been a waste of time. We had tried the psych ward, but it just wasn't a fit for Tiara. Now what?

CHAPTER 28

Lasting Memories

I stopped writing the blog full-time and posted updates on Tiara once in a while. My loyal readers kept reaching out and asking how she was, so I posted the updates for them. I couldn't stand to write about my life anymore because nothing changed from late July 2014 until November 2014.

As the holidays drew near, Tiara was no longer able to walk most of the time. When she wanted to move around, she crawled. Tiara now weighed more than three hundred pounds and wore her oxygen mask all day. If she wanted to go for a drive or to McDonald's, I wheeled her to the car and pulled her portable oxygen tank behind us. Most of her time was spent on the couch. She no longer enjoyed coloring, tearing up magazines, or watching television much. She just wanted me to lie beside her on the sofa, read her books, and hug her while she dozed or listened to her iPod. She didn't even have the energy to hurt me, except for the occasional hair pulling.

I didn't know what brought on the sudden change in her health but started on a quest to figure out, what, if anything, I was missing. Was she in heart failure? Did she have diabetes or high blood pressure?

In my heart, I knew her body was slowly shutting down but had to make sure I wasn't missing something that could buy her more time.

I started at the pediatrician's and asked him to order labs and to check all the basics. Despite her severe obesity, Tiara's blood sugar was low, and she didn't have high blood pressure. Next, we saw her cardiologist, and he ordered a few tests, which I never got completed. Then we went to UCLA to see her neurologist, pulmonologist, and nephrologist. They ordered an MRI of her kidneys and a CT of her lungs, to be completed in the upcoming months, but none of them saw an immediate issue that could explain her current state. I kept telling them all my daughter reminded me of an elderly patient with dementia or Alzheimer's.

I thought I was getting close to an answer when Tiara came down with a cold. I heard a single cough, and within hours she was in full-blown respiratory distress, despite being on oxygen twenty-four hours a day. Once in the ICU at CHOC, I spoke to Dr. Knight, who had treated Tiara for years. I described how worried I was about Tiara's declining health. I told him what I felt in my heart—she was dying.

He looked at me and said: "I have never heard you talk like this. We know you here and want to support you both the best that we can. Maybe we should talk about not intubating Tiara if she needs it this time."

I shook my head as tears formed in my eyes. "I'm not ready to let her go yet."

"Okay, we will talk about it when you are," he said. He was so kind and understanding, but after he left, I thought about what he had said. I wasn't crazy thinking she was fading away, or he wouldn't have said that to me. I called Lou and told him what the doctor had said. He cried and said he wasn't ready either. In the end, Tiara didn't need to be intubated, and after a week, she was ready to go home. Upon our departure, I had a conversation with Dr Cherin, who said to me, "We may need to have a conversation soon."

"I know," I said somberly.

I warned our family that it would probably be Tiara's last Christmas and to make the most of their time with her. I called Mara, my BF from college, who was also a photographer, and asked her to take our family portrait before it was too late. She did, and I will be forever grateful for the shots she captured of Tiara and our entire family. The picture on the cover is from that last photoshoot.

We had a very special Christmas, which I will remember as the best Christmas of my life. I love big family gatherings, but often, not everyone invited, can attend. Every parent, aunt, uncle, cousin, sister, and friend I invited to Christmas Day showed up. Sarah had said her family couldn't make it to the party because they were spending the day with Ray's brother and his family. They surprised us by showing up late, which made my day. My cousin Danie and Aunt Joan, who had moved away to Rancho Santa Fe and could no longer attend holidays because of their horse and dog commitments, also surprised me by coming to Christmas Day. I started crying when they walked in the door. Every person I hoped would attend made it. There was so much laughing and reminiscing; it was truly magical. I knew God was giving us this gift.

Two days after Christmas, I had to bring Tiara back to CHOC. I knew she was sick again, but this time she didn't get the same care in the emergency room. She wasn't wheezing, and even though I knew she had pneumonia, the ER doctor took five hours to come to this conclusion. After deciding we should spend the night, she tried to send us to the floor. I begged her to call the ICU and ask them if Tiara could go to the sixth floor. When they heard Tiara was back, they offered her a bed in the ICU, her home away from home. I knew Tiara's pneumonia was most likely bacterial, not viral, because she was unable to swallow correctly. She was continually choking and aspirating food and liquids into her lungs. During rounds the first day, I asked Dr. Cherin what he thought about hospice. I had been researching it ever since she had been discharged early in December.

He paused and said, "I think it's probably time. We can't do anything medically to get her better. She is going to be in here every week at this point, but she is a fighter, and this could go on for a long time."

He graciously offered to let us stay in the ICU until hospice was arranged. We went home on New Year's Eve.

Tiara still showed moments of her feisty self several times each day. The hospice team came to meet with us and decided she needed to see the nurse once a week at that point. Lou and I decided to cancel all the caretakers, since she hated when I left her with them—and really, what errands did I have to do that were so important at this point? None. Lou shortened his schedule at work to help take care of her, and friends started bringing food over. Grandma Cindy showed up every day, instead of every other day, to help me take care of her. Tiara no longer liked visitors, loud talking, or laughing like she had before. She was so anxious; she couldn't stand too much activity going on around her. She just wanted to lie on the couch quietly with me or someone from our family.

One evening, Lou came home from work, and I told him I needed to take a walk. I hadn't been outside in two days, and it was starting to get to me. Tiara overheard our conversation, and the second I walked out the door she started asking Lou to go on the trampoline. "Jump, Jump, Jump."

He convinced her to wait until I got home because he knew I would freak out if he took her on the trampoline, since she could barely walk. When I got home, she started asking again. She was adamant. I knew she needed to jump one last time, so I said, "Let's do it."

Trinity walked out first, Lou helped support Tiara, and I followed with the oxygen tank. We stopped at the swing for Tiara to sit and rest. While she was catching her breath, we tried to convince her swinging was enough activity, and we should go back inside. She wouldn't hear of it. She pulled herself up and headed for the trampoline. Trinity got in first, Tiara followed with Lou pushing her up, and then me. She started jumping, and all four of us held hands as she slowly went up and down. I was praying the trampoline wouldn't break, since we were doubling the weight limitations, but once again, God provided. After a few short minutes, she stopped, and we got our smiley, glowing girl safely back inside the house.

That was the last time she ever jumped on her trampoline.

A few days later, I called our priest to give her another Anointing of the Sick. It was Sunday, January 11, and Tiara was talking and moving around the sofa so much, the priest seemed very confused as to why I had called him. She didn't look sick enough for him to perform the sacrament. I assured him she was that sick, and he performed the ceremony, while Tiara kept interrupting him to ask for her music. Oh, TT.

The next morning, I knew something had changed with her. I called my family and told them they needed to start coming over every day because Tiara was dying. The next day Ray came to visit and see how sick Tiara really was. After seeing Tiara, he knew I wasn't exaggerating. The situation was dire. He returned later that day with Sarah and their kids. From that moment on, the entire family arrived, and we sat vigil with Tiara. There were between thirteen and eighteen of us at all times, except when people went home to sleep.

Tiara ate her last meal of hummus and crackers on Tuesday, January 13, at two thirty in the afternoon. She could barely swallow. She kept falling on her elbows when she tried to crawl. The hospice nurse came over, and we decided, for Tiara's safety, we should sedate her. Hospice usually likes to keep the patient awake as much as possible, but because Tiara refused to stay put or stop eating, it was time. We tried Ativan, but it didn't work well enough. We then tried phenobarbital, which started to calm her. We gave her a double dose at seven o'clock that night. She shouldn't have woken up again, but by some miracle, she did.

She woke up while lying in the king-size bed she shared with Lou and me, surrounded by her family. She reached her hand back to the headboard and started knocking. That was the game she played with Lou every day. She would knock, and he would pretend someone was at the door and answer it. She always thought she was tricking him. She played that game with the whole family for a few minutes, and then we started singing "Happy Birthday" and pretending we were at her party. She loved it. After about ten minutes, she began to get upset, and I knew she'd had enough. I kicked everyone out of her room so that I could give her another dose of medication rectally. That was the last time we heard her voice.

All through Wednesday, we took turns lying by her head or her feet, and holding every part of her body as we prayed for her to pass. She was no longer wearing her oxygen and was struggling to breathe. I kept suctioning her to help with the secretions, but her body was shutting down. Early Wednesday evening, her soul left her body; I don't know the exact moment. I just know that when Tabitha and I slept with her that night, we couldn't feel her. It wasn't like it had been the previous nights when I slept next to her, clinging to every ounce of her being.

As we watched her struggle to breathe, I sent a text to my family that said, "Her soul is already gone, but her body has not finished the process yet."

I hit send and looked over at her. She took her last breath at 8:18 a.m. She was sixteen years old.

The hospice nurse showed up forty minutes after she passed, with an amazing art project for us. She brought a canvas and some paints. We gathered around Tiara's bed and I dipped Tiara's hand in blue paint and placed her handprint in the center of the canvas. We then took turns dipping each of our hands in a different color paint and layered our handprints around Tiara's The finished project is the most valuable piece of art I will ever own.

We celebrated a Mass for her at Our Lady of Mount Carmel Church on Wednesday, January 21, 2015. I think nearly four hundred people showed up to support Tiara and our family. I gave the eulogy, my final gift to her, and then we buried her, in the coolest turquoise casket you have ever seen, at Pacific View Memorial Park in Corona del Mar. Lou and I bought the space next to her grave, so we will be buried with her when it is our time to see her again in Heaven.

Our Last Family Photo

Tabitha (22), Tiara (16) and Trinity (12 ½)

Original image taken by Mara Blom Schantz

www.artisticimpressionsbymara.com

EPILOGUE

I have found the quiet. At forty-five years old, my life's mission was complete. If I died tomorrow, I would be proud of the life I lived. I was born a caretaker, and God gave me the ultimate challenge in caring for Tiara, and now she is in Heaven. No more suffering.

So, how did we all move forward after losing the center of our lives? Let's start with the girls. Tabitha went back to work and moved out of her apartment, into a beach house with several roommates, enjoying a party lifestyle. She started therapy but suffered the most, emotionally, because she held in her pain. Nine months after Tiara passed away, Tabitha, at twenty-one years old, needed a change and decided to stop working for Sarah. She started working at Nordstrom and became an all-star employee in six months, which was a huge accomplishment. She stayed at Nordstrom for several years, until she was ready to retire from the demands of retail after reuniting with Chandler, her high school love. Their love for one another seemed to save them both, and I can't wait until he is officially my son-in-law. He is like a son to Lou and me, a brother to Trinity, and everything Tabitha needs to be the best version of herself. Tabitha now runs the sales team at Simply Straws, a glass straw company started by Aunt Cyndi's family in 2012. She works a few miles from their apartment in Eastside Costa Mesa, and we talk on the phone at least once a day, as she calls me on her way to work, at lunch, and on her way home.

Trinity was able to talk about her feelings better than Tabitha, but suddenly our quiet home felt uncomfortable to her. She was used to a loud, chaotic home life, and now it was silent. She tried filling the void by always making plans with friends away from the house. The year Tiara died, Trinity graduated eighth grade, and her best friend moved back to Japan. She decided to attend Mater Dei High School, the "ra-ra school" Tabitha refused to consider, and is currently a senior. Like Tabitha, Trinity ended up playing volleyball and loved every minute of it I got to be a volleyball mom again and was thrilled.

Trinity got her driver's license on her sixteenth birthday and has rarely been home since. We talk about how she didn't receive the attention she deserved as a child, but now she has all my attention. She has turned into a mini-me, and we spend lots of time talking about everything. Even though she doesn't enjoy reading, she's the only one in our family who has read the manuscript and claims to love it. She isn't planning on attending college after graduation this year, but will most likely work in the car business, like her dad. She loves cars and helping people. If the car business doesn't work out, she is contemplating becoming a psychologist, if she can endure the schooling. Luckily, she has all the time in the world to decide.

As for Lou, he washed anything he could find with a speck of dirt the day Tiara passed away. I remember watching him strip our room bare until there was nothing left to clean. After a week, he returned to work. Life continues, even when your heart is broken. It seems as if the world should stop, but it doesn't. I'm not sure how he dealt with customers who haggled him for three dollars a month on a lease for a $75,000 car, but he did. While at work, he put aside his pain and negotiated deals for new luxury vehicles all day. He never stopped providing for our family. After work, he drank too much wine, and his days off were spent praying, reading the Bible, and going to the gym. He started doing woodworking and has built some beautiful things, including a bench for the TSC auction each year. He keeps busy around the house by cooking dinner a few nights a week, washing the cars, and making repairs to our home. We still live in the house we rented when Tiara was alive and are hopeful to purchase it someday.

As for myself, immediately after her funeral, I slept. I was more exhausted than I could ever describe, and my body was desperate for rest. I slept long hours each night and took long naps every day until I finally felt rested. After a few weeks, I got busy cleaning and organizing every room in the house. I took long walks, started Pilates, and worked on tons of house projects. I refinished the dining room table and painted the dining room chairs, all the outdoor furniture, and Tiara's desk turquoise, which I'm using right now. Whatever work I could find around the house that would keep my mind and body busy to the point of exhaustion, I did it. After a few months, I ran out of projects and realized I needed to figure out what I was going to do with the rest of my life.

Like Trinity, the quiet made me uncomfortable. I bought a canary two weeks after Tiara died, but Mickey (we named him after Tiara's favorite food place) didn't make enough noise or mess. We needed more chaos, so Trinity and I decided we should adopt a dog. Bailey, our poodle, had died from cancer two years before Tiara, and Tabitha had never quite gotten over losing him. I went against all the grieving advice of not making any significant changes and started researching rescue shelters. Trinity and I adopted Stella, a timid, two-year-old female poodle mix, who helped fill the void in our quiet household. Tabitha was hesitant to meet Stella because she didn't want to get her heart broken again but fell deeply in love with her after ten minutes. Stella is still with us but developed a rare autoimmune disorder a year ago, which required a blood transfusion and constant vet appointments. In my typical fashion, I charted her medications, reviewed and compared her blood results, and have managed to keep her alive, despite the grim odds. After months of almost daily appointments, our vet would get a kick out of asking me, "What should we do?" And I would give him the answer.

It seemed as if everyone, except Lou, Tabitha, and Trinity, were waiting for me to fall apart and suffer extreme grief, but I didn't.

How could I not fall apart after losing a child?

It was because I always knew Tiara would die before me, and I had planned my life around this reality. I started grieving her death the moment she was diagnosed with TSC at eight months old. I grieved her entire life, knowing she would live on this earth for a short amount of time, so I didn't cry and mourn as everyone expected. I gave Tiara everything I could give another human being, so when she passed away, I was also at peace.

I missed Tiara, but I didn't miss being afraid. I no longer needed a blog to reach the outside world. I could get in my car and drive anywhere I wanted to go, without worry. Her death gave me my life back. I could do or be anything I wanted and not feel an ounce of guilt. I sacrificed my life for her, and now it was my turn.

A few months after Tiara passed away, I went to lunch with a few of my high school friends. During the lunch, one of my friends, Shelly, who I wasn't as close to during high school, asked if I could teach her to cook. Shelly offered to pay me $25 an hour, but I felt weird accepting her money, even though I needed it, so I said, "I'll think about it." She reached out to me a week later and asked again. We agreed to meet at her house the following week. Once I arrived and saw the state of her home, I told her she needed more than cooking lessons. Shelly was beyond disorganized. She lived in a gorgeous house with a fantastic style, but she was struggling emotionally with different issues, and as a result, her home was a bit of a disaster. Once we walked through every room, and I made suggestions, she asked if I would help her get organized and fix her life.

I agreed, and we started working together three times a week for months. It was emotionally exhausting but extremely fulfilling for both of us. I helped change every aspect of her life in four months, and she brought me closer to God. Her spirituality was contagious, and soon after working with her, I started attending daily Mass. We became close friends. After organizing her house and calendar, helping her get rid of a crappy boyfriend, helping her rebuild relationships with her family, and teaching her how to take care of her emotional self better, it was time to end our financial relationship and just be friends.

During this time, I started receiving job offers from people who had followed me on Facebook or were readers of my blog. Our real estate agent asked me to work on his team as a consultant. When he received a new listing, he wanted to pay me a hundred dollars to meet with the sellers, walk through their home, and then provide them with a detailed list of recommendations to help them get their house market ready. The sellers could follow my suggestions themselves or hire me to make the changes. I loved the idea and gave it a try.

Nine months after Tiara passed away, I was being pulled in several directions and wasn't sure which path to choose. I was trying to decide between starting a business of selling certain items to hospital gift stores, becoming a full-time life coach, or becoming a home stager based on my friend's concept. I was feeling torn. It was my birthday, and I had received some birthday money. I went to church on Sunday and put half of my birthday money in the collection plate, about $300, and prayed to God to show me which way to proceed. I got home from church and was sitting at my computer when my phone rang. I picked it up, and it was one of my best friend's daughters, who happened to be a real estate agent. I had run into her at Pilates the week before and had mentioned my home staging idea to her.

We started talking, and she said, "You remember that idea you told me about last week? Well, I have this client that wants to sell her house, but it needs a lot of work to get it ready, and she needs help. The house was remodeled a few years ago, but she never finished the decorating part. I told her about you, and she wants to meet you. She needs help with decluttering, picking out art for the walls, and accessorizing the spaces."

It was a sign from God, and I knew it.

I met the woman the next day, and we started working together. She paid me an hourly fee to help her complete everything on her long list. The agent put the house on the market, took professional pictures, and everyone loved the house. After that job, I got another large job from the same agent and made a massive transformation on the next home. I used the professional real estate photos from both listings to create a website I designed myself, picked a business name with the help of my Uncle Stephen, designed a logo, applied for a business license, and opened a business account. That's how my home-staging business started.

How did I get my clients? On a suggestion from a Facebook friend, Monica, I sent out a funny email to over a thousand local real estate agents and described my services, which were a bit different than other stagers. I landed a few clients from that first email, and I soon had a booming business solely from referrals. I kept my prices low and worked harder and faster than most stagers. For the first six months, I only staged homeowner-occupied homes, which required me to purchase only pillows and accessories. As more of my agents requested staging for empty properties, I took the plunge and started investing in furniture, with the money I brought in. It was exhausting and fulfilling work, which is what I was looking for at the time. I got so busy that at one point I had ten houses on the market at once. I was proud of my work, but after three years, I realized I was exhausted from all the physical labor, and the real estate market was starting to slow. I hardly ever hired movers because then I wouldn't make as much money, so I did everything myself or begged help from Lou and the girls.

While staging, I became the designer for several remodels and loved the work. Because of my inexperience, I was sometimes scared to take a design job, but I did it anyway. Picking out tile, countertops, flooring, and fixtures for multimillion-dollar homes was stressful, but I always reminded myself not to let fear stop me. If I could take care of Tiara, I could do anything.

Last year, when the real estate market started to slow down and I was tired of being a "glorified slave," as Lou liked to describe my job, I decided to sell off half my inventory so I would only have one large storage unit to pay for each month. I wanted to focus on getting more design jobs, which aren't so physically taxing, and scale down my staging business. I raised my prices, and for the first time, did not receive every job I bid. I started writing again and decided I wanted to finish the book I kept promising all my former blog readers—and myself—I would finish.

So here I am, four and a half years after Tiara passed away: a retired home stager, interior designer, blogger, and now a published author. I'm hoping that soon I will be a full-time author and nothing else—except a wife to Lou and mom to my grown girls.

As for the rest of my life—Lou and I are still happily married—which we both find miraculous. After not having a social life for most of our marriage, we continue to be homebodies, now out of choice, not necessity. Going to social functions causes us both anxiety, so we opt to sit at home together, drinking chardonnay while watching TV. We try pushing each other to be more social, and we have improved, but we have more work to do in this area. We rarely argue, but when we do, it's usually about Lou's drinking or me throwing away some keepsake of his I have deemed trash. Yes, he leaves his underwear on the floor, black hair in the sink, shoes in the living room, and dishes in the sink, but I don't nag him. I either clean it up, or I leave it, depending on my mood. When he comes home from work, and there is no food because I've been working myself, he doesn't complain. When I took over the entire garage and sunroom for my staging business, he didn't get mad. We both take turns cooking dinner and doing the laundry, but he does all the sewing. We weren't always this gracious to one another, but somewhere along the way, we learned how to be kind to one another and have compassion for the other person's feelings. We have both evolved as humans over the past twenty-eight years, luckily, in the same direction. Despite being complete opposites, we have the same core values and immense trust for one another, which is why we are probably still happy together.

As for everyone else—Grandma Cindy married a wonderful widower twenty days before Tiara passed away, and they live in Newport Beach. We see them often, spend most of our holidays together, and have even traveled together. Grandma Cindy was my Tiara savior. She saved me physically and emotionally by taking care of Tiara more times than I could ever count. Tiara loved every minute she spent with her Grandma Cindy, and I'm not sure I could have done it without her. I know Grandma Cindy misses Tiara every day, but she, too, doesn't have regrets.

As for my parents, losing Tiara was devastating for them. I can't speak to their grief or how they felt, but it seemed as if they suffered a loss greater than mine. We were in different places emotionally, and Tiara's dying created an even larger divide between us. I was often frustrated because I felt like I needed to comfort them, and they didn't know how to support me. Two weeks after Tiara died, Mom delivered a pair of Tory Burch thongs to me. I loved them, but I needed more, and Mom didn't know how to give me what I needed. She often brought gifts to Tiara's grave, but in my mind, Tiara wasn't there, so it seemed weird. Dad was even more inconsolable than Mom, and together, their grief took up all the space in the room, leaving none for me. We had a hard time communicating because I wasn't falling apart, like them. They enrolled in a grief class, and Mom declared, "I wasn't receiving the help I needed." The grief counselor gave them permission to be selfish during the grieving process. This permission, along with Tabitha leaving Sarah's store, was the end of my nuclear family, as it once existed.

While Tiara was dying, Sarah showed up and supported me, like the sister I once had. She helped Lou and me with every aspect of the funeral, including hosting the reception after the service. It was like I had my sister back. Through the years, Sarah and I had drifted apart for many reasons. I could write a book explaining how we went from being best friends to not speaking, but the most simplistic version, in my opinion, is this: Mom, Ray, and I are all controlling people. Sarah couldn't handle us all, so she picked Ray. Ray encouraged the separation from our family, and by the end of Tiara's life, we had drifted worlds apart. Sarah, Mom, and Tabitha all worked together in Sarah's store while I was at home trying to survive my life with Tiara and blogging about it.

Tabitha was stuck between both worlds and needed to find her own life, separate from ours, which is why she quit working for Sarah. The day Tabitha quit, Ray declared her leaving was my fault and said:

"We are no longer family." Mom sided with Sarah, and somehow everything became my fault. Losing them was harder than losing Tiara because it was so unexpected. My family is far from perfect, but I never imagined they would abandon us after Tiara's death.

Thanksgiving was always at Sarah's, so we had to find somewhere else to spend our first big holiday without Tiara. I invited Mom and Dad to spend the holiday with us, but Mom said no. She claimed it was too painful for her and Dad after losing Tiara. I begged her to reconsider, but she had permission from her grief counselor to take care of herself, which meant not spending Thanksgiving with us. Dad does whatever Mom demands; otherwise, he suffers additional abuse. Mass on Christmas Eve, followed by dinner at my parents', was instead spent at my best friend, Laura's, house. I still hosted Christmas Day, but my parents and Sarah's family didn't come. The divide has only gotten worse with time.

As for the rest of our family and friends, they have helped us survive over the past four and a half years. Without our aunts, uncles, cousins, and friends, we would have been lost. This includes our TSC community. The TS Alliance asked me to speak and share Tiara's story at Comedy for a Cure, following her death. They then highlighted her story on the cover of their quarterly magazine, *Perspective*, and renamed the annual Southern California picnic after her. While Tiara was alive, I had put on the picnic for ten years, only to stop a few years before her death, for obvious reasons. I continue to put on the annual family picnic every summer for all our local TSC families and have taken on the role of auction chair for the annual Comedy for a Cure event. This way, I stay connected to all my TSC family and can help raise money to find a cure for this devastating disorder.

And last, my current relationship with Tiara. Tiara works hard to make herself known to me and everyone in our family. She flashes lights; leaves me coins with her birth year on them; shows up as a butterfly and lands on our hands; rearranges the pillows on my couch in the middle of the night; and the list goes on and on. I have been to a medium twice, and both times Tiara came through loud and clear. Tiara knew about my staging business and said she went with me to all the houses. She knew about Stella, Trinity getting braces, and last but not least, she told me I had to finish the book because it was going to help lots of people. Once I heard that, I decided I would have the first draft completed by my fiftieth birthday, September 11, 2019. It would be my gift to us both, and a way to commemorate living half a century. I completed my goal, which is why you just finished reading *Loving Tiara*.

I hope you've enjoyed reading about our journey.

xoxo

Tiffani Goff

Made in the USA
Las Vegas, NV
20 May 2021